THE CHICANO HERITAGE

This is a volume in the Arno Press collection

THE CHICANO HERITAGE

See last pages of this volume for a complete list of titles.

THE MEXICAN-AMERICAN WORKERS OF SAN ANTONIO, TEXAS

Robert Garland Landolt

ARNO PRESS

A New York Times Company

New York — 1976

Editorial Supervision: LESLIE PARR

First publication in book form, 1976
by Arno Press Inc.

THE CHICANO HERITAGE
ISBN for complete set: 0-405-09480-9
See last pages of this volume for titles.

Manufactured in the United States of America

Library of Congress Cataloging in Publication Data

Landolt, Robert Garland.
The Mexican-American workers of San Antonio, Texas.

(The Chicano heritage)
Reprint of the author's thesis, University of Texas.
1. Mexican Americans--Employment--San Antonio.
2. Discrimination in employment--Texas--San Antonio.
3. Mexican Americans--Economic conditions--San Antonio. I. Title. II. Series.
HD8081.M6L3 1976 331.6'3'68720764351 76-1291
ISBN 0-405-09509-0

THE MEXICAN-AMERICAN WORKERS OF SAN ANTONIO, TEXAS

DISSERTATION

Presented to the Faculty of the Graduate School of
The University of Texas in Partial Fulfillment
of the Requirements
For the Degree of

DOCTOR OF PHILOSOPHY

By

Robert Garland Landolt, B.A., M.A.
Austin, Texas

August 1965

P R E F A C E

The central Texas community in which I was born and reared had a "Mexican Town" across the railroad tracks from the Anglo residential section. The men of this group all worked in unskilled labor jobs at the Santa Fe tie and lumber preserving plant.

We "white" teenagers, having no baseball diamond of our own, frequently accepted the generous invitations of the young Mexican-Americans to play with them on a field they had laid out in a corner of the railroad property. We were, at first, surprised to find these foreigners intelligent and good ball players as well as friendly. These baseball games were, however, our only contacts with our Mexican friends, for we were not permitted to mix with them socially, and the little town of barely 2,000 inhabitants provided three separate schools--for "Whites," Negroes, and Mexicans, respectively--and the inferior quality of the latter two was considered both adequate and prudent as preparation for the rigidly circumscribed unskilled occupations which the mores of the 1920's decreed as suitable for these ethnic groups.

These social distinctions seemed unfair even to a high school boy, and when I later became interested in labor economics, the waste in productive potential became significant. It is in this wider scope of utilization of human resources that this investigation is made. As a safeguard to the intrusion of personal bias, I have sought carefully to limit myself to a single preconception: in our accelerating technological development, the long-term economic prosperity of a city, state, or country is increasingly dependent on the degree to which it is successful in utilizing the productive potential of all its citizens

San Antonio was considered a natural locale for the focus of the research. This third largest Texas city has long been the historical center of Texas-Mexican life and culture; its Mexican racial stock constituted nearly half of its total inhabitants and more than one-sixth of the persons of this ethnic group in the entire state; its distance from Mexico is sufficient to eliminate the problem of statistical bias due to the Mexican commuter traffic common to border towns.

While library sources were freely used for historical and cultural information, the most significant insights were obtained through field research in San Antonio during the summers of 1962, 1963, and 1964.

My heartfelt thanks go to all the leaders of government and private organizations, employers, representatives of organized labor, and individual citizens who so graciously contributed of their knowledge and experience.

Special gratitude is expressed for the invaluable assistance of the following: Mr. Melvin Sisk, executive vice-president of the San Antonio Chamber of Commerce; Mr. C. F. Motsch, executive secretary of the San Antonio Manufacturers Association; Mr. Jack A. Martin, president of the San Antonio Building and Construction Trades Council; Mr. J. S. Strauss, district director of the Texas Employment Commission and his staff; the Reverend John A. Wagner, executive secretary of the Bishop's Committee for the Spanish-Speaking; and Mr. E. G. Luna, director of the Inman Christian Center.

I want to express my particular appreciation to Professor F. Ray Marshall for his general assistance and leadership in the preparation of this paper, and to Professors C. C. Thompson, H. H. Liebhafsky, and F. S. Brandt for serving on my dissertation committee.

R. G. Landolt

The University of Texas
Austin, Texas
July, 1965

TABLE OF CONTENTS

TABLES AND MAPS

Table Page

CHAPTER I

INTRODUCTION

Objectives and Methodology

A major economic problem of the 1960's is the development of an active labor force capable of meeting the needs of the accelerating technology. Central related issues involved in the attack on this problem are the provision of effective measures to give equal economic opportunity to all persons, particularly members of minority groups, and the planning and administration of programs to combat the root causes of poverty. Efforts aimed at solution of these socioeconomic problems have been largely focused on the Negro population, with relatively little attention given to the needs of Mexican-Americans, who constitute the largest minority group in the five southwestern states, and who outnumbered Negroes in Texas by 1,417,810 to 1,185,476, according to U.S. Census reports for 1960. Four-fifths of the Mexican-Americans in Texas resided in urban communities.

The objectives of this research have been to determine the nature and extent of the utilization of the Mexican-American segment of the labor force in San Antonio and other Texas cities, to examine the probable causes of ethnic imbalances in employment and incomes, and to evaluate programs designed to accelerate the assimilation of the economically disadvantaged. It is hoped that this research will be of value in the implementation of such laws as the federal Economic Opportunity Act of 1964 and the Civil Rights Act of 1964, and the appraisal of such proposed legislation as amendments to the Fair Labor Standards Act and provisions for expansion of federal education and housing programs.

The study has been intensive rather than extensive, in order to secure the firsthand information considered necessary to an understanding of the problems of this ethnic group; however, the findings are considered relevant for other southwestern cities, particularly the large urban communities of Texas. Analysis of comparable data is presented for Texas' four largest cities--Houston, Dallas, San Antonio, and Fort Worth--and the two other cities with the largest numbers of Mexican-American residents--Corpus Christi and El Paso. Field research was concentrated in San Antonio. This included detailed employment data and related information secured from executives of 31 selected private firms and government agencies, plus equivalent material concerning the memberships of the major labor union locals. The roles of politics, education, housing, health, and cultural and other social factors were examined. Information was obtained from records and publications of numerous government organizations, civic and religious groups, newspaper files, and, through scores of personal contacts, the experiences and observations of outstanding leaders from each of these fields.

Evolving interethnic relationships and changes in population components have played important roles in forming the present economic circumstances of San Antonio's Mexican-Americans; hence, historical backgrounds in these areas are provided. Otherwise, emphasis has been given to the years since 1940. This period encompasses those recent major economic developments and social changes incident to the close of the great depression, the impact of two wars and their aftermaths, and varying levels of cold-war military preparedness.

Explanation of Terms

Numerous designations are used to distinguish members of the Mexican ethnic group from other white persons. In addition to Mexican-Americans, they refer to themselves and are commonly called by others: Mexicans,

Latin-Americans or simply Latins or Latinos, Spanish, and Spanish-speaking.

These terms are freely interchanged but some people differentiate between pairs of them to denote distinct levels of social acceptance by other white persons. The very dark-skinned agricultural worker or unskilled laborer, who is uneducated and economically poor, is most often considered Mexican. By contrast, the individual who is of lighter complexion, is better educated, speaks English fluently, has a regular job and has some degree of social acceptance, is spoken of as Spanish. It is not unusual for persons who refer to themselves as Mexican among their own ethnic group to describe themselves as Spanish when talking with other whites and Negroes.

The writer's observation after talking with many of the ethnic group in San Antonio is that, with the exception of some of the least educated, they are unconcerned as to which of the above terms is used so long as they are addressed with respect. When asked their preference, they are likely to grin and make a joking reply, such as: "A Latin-American is a Mexican who has paid his poll tax"; or "A Latin is a Mexican who buys bread at a store"; or possibly "The Spanish are the Mexicans who have moved to the North Side."

In this paper, Mexican-American will denote all U.S. citizens of Mexican descent in preference to the less precise Latin-American. Mexican and Spanish will be terms applied only to citizens of those countries. In fact, since they are relatively small in number and since most information sources do not distinguish them, Mexican aliens who are residents of San Antonio will be included in data on Mexican-Americans unless separately specified.

Happily, the term Anglo-American, or its shorter version Anglo, is universally used to designate all whites other than Mexican-Americans.

The U.S. Bureau of the Census in 1930 distinguished "Mexicans" in its enumeration as "all persons born in Mexico, or having parents born in Mexico, who were not definitely white, Negro, Indian, Chinese, or Japanese." This definition led to substantial understatement of Mexican-Americans, many of whom, particularly third and fourth generations, were enumerated as "white."[1]

Partly because of the shortcomings of the 1930 designation and partly because of the strong resentment

---

[1]H. T. Manuel, "The Mexican Population of Texas," Southwestern Social Science Quarterly, Vol. XV, No. 1, June, 1934, p.51. Manuel estimated that Mexican population of Texas in 1930, enumerated as 683,681, was probably as high as 790,000.

of Mexican-Americans to being categorized as a race other than white, the Bureau of the Census in 1940 classified all persons of Mexican descent as white. "Mother tongue" was substituted as the criterion for distinguishing the Mexican-American population. This designation was intended to include all persons from Spanish-speaking countries and descendants of persons from Spanish-speaking countries. Substantial understatement in the enumeration of Mexican-Americans again resulted, especially among the more highly assimilated native born who chose to give English as their native tongue.

In the censuses of 1950 and 1960, white persons of Spanish surname were distinguished separately in the five Southwestern States of Arizona, California, Colorado, New Mexico, and Texas. Dr. Carl Rosenquist, the eminent demographer of the Department of Sociology at The University of Texas, lauds this as the best possible means of mass gathering of data on Mexican-Americans. Of particular value is the fact that, for the first time, truly comparable statistics of decennial censuses are made available.

The Spanish surname classification, although far superior to other criteria, does have some shortcomings which result in a degree of underenumeration of Mexican-Americans. In the first place, some changing of names, for the most part anglicization, does occur. Father John A. Wagner, executive director of the Bishops' Committee for the Spanish Speaking in San Antonio, stated in an address in 1961: "The reaction of the person who wants to become an American as quickly as possible, frequently will change his name, move away from the old Mexican community, get away so that he might identify himself as quickly as possible with the American community."[2] Other local social authorities verified that such action is observed; however, there was fairly general agreement that the practice is considerably less prevalent than this quotation would seem to indicate. Thus, one can only conclude that a small but indeterminate underenumeration results.

A more significant shortcoming of the use of Spanish surname as the basis for identification of Mexican-Americans arises from interethnic marriage, which from the first appearance of Anglo-Americans in San Antonio has been markedly more frequent between Anglo males and Spanish surname females than between Spanish surname males and Anglo females.

One long-term observer of ethnic relationships in San Antonio, who taught school there from 1887 to 1918,

---

[2]"Community of Tomorrow," John A. Wagner, Address delivered at Christ the King Church, Lubbock, Texas, July 9, 1961.

noted that intermarriages were rather popular from 1835 to 1880 but then gradually dropped off, with the new Anglo-Americans forming their own exclusive society.[3]

Benjamin Bradshaw, in an examination of a 10% random sample of marriage licenses issued during the period 1940-1955 in Bexar County, of which San Antonio is the county seat, secured the information shown in Table 1.[4]

In the 16 years covered by the study, Bradshaw found a total of 5,920 Anglo-Spanish surname marriages, an average of 5.8% of all marriages. Of the total mixed marriages, 4,250 or 4.2% of all marriages were of Anglo males, with the remaining 1,670 or 1.6% of Spanish surname males. Thus, there was a net difference of 2,580 family units formed in which a Spanish surname partner lost her statistical identity, some 2.6% of all marriages. The only discernible sustained change during the period was the postwar decline in marriages involving Spanish surname males and Anglo females.

Racial intermixture between Mexican-Americans and Negroes, either through marriage or cohabitation, is

---

[3]William J. Knox, The Economic Status of the Mexican Immigrant in San Antonio, Texas, University of Texas, Unpublished Master's Thesis, Austin, 1927, p. 16.

[4]Benjamin S. Bradshaw, Some Demographic Aspects of Marriage, University of Texas, Unpublished Master's Thesis, Austin, 1960, p. 52.

TABLE 1

EXOGAMOUS MARRIAGES BY ETHNIC COMBINATION, BEXAR COUNTY, 1940-1955

	Both Classes		Anglo Male-Sp. Female		Span. Male-Ang. Fem.	
Year	Marriages	% All Mar.	Mar.	% All Mar.	Mar.	% All Mar.
1940	290	6.3	220	4.8	70	1.5
1941	270	4.3	220	3.5	50	.8
1942	420	3.6	260	2.6	160	1.0
1943	510	5.9	370	4.3	140	1.6
1944	450	6.6	300	4.4	150	2.2
1945	350	4.5	200	2.6	150	1.9
1946	470	5.1	330	3.6	140	1.5
1947	320	4.7	220	3.2	100	1.5
1948	430	7.1	350	5.8	80	1.3
1949	420	7.9	270	5.1	150	2.8
1950	300	5.2	220	3.8	80	1.4
1951	340	5.5	260	4.2	80	1.3
1952	240	4.1	160	2.7	80	1.4
1953	410	7.5	330	6.0	80	1.5
1954	360	7.1	280	5.5	80	1.6
1955	340	6.9	260	5.3	80	1.6

Source: Benjamin S. Bradshaw, Some Demographic Aspects of Marriage, University of Texas, Unpublished Masters Thesis, Austin, 1960, p. 52.

extremely rare. Intermarriage would be in conflict with Texas' miscegenation law. The much more controlling barriers to such unions are, however, the differences in cultural backgrounds, religion, and language.

The possible overenumeration of Mexican-Americans through counting of all Spanish surname persons is actually of very little statistical consequence, since the number of persons distinctly of Spanish descent is small and becomes relatively less a factor each year, and since there are virtually no residents from any other Spanish surname country.

Unless otherwise specifically indicated, quantitative data on Mexican-Americans throughout this paper will be on the basis of Spanish surname.

Inevitably, questions involving "discrimination" will arise in a study such as this. The term will be used here only in the narrow sense in which objective evidence may indicate that persons of ethnic origin are or have been refused employment, equal pay for equal work, or advancement solely because of ethnic background. Absence or low proportion of Mexican-American workers in any occupation for any employer, or failure of workers of this ethnic group to advance will not necessarily be evidence of discrimination, since they may not have sought such employment or those Mexican-Americans seeking employment or advancement may be otherwise less qualified than others. Refusal of employment or advancement solely because of racial extraction will be considered as discrimination even though the employer's decision is due not to personal bias but from fear of damage to the interests of the enterprise because of adverse reaction of employees, unions, customers or others; however, no value judgment will be made regarding justification of such action.

CHAPTER II

SAN ANTONIO'S ETHNIC HERITAGE

The rounded hills of the Balcones Escarpment, which forms the border of the Edwards Plateau, sweep due east from the Rio Grande and then swerve northward to the Colorado River. On a beautiful site at the southeast edge of the escarpment lies the city of San Antonio, marking a natural juncture of East, West, and South Texas. To the north and northwest of the city, the elevation rises abruptly into the rugged hill country; to the east spread the fertile coastal plains, and to the south stretch the dry prairies and brush country of the Rio Grande Plain. The Mexican border and the Gulf of Mexico are each about 150 miles at their closest points.

San Antonio occupies the site of an Indian village where a small Spanish military post was built in 1691. The city was officially founded in 1718, when the garrison was enlarged and the mission San Antonio de Valera was established. San Antonio has continued to grow as a military center.

Texans have within the past four and one-half centuries been subject to the sovereignty of six nations:

Spain, 1519-1685; France, 1685-1690; Spain again, 1690-1821; Mexico, 1821-1836; the Republic of Texas, 1936-1845; the United States, 1845-1861; the Southern Confederacy, 1861-1865; the United States again, 1865 to the present.

San Antonio has served as a colorful and frequently tumultuous focus of military and political activity under each of these nations except France. Due to this unusual background and the additional impact of German and Irish immigration, the socioeconomic consequences of ethnic relationships is notably important to an understanding of the present circumstances and future possibilities of the Mexican-American workers of San Antonio.

The following gives in roughly chronological sequence some of the more significant historical ethnic relevancies that underlie the present economic environment of San Antonio's Mexican-Americans.

Period of 1718-1836

The more than century-long span of Spanish sovereignty reflected the cultural and economic patterns developed by Spanish conquistadores and Catholic missionaries in their conquest and control of Mexico. To decimate the Indians and drive the remainder into reservations as was done in the United States was unthinkable to either the sons of feudal Spanish nobility or to the clergy, although the end result was hardly more commendable. Concerned with finding gold and gaining other riches, the secular leaders and soldiers in Mexico found it much more expedient to exploit the nominally free Indians to the point of virtual slavery. This condition was brought about by the "repartimiento" system, by which Spanish nobles, priests and soldiers were granted tracts of land together with all the Indians living on them. Strict class distinctions resulted in relatively little racial intermixture, particularly in the 18th century. The position and power of the Catholic Church in the close church-state political system, as well as the dedication of priests, contributed to the settlement pattern of Texas. Thus, priests accompanied expeditions and established numerous missions either in conjunction with military posts, as was the case of San Antonio, or, in places without garrisons, serving as symbols of Spanish rule and temporary forts as the need arose.

The Spanish government's offer of free land to colonists in the new world was directed primarily to

Spaniards and limited to Catholics, and the plan proved to be not particularly successful.

The combination of the above factors resulted in relatively little immigration, and the population of the entire Province of Texas was estimated at only 4,000, exclusive of Indians, in 1820.[1]

Of greater significance than numbers were the racial stock and status of these early immigrants from Mexico. Almost without exception, they were of pure Spanish lineage and they included the government, social and economic leaders of San Antonio.

The first and most important group of colonists to come to San Antonio during the Spanish domination was composed of sixteen families, totaling 52 persons, which arrived in 1731 from the Canary Islands by way of Mexico. They were welcomed with great honor by the capitan of the presidio and, by direction of the king's viceroy, each of the settlers was proclaimed "Hijo Dalgo" or "Hidalgo," literally "son of noble lineage." The title carried with it all the honors granted to founders of new settlements. The descendants of these Canary Islanders still form,

---

[1]Frederick C. Chabot, San Antonio and Its Beginnings, Artes Graficas Printing Co., San Antonio, 1936, p. 10.

together with a few select "old families," the small, aloof elite of the Spanish-speaking of San Antonio.[2]

Ironically, the period following Mexico's final achievement of independence in 1821, marked the beginning of the decline in the relative numbers and influence of Mexican-Americans in San Antonio and the remainder of Texas.

Mexico's land policy, which not only granted free land to settlers but also provided for generous special grants to "empresarios" who contracted to settle at least 200 families, attracted a wave of immigrants to Texas. The great majority of these were brought from the United States through American empresarios, beginning with Austin's first colony in 1821. A small proportion came from Mexico, and this period saw the small beginnings of the tremendously important German as well as Irish and other European immigrations.

In 1830, the Mexican government sought to stem the tide of Americans to Texas. A law was enacted which forbade further immigration except in two colonies. It

---

[2]Frances J. Woods, Mexican Ethnic Leadership in San Antonio, Texas, Catholic University Press, Washington, 1949, p. 12; Chabot, p. 8.

also provided for the establishment of Mexican convict colonies. Duties were levied on all foreign imports. This, together with Mexico's retention of the requirement of acceptance of Catholicism by settlers, failure to provide for them trial by jury and other civil protections, and the constant disagreements with the ever-changing Mexican government leadership (from 1824 to 1876, Mexico had fifty-seven presidents and an emperor) led Mexican-Americans as well as Anglo-Americans in Texas to seek independence.

Period of 1836-1900

For a very brief time after Texas had won its independence, some of the leaders of Mexican extraction continued to serve in high government positions. The highly esteemed Mexican empresario, Don Lorenzo de Zavala, became the first vice-president of the Republic of Texas, and others were members of the Congress.

In 1837, Bexar County was created by an Act of the Congress of the Republic of Texas. The city of San Antonio was incorporated the same year, and through 1842 the proceedings of the city council were conducted and the minutes written in both English and Spanish.[3] An examination of the roster of San Antonio's mayors revealed that Antonio Menchaca served as mayor pro tem from July, 1838, to January, 1839, and that Juan N. Seguin was mayor from January, 1841, to April, 1842; in the nearly a century and a quarter since, there has not been a single Spanish-surname mayor.

The land policy of the Republic of Texas was almost identical to the empresario system of Mexico, except that acceptance of Roman Catholicism was no longer required. There were, however, major differences in the numbers, origins, and character of immigrants. Largely through contractors, as empresarios were called after independence from Mexico, Texas gave grants of lands to encourage immigration totaling 46,218,434 acres, as compared to the aggregate prior grants in Texas by Spain and Mexico of 26,280,000 acres.[4]

Tremendous acceleration of immigration from Europe, particularly during the 1840's and 1850's, overshadowed the continued flow from other American

---

[3]Edward W. Heusinger, A Chronology of Events in San Antonio, Standard Printing Co., San Antonio, 1951, p. 19.

[4]Texas Almanac, 1961-1962, A. H. Belo Corp., Dallas, 1962, p. 250.

states and slower movement from Mexico. Immigrants came from throughout Europe, but in order of their numbers and influence on ethnic relationships and economic environment of San Antonio, the three most important national groups were the Germans, Irish, and French.

Toward the end of the 18th century and during the early part of the 19th century, small numbers of Frenchmen came to San Antonio, nearly all by way of New Orleans. With few exceptions, these early arrivals married Spanish-Mexican natives and became for the most part homesteaders.[5] In 1844, the French empresario, Henri Castro, founded Castroville, 20 miles to the west of San Antonio, with 600 families of Alsacians, and by 1847 had introduced 2,134 French and German colonists.[6] With their common Catholic faith and somewhat similar language and cultural backgrounds, ethnic problems between the French and the Mexican elements were relatively slight, even though intermarriage became increasingly rare after 1850. Many of Castro's settlers gravitated to San Antonio,

---

[5]Frederick C. Chabot, With the Makers of San Antonio, Artes Graficas Printing Co., San Antonio, 1937, p. 255.

[6]Julia Nott Waugh, Castroville and Henri Castro, Standard Printing Co., San Antonio, 1934, p. 116.

where they became most prominent in wholesale and retail trade establishments.

Irish colonists in Texas, unaffected by the Mexican religious requirements since they also were Catholic, were brought over under Mexican contracts, for the most part between 1829 and 1834, by two pairs of empresarios, James Hewetson and John Power, and John McMullen and James McGloin. The grants to Hewetson and Power were north and west from the Gulf coast. The McMullen settlements stretched northwest of them to the Medina River in Bexar County. Over the next several decades, considerable numbers of immigrants in these colonies, including McMullen, moved into San Antonio. As in other American cities, the Irish became most notable as politicians, quickly gained control of the dominant Democratic Party in both San Antonio and Bexar County, and built a powerful, ultraconservative and nonprogressive political machine, whose leaders did little to solve the mounting problems of the Mexican-American segment of the population. In addition to their political leadership, the Irish became ranchers, merchants, and bankers.[7]

---

[7]Most comprehensive sources on Irish immigrants are: William H. Oberste, Texas Irish Empresarios and

The largest and by far the most momentous immigration during the period from Texas independence to the beginning of the Civil War was that of the Germans, whose settlements west of the Colorado River began in 1844. Most prominent among the several organizations which brought Germans to Texas was the Adelsverein, or Association of Noblemen, organized and financed in 1842 by 21 German noblemen, "for the purpose of purchasing land in the free state of Texas." In 1844, the purpose was changed to "the protection of German emigrants to Texas." Under the leadership of Prince Carl Solms-Braunfels, settlements developed rapidly north and east of San Antonio, which, together with the many Germans at Castroville, formed about the city a semicircle of German settlements. New Braunfels was founded in 1845, Fredericksburg and Comalstadt in 1846, Sisterdale and Boerne in 1847, Mayersville in 1849, Bandera in 1850, and Comfort in 1854. From all these and later settlements, Germans were drawn in large numbers to the business and social center of San Antonio.[8]

Their Colonies, Von Boeckmann-Jones Co., Austin, 1953; and Chabot, With the Makers of San Antonio, pp. 271-348.

[8]Most valuable sources on German immigrants are: G. G. Benjamin, The Germans in Texas, University of

By 1856, it was estimated that nearly one-third of the inhabitants of San Antonio were German.[9] The first city directory, published in 1879, gave the following division of nationality groups: Americans, English, and Irish, 7,800; Germans, 7,610; Mexicans, 3,470; Spaniards, 25; Italians, 25; French, 310; Swiss, 60; Hungarians, 17; Dutch, Belgians, and Swedes, 32; Poles, 178; Chinese, 2; Negroes, 2,178; a 35% German representation as compared to 16% Mexican and Spanish.[10]

Their character, even more than their numbers, distinguished the German immigrants and quickly made them the dominant ethnic power in San Antonio. A large proportion were intellectual liberal idealists of varying socialist leanings who had, particularly after the failure of the Frankfurt Assembly, despaired of the prospects of a united Germany under a liberal, constitutional government.

Pennsylvania Publications, Philadelphia, 1909; R. L. Biesele, The History of the German Settlements in Texas, 1831-1861, Von Boeckmann-Jones Co., Austin, 1930; Chabot, With the Makers of San Antonio, pp. 297-373.

[9]Boyce House, City of Flaming Adventure, The Naylor Co., San Antonio, 1947, p. 42.

[10]Leah C. Johnston, San Antonio, St. Anthony's Town, The Naylor Co., San Antonio, 1947, p. 42.

They included sorely needed professional men--medical doctors, dentists, lawyers, musicians, and teachers; dynamic experienced businessmen; as well as skilled craftsmen and farmers. Although they transplanted and quite rigidly followed the traditions and customs of the Fatherland, establishing their own German-language schools and newspapers and exclusive social organizations, and in spite of their liberal political tenets, the Germans were welcomed and accepted as economic and social leaders of the community. Grateful to the Germans for providing for their medical and other professional needs, and impressed by the Germans' abilities, work, and neat and sturdy homes and buildings, the Anglo-Americans saw in them the exemplification of the dauntless and triumphant American frontiersman.

By contrast, a goodly portion of the Mexicans who came to San Antonio during the latter part of the century were political expatriates of Mexico's almost continuous revolutionary activities, and frequently they distinguished themselves as participants in drunken brawls and knifings, and as procurers of Mexican entertainers and prostitutes for the dance halls, gambling establishments, and brothels that grew in the already Mexican

West Side. As the actions of these attention-gatherers became attributed to the entire ethnic group, the Mexican-Americans of San Antonio were measured against the German-oriented criteria for excellence and were found wanting. Persons of Mexican extraction were increasingly stereotyped as morally weak and untrustworthy, unsanitary and in ill-health, lazy and unambitious, and capable of performing only the most menial labor.

Lutheran Germans and Catholic Mexican-Americans found each other's cultural motivations and responses largely incomprehensible. The former came generally to accept the stereotype of the latter, who, in turn, lacking the leadership for an effective counteraction, resentfully assumed the role of second-class citizen. The Canary Islanders and "old families" chose to stand aloof, satisfied to act as caretakers of the glorious culture of the past, more closely associated with, but never quite a part of, the Anglo-American community.

As early as 1854, Gleason's Pictorial Drawing-Room Companion reported:

> The greatness of Bexar is being developed under the brighter auspices of Anglo-American energy and enterprise. And, although the Spanish idioms and customs are still tenaciously maintained among the

> Mexican population here, the chapeau vies with the sombrero, and the chaste attire of the American ladies presents a not unpleasant contrast to the mantilla and rebozo of the dark-eyed senoritas . . . . The Mexican will soon disappear altogether.[11]

Gleason's poetic comment on San Antonio may have been an apt observation of the contemporary ethnic scene, but he could hardly have made a greater error in judgment than in his prediction of the future of Mexican-Americans in the city, as will be seen in the succeeding chapter.

---

[11]Charles Ramsdell, San Antonio, A Historical and Pictorial Guide, University of Texas Press, Austin, 1959, p. 40.

CHAPTER III

TWENTIETH CENTURY POPULATION MOVEMENTS

San Antonio became Texas' most populous city in the 1850's, displacing the port city of Galveston in the U.S. Census of 1860. Although nosed out by Dallas in 1890, San Antonio regained its lead in 1900 through timely expansion of its military operations, and retained the top position until the census of 1930. By that time, Houston, which had become a major port with the completion of its ship channel to the Gulf of Mexico and was rapidly developing as an industrial center around the booming oil industry, took over as Texas' largest city and has continued to extend its lead. By 1930, Dallas, with the aid of the collective talents of an outstanding group of business and civic leaders, had developed a broad-based economy and was able to retain its second place, leaving San Antonio an apparently permanent third.

Table 2 shows, for each decennial census since 1890, population and percentage increase over each preceding census for the three most populous Texas cities, the fourth largest, Fort Worth, and the two which, next

TABLE 2

POPULATIONS OF TEXAS AND SELECTED TEXAS CITIES
1890 - 1960

Year	Texas	San Antonio	Dallas	Houston	Fort Worth	Corpus Christi	El Paso
1890	2,235,527	39,673	38,067	27,557	23,076	4,387	10,388
1900	3,048,710	53,321	42,638	44,633	26,688	4,703	15,906
1910	3,996,542	96,614	92,104	78,800	73,312	8,222	39,279
1920	4,663,228	161,379	158,976	138,276	106,482	10,522	77,560
1930	5,824,715	231,542	260,475	292,353	163,447	27,741	102,421
1940	6,414,824	253,854	294,734	384,514	177,662	57,301	96,810
1950	7,711,194	408,442	434,462	596,163	278,778	108,287	130,485
1960	9,591,508	587,718	679,684	938,219	356,729	167,690	276,687

PERCENT POPULATION INCREASE OVER PRECEDING CENSUS

Year	Texas	San Antonio	Dallas	Houston	Fort Worth	Corpus Christi	El Paso
1890	40.4	83.3	267.5	66.9	246.3	34.7	1,304.6
1900	36.4	41.5	12.0	62.0	15.7	7.2	53.9
1910	27.8	81.2	116.0	76.6	174.7	74.8	146.9
1920	19.7	67.0	72.6	75.5	45.2	28.0	97.5
1930	24.9	43.5	63.8	111.4	53.5	163.6	32.1
1940	10.1	9.6	13.2	31.5	8.7	106.6	-5.5
1950	20.2	60.9	47.4	55.0	56.9	89.0	34.8
1960	24.2	43.9	56.4	57.4	28.0	54.9	112.0

Sources: 17th Census, 1950, Population, Vol. I, _Number of Inhabitants, Texas_, pp. 11, 12.

U.S. Census of Population: 1960, _General Social and Economic Characteristics, Texas_, pp. 312, 313.

to San Antonio, have the largest number of Mexican-Americans, Corpus Christi and El Paso.

San Antonio's 60.9 percent increase in population from 1940 to 1950, higher than either of the others of the "big three" and three times that of Texas as a whole, must be attributed primarily to retention of the greater part of the buildup of the military installations during World War II. While the increase in the decade 1950-1960 was a still husky 43.9 percent, this was substantially less than that of Houston and Dallas, both of which enjoyed population growth rate increases greater than for the previous decade.

San Antonio's tourist guides refer to the city as "The Capital of Mexico in the United States" with considerable justification. In addition to its roles as the seat of Spanish and Mexican provincial government and as the center of early Spanish-Mexican culture in Texas, San Antonio has been the residence of more Mexican-Americans than any other city outside Mexico for the greater part of the twentieth century. The city's 243,627 Spanish surname inhabitants in 1960 constituted 41.5 percent of its total population, and only five cities in Mexico had larger total populations.[1]

---

[1]Mexico City, 4,829,402; Guadalajara, 737,346; Monterey, 596,993; Puebla, 287,952; Juarez, 261,683;

Los Angeles, riding the swell of California's surging growth, supplanted San Antonio as the home of the most Mexican-Americans with 260,389 in the census of 1960.[2] This amounted, however, to only 10.5 percent of Los Angeles' total enumeration.

Texas had five of the first ten United States cities in Spanish-surname population: San Antonio, second, 243,627; El Paso, third, 125,745; Houston, fifth, 63,372; Corpus Christi, sixth, 59,859; and Laredo, on the Mexican border, eighth, 49,819.[3]

San Antonio, in the 1960 census, had 17.2% of Texas' 1,417,810 persons of Spanish-surname, and 7.0% of the United States total.[4]

While the Anglo-Americans of San Antonio retained the economic and political power which they had taken over from the Mexican-Americans before the middle of the nineteenth century, their numerical ascendancy

---

World Almanac, New York World Telegram and Sun, New York, 1963, p. 779.

[2]U.S. Census of Population: 1960, Persons of Spanish Surnames, p. 173.

[3]From examination of data, U.S. Census of Population: 1960, Persons of Spanish Surnames, pp. 170-183.

[4]Ibid., p. ix.

began a relative reversal after 1900. This was the result of a number of contributing factors.

European immigration began to decline in the latter part of the nineteenth century as the availability of cheap land dried up, qualitative immigration requirements were tightened, and finally the quota system was established in 1921.

In Mexico, the rapidly growing mestizo class, the intermixture of Spanish and Indian, was rising up against the almost feudal control of the dictator Diaz and finally overthrew his regime in 1910. In the meantime, across the Rio Grande, greatly increased production of cotton, citrus fruits, vegetables, and sugar beets, together with railroads and mining, offered good employment compared to their meager existence in Mexico. Immigration of Mexican citizens is not restricted by quota.

As a further measure to get badly needed workers during World War I, the United States suspended until 1921 the literacy test, the payment of the head-tax, and the contract labor regulations for Mexicans. While employers of laborers under these provisions were responsible for their return to Mexico, incomplete records showed that only about 2,000 of the 14,318 Mexicans imported in this manner returned to Mexico.[5]

Legal immigration from Mexico rose sharply in the 1920's, fell to a trickle in the depression of the 1930's, rose again slowly in the 1940's, and shot up again after mid-century. Decennial records of immigration from Mexico to the United States from 1820 to 1962 are shown in Table 3.

Many thousands of Mexicans have entered the United States illegally and a large proportion of them are never apprehended. These "wetbacks" simply cross the loosely guarded Rio Grande, get a job and take up residence. They enter illegally instead of becoming authorized immigrants either because they cannot pass the literacy test or other requirements for admission, or they do not have the money to pay for the $25.00 visa fee plus Mexican costs for birth certificate, passport, transportation, room, board, and the extralegal "mordida" to officials for expediting the procedure. This sometimes amounts to as much as $200.

---

[5]Ruth A. Allen, Chapters in the History of Organized Labor in Texas, University of Texas, Austin, 1941, p. 228.

TABLE 3

MEXICAN IMMIGRATION TO THE UNITED STATES

1820 TO 1962

Years	Number	Years	Number
1820-30	4,818	1891-00	971
1831-40	6,599	1901-10	49,642
1841-50	3,271	1911-20	219,004
1851-60	3,078	1921-30	459,259
1861-70	2,191	1931-40	22,266
1871-80	5,162	1941-50	60,589
1881-90	1,913	1951-62	397,173

Sources: *Annual Report, Commissioner General of Immigration, 1928*, p. 190; *Statistical Abstract of the United States, 1963*, p. 100.

The United States government has been lenient with the "wetback" in many ways. If apprehended, his penalty is only return to Mexico. If he is not apprehended for seven years, has no police record and meets the minimum qualifications for admission, he is allowed to remain as a legal resident. Literacy and other tests are frequently waived for parents of children born in the United States who want to become naturalized citizens.[6]

After World War II, complaints about "wetbacks" brought a crackdown, with the number of apprehensions in Texas rising from 16,500 in 1943, to 197,500 in 1948, and 875,318 in 1953, after which the problem was brought pretty well under control by 1955.[7]

In addition to legal and illegal immigrants, Mexican alien "braceros" were employed as agricultural laborers, under Public Law 78, when the Secretary of Labor certified that sufficient domestic employees were not available. Congress voted not to renew Public Law 78,

---

[6]George I. Sánchez, Wetbacks, Preliminary Report to Advisory Committee, Study of Spanish-speaking People, University of Texas (mimeo., 1949), pp. 21, 22.

[7]What Price Wetbacks?, American G. I. Forum of Texas and Texas State Federation of Labor, Austin, 1953, p. 31; Down in the Valley, Texas State Federation of Labor, Austin, 1955.

and the bracero program was terminated December 31, 1964.

The economic significance of legal immigration, wetbacks, and braceros to the Mexican-American workers will be discussed later.

Legal immigrants of Mexican birth who gave San Antonio as their destination, for the years 1953 through 1962, are shown in Table 4.

The causes for the recorded drop in the number of immigrants of Mexican birth destined for San Antonio during the latter half of the decade 1953-1962 cannot be specified with a high degree of confidence. In the first place, consistency in the reporting practices of the Immigration and Naturalization Service, particularly for data involving individual cities, is not found. The difference here may very well result from a stricter interpretation of "destined for San Antonio."

While the total number of Mexicans arriving in the United States in the years 1958 and 1959 was somewhat lower than in the years immediately preceding, immigration rose strongly in 1960-62. A possible explanation for the reported decline in immigration to San Antonio is the likelihood of a compensating increase in "wetbacks" with the easing of pressure in apprehending them after the big

TABLE 4

IMMIGRANTS OF MEXICAN BIRTH DESTINED FOR SAN ANTONIO, TEXAS, YEARS ENDING JUNE 30, 1953-62

Year	Number
1953	1,123
1954	1,863
1955	1,886
1956	1,822
1957	1,348
1958	376
1959	561
1960	867
1961	919
1962	798
Total, 1953-62	11,563

Source: Letter, Immigration and Naturalization Service, U.S. Dept. of Justice, Washington, D.C., June 12, 1963.

drive in 1953 and 1954. Cutbacks totaling about 4,500 in civilian military employment during 1958-1962 may have been a material influence in the immigration drop.

Table 5 gives a comparison of the U.S. Census data of 1950 and 1960 for population by race and for persons of Spanish surname in San Antonio and five key Texas cities.

In every city with the exception of the rapidly growing border town of El Paso, the percent increase in Spanish surname persons was substantially higher than for total white persons. This was most notable in Dallas, where the rate of increase for Spanish surnames was more than five times that for all whites; at Houston, the rate of increase for Spanish surnames was about 50 percent higher than the rate of increase for all whites during the decade.

The rate of increase shown for Spanish surname persons was greater than that for Negroes in each of the six cities, even though, except for Corpus Christi, the rate of growth of Negroes was larger than that for the total white population.

It is interesting to note that in the three cities with high concentration of Mexican-Americans--

TABLE 5

POPULATION BY RACE, AND PERSONS OF SPANISH SURNAMES
SELECTED TEXAS CITIES, 1950 AND 1960

1950	San Antonio	Corpus Christi	Dallas	El Paso	Ft. Worth	Houston
Total Population	408,442	108,287	434,462	130,485	278,778	596,163
White	378,897	101,123	377,199	127,033	241,651	470,503
Negro	28,729	7,101	56,958	3,116	36,933	124,766
Other Races	816	63	305	336	194	894
Spanish Surnames:	160,420	36,501	8,615	63,976	8,139	34,363
Native	135,760	32,846	7,102	45,802	6,680	28,732
Foreign Born	24,660	3,655	1,513	18,174	1,459	5,631
1960						
Total Population	587,718	167,690	679,684	276,687	356,729	938,219
White	544,497	158,363	548,473	269,263	299,346	720,547
Negro	41,605	9,156	129,242	5,944	56,440	215,037
Other Races	1,616	171	1,969	1,480	482	2,635
Spanish Surnames:	243,627	59,859	29,464	125,745	16,322	63,372
Native	213,328	54,981	25,517	91,295	14,552	54,016
Foreign Born	30,299	4,878	3,947	34,450	1,770	9,356
Percent Increase						
Total Population	43.9	54.9	56.4	112.0	28.0	57.4
White	43.7	56.6	45.4	112.0	23.9	53.1
Negro	44.8	28.9	126.9	90.8	52.8	72.4
Other Races	98.0	171.4	545.6	340.5	148.5	194.7
Spanish Surnames:	51.9	64.0	242.0	96.6	100.5	84.4
Native	57.1	67.4	259.3	99.3	117.8	88.0
Foreign Born	22.9	33.5	160.9	90.0	21.3	66.2

Sources: U.S. Census of Population: 1950; Vol. II, Characteristics of the Population, Part 43, Texas, pp. 100-103, Special Reports, Persons of Spanish Surname, p. 46.

U.S. Census of Population: 1960; Census Tracts, Respective Cities, Table P-1.

San Antonio, Corpus Christi, and El Paso--the proportion of Negroes was very low. Conversely, in Dallas, Fort Worth, and Houston, all of which had relatively large Negro populations, the percentage of Mexican-Americans was quite low.[8] To a considerable extent this was simply due to the greater distance of the latter three cities from the Mexican border. For another reason, the Spanish settlers and the German immigrants in Southwest and West Texas were known for rarely owning slaves.

A smaller proportion of Mexican immigrants become naturalized citizens of the United States than do immigrants from any other country. A prime factor in this situation is the proximity to the mother country. With no quota restrictions, Mexican immigrants can return to Mexico and move back to Texas at will and with little expense. The Mexican-born person is likely to consider his United States residency as temporary, even after many years in this country, and his loyalties and cultural ties

---

[8]Simple correlations of ethnic population relationships among the six cities showed the following coefficients of correlation: Percentage of Negroes and percentage of Spanish surname, negative (-.94); Negroes and percentage increase in Negroes, positive (.41); Spanish surnames and percentage increase in Spanish surnames, negative (-.50).

tend to remain with his native land, especially when he is convinced that naturalization will not result in material changes in his social and economic status. Since a Mexican citizen can call on the Mexican consul for assistance in solving his problems, he is loath to relinquish his Mexican citizenship.

Table 6 shows the distribution of foreign-born Mexican-Americans as between naturalized citizens and aliens for San Antonio and five major Texas cities in 1950.

Since the great majority of foreign-born residents not distinguished in the reports were most likely aliens, the actual ratio of aliens to naturalized citizens is somewhat higher than the figures shown in Table 6.

Changes in San Antonio's ethnic composition, as between Mexican-Americans, Anglo-Americans, Negroes, and persons of other groups, based on U.S. Census data during the period 1900 through 1960, are shown in Table 7. These figures are considered reasonably comparable in spite of changes in techniques in collecting data on Mexican-Americans--Mexican birth and parentage from 1900 through 1920, "Mexican" in 1930, mother tongue in 1940, and Spanish surname in 1950 and 1960. Since there were relatively few third generation (and more) Mexican-Americans up to 1920, understatement in the earlier data is not great.

TABLE 6

FOREIGN-BORN MEXICAN-AMERICANS, NATURALIZED CITIZENS AND ALIENS, SELECTED TEXAS CITIES, 1950

City	Total	Naturalized	Alien	Not Reported
San Antonio	24,660	7,363	16,450	847
Corpus Christi	3,655	1,231	2,275	149
Dallas	1,513	449	933	131
El Paso	18,174	3,212	12,360	1,602
Fort Worth	1,459	341	942	176
Houston	5,631	2,181	2,760	690

Source: U.S. Census of Population: 1950, Special Reports, Persons of Spanish Surname, p. 46.

TABLE 7

POPULATION AND PERCENT OF POPULATION, BY ETHNIC GROUP
SAN ANTONIO, TEXAS, 1900 - 1960

Year	Total Pop.	Mexican-American		Anglo-American		Negro		Other	
		Number	Percent	Number	Percent	Number	Percent	Number	Percent
1900	53,321	13,722	25.7	32,000	60.0	7,538	14.2	61	.1
1910	96,614	29,480	30.5	56,321	58.3	10,716	11.1	97	.1
1920	161,379	59,970	37.2	86,829	53.8	14,341	8.9	239	.1
1930	231,542	82,373	35.6	130,737	56.5	17,978	7.7	454	.2
1940	253,854	103,000	40.6	131,221	51.6	19,235	7.6	398	.2
1950	408.442	160,410	39.3	218,487	53.5	28,729	7.0	816	.2
1960	587,718	243,627	41.5	300,870	51.2	41,605	7.0	1,616	.3

Sources: U.S. Censuses of Population and Housing: 1960, _Census Tracts, San Antonio, Texas_, p. 13.

U.S. Census of Population: 1950, Vol. II, _Characteristics of the Population, Part 43, Texas_, pp. 100-103. _Special Reports, Persons of Spanish Surname_, p. 46.

T. N. Picnot, _An Economic and Industrial Survey of San Antonio, Texas_, Public Service Company, San Antonio, 1942, p. 167.

The most significant relationships in the data in Table 7 are the persistent increase in the proportion of Mexican-Americans and the decline in the proportion of Anglo-Americans of the total population. Should their respective decennial rates of increase in 1960 over 1950 (Mexican-Americans, 51.9% and Anglo-Americans 37.6%) be maintained, the numbers of Mexican-Americans and Anglo-Americans would be virtually identical by 1980.

While the number of Negroes continues to increase, this small segment of the population of San Antonio is very slowly declining as a percentage of the total population.

Populations of Bexar County and San Antonio in 1960 by race and by country of origin are shown in Table 8.

Bexar County residents living outside San Antonio numbered 99,433, and made up 14.5 percent of the county population. The bulk of these people are made up of the approximately 50,000 military personnel and their families, who reside at and around the large military installations, and residents of the five incorporated towns located in the northern part of San Antonio--Alamo Heights, Balcones Heights, Castle Hills, Olmos Park, and Terrell Hills--with a combined population of 19,153. Since all of these

TABLE 8

POPULATION BY RACE AND COUNTRY OF ORIGIN
BEXAR COUNTY AND SAN ANTONIO, TEXAS, 1960

Race and Country of Origin	Bexar Co.	San Antonio
Total Population	687,151	587,718
White	369,756	544,497
Negro	45,314	41,605
Other Races	2,081	1,616
White: Spanish Surname:		
Native	225,572	213,328
For. Born	31,518	30,299
Total Foreign Stock	154,600	141,147
Foreign Born	43,259	39,784
Native: Foreign or Mixed Parentage	111,341	101,363
United Kingdom	4,745	3,748
Ireland	1,680	1,354
Norway	391	318
Sweden	763	669
Germany	12,999	10,376
Poland	2,250	1,840
Czechoslovakia	1,385	1,160
Austria	1,265	1,073
Hungary	488	386
U.S.S.R.	1,824	1,448
Italy	2,743	2,152
Canada	2,982	2,041
Mexico	110,314	105,889
All Other and Not Reported	10,771	8,693

Source: U.S. Censuses of Population and Housing: 1960, Census Tracts, San Antonio, p. 13.

groups are very predominantly Anglo-American, the proportion of Mexican-Americans in the entire county is only 37.4%, as compared to 41.5% in San Antonio.

San Antonians of Mexican origin constitute three-fourths of the total foreign stock, the foreign born plus the native born of foreign or mixed parentage. Persons of German foreign stock, although only one-tenth as numerous as Mexicans, are still nearly three times the number of the foreign stock of the United Kingdom, the next largest group.

Using data from Table 8, the number of San Antonio's second generation Mexican-Americans can be obtained with reasonable accuracy by subtracting the number of foreign born with Spanish surnames (30,299) from the total Mexican foreign stock (105,889). Third and older generations are then obtained by subtracting the number of the second generation (75,590) from the total of native Spanish surname persons (213,328). Distribution of Mexican-Americans in 1960 is thus found to be as follows:

First Generation (foreign born)	30,299
Second Generation	75,590
Third Generation and over	137,738
Total Mexican-Americans	243,627

The Mexican-Americans are highly concentrated in southwestern and west central San Antonio, commonly called the West Side. Much of this area is a vast slum, characterized by poverty, dilapidated housing, woeful lack of sanitary facilities, ignorance, disease, and despair.

Appendix A provides data on total population, Mexican-American population, and percent Mexican-American by census tract for all census tracts in the San Antonio Standard Metropolitan Statistical Area, Bexar County, with 400 or more persons with Spanish surnames in the 1960 U.S. Census.

A map of the census tracts in the San Antonio SMSA, distinguishing various levels of concentration of Mexican-Americans, is placed just inside the back cover. Census tract data grouped by levels of Mexican-American concentration are shown in Table 9.

Well over one-half of all Mexican-Americans in Bexar live in 22 census tracts, in each of which they constitute more than 70 percent of the total population. At the other extreme, in the 69 tracts having less than 25 percent Mexican-American residents, are found less than one-eighth of the total Mexican-American population.

The much smaller Negro segment of the population is also rather highly concentrated, with 86.7% of their total living in the 16 census tracts in which Negroes

TABLE 9

LEVELS OF CONCENTRATION OF MEXICAN-AMERICANS BY CENSUS TRACTS, SAN ANTONIO AND BEXAR COUNTY, 1960

Spanish Surname Percent of Pop.	No. of Tracts	Number of Spanish Surnames	Percent all Spanish Surnames in County
90 and over	9	75,672	29.4
80 to 89.9	8	40,112	15.6
70 to 79.9	5	27,800	10.8
60 to 69.9	4	16,902	6.6
50 to 59.9	6	20,194	7.9
25 to 49.9	26	45,797	17.8
Under 25.0	69	30,613	11.9
Totals	127	257,090	100.0

Source: Appendix A.

comprise more than 10% of all residents as shown in Table 10.

Negroes are concentrated mostly in the east central part of the city. Smaller Negro groups are found in the predominantly Mexican-American West Side tracts numbered 34, 35, and 38. A Negro public housing project, Lincoln Heights Courts, is situated in tract 35.

On the whole, Mexican-Americans tend more to live in mixed neighborhoods with Negroes than do Anglo-Americans. In all census tracts in which Negroes comprised 20 percent of the total residents, there were more Mexican-Americans than Anglo-Americans, except in tracts 27 and 52. However, calculation of the coefficient of correlation of the percentage of Negroes and the percentage of Mexican-Americans revealed a negative coefficient of -.63.

The influence of the massing of the great majority of San Antonio's Mexican-Americans on the West Side upon the retardation of the economic advancement of this ethnic group will be discussed in succeeding chapters.

TABLE 10

NEGROES BY CENSUS TRACT WITH AT LEAST TEN PERCENT NEGRO POPULATION, BEXAR COUNTY, TEXAS, 1960

Tract No.	Total Population	Number Negroes	Percent Negroes	Percent Spanish Surname
10	4,522	642	14.2	48.7
27	11,165	3,492	31.3	5.4
28	4,478	2,111	47.1	34.2
34	12,194	1,495	12.2	79.0
35	14,193	3,740	26.4	62.8
38	8,927	2,077	23.3	59.4
47	2,734	1,137	41.7	39.5
48	6,128	2,318	37.8	33.7
49	6,807	5,763	84.7	8.3
50	8,959	6,825	76.2	10.9
51	2,833	2,453	86.6	*
52	4,341	1,906	43.9	19.0
53	2,830	324	11.4	36.4
54	9,539	1,161	12.2	53.9
69	8,857	2,715	30.7	37.0
70	6,735	1,142	17.0	*
Other		6,013		
Total		45,314		

*Tracts with less than 400 Spanish Surnames.

Source: U.S. Censuses of Population and Housing: 1960, _Census Tracts, San Antonio, Texas_, pp. 13-18.

CHAPTER IV

LABOR FORCE, EMPLOYMENT AND INCOME

In this chapter will be examined data on labor force characteristics, on employment by occupational and industry groups, and on levels of incomes. The data presented will be for standard metropolitan statistical areas, unless otherwise indicated, since more comprehensive information is available on this basis.

To discover indications of general employment patterns or dissimilarities, comparisons will be made between the information on the San Antonio Standard Metropolitan Statistical Area, representing Bexar County, and the metropolitan areas of five other Texas cities.

Labor Force and Employment by Ethnic Group

Table 11 provides 1960 labor force and employment data on persons of Spanish surname for the standard metropolitan statistical areas of San Antonio, Dallas, El Paso, Houston, Fort Worth and Corpus Christi.

While there are no great disparities in the labor force participation of Mexican-American males, it is noteworthy that the three cities with heavy Mexican-American

TABLE 11

EMPLOYMENT STATUS, PERSONS OF SPANISH SURNAME, BY SEX
SIX TEXAS STANDARD METROPOLITAN STATISTICAL AREAS, 1960

	San Antonio	Dallas	El Paso	Houston	Fort Worth	Corpus Christi
Male: 14 years and over	71,467	10,631	37,044	21,540	6,402	22,572
Labor Force	54,517	8,479	29,033	17,346	5,080	17,312
Percent of Total	76.3	79.8	78.4	80.5	79.4	76.7
Armed Forces	1,699	28	1,150	48	145	89
Civilian Labor Force	52,818	8,451	27,883	17,298	4,935	17,223
Employed	48,729	8,017	25,133	16,321	4,680	15,515
Unemployed	4,089	434	2,750	977	255	1,708
Percent of Civilian Labor Force	7.7	5.1	9.9	5.6	5.2	9.9
Not in Labor Force	16,950	2,152	8,011	4,194	1,322	5,260
Inmate of Institution	1,211	110	191	108	*	*
Enrolled in School	7,404	927	4,383	2,041	*	*
Other, Under 65 Years old	4,875	686	1,807	1,244	*	*
Other, 65 years and over	3,460	429	1,630	801	*	*
Female: 14 years and over	79,327	11,044	43,746	21,610	6,089	24,307
Labor Force	20,947	3,613	14,707	5,899	1,826	5,932
Percent of Total	26.4	32.7	33.6	27.3	30.0	24.4
Employed	19,220	3,422	13,693	5,421	*	*
Unemployed	1,665	191	1,003	478	*	*
Percent of Labor Force	7.9	5.3	6.8	8.1	*	*
Not in Labor Force	58,380	7,431	29,039	15,711	*	*
Inmate of Institution	704	13	29	36	*	*
Enrolled in School	8,033	1,187	4,887	2,017	*	*
Other, Under 65 years old	44,250	5,680	21,396	12,567	*	*
Other, 65 years and over	5,393	551	2,727	1,091	*	*

* Data Not Available

Sources: U.S. Census of Population: 1960, Persons of Spanish Surname, p. 164; Census Tracts, Corpus Christi, p. 29; Census Tracts, Fort Worth, p. 62.

concentration, San Antonio, El Paso and Corpus Christi, have smaller proportions of males in the labor force than any of the other three. Indeed, when adjusted to exclude the armed forces personnel from consideration, the distinction is slightly higher; the percentages of civilian males in the civilian labor force being: San Antonio, 75.7; El Paso, 77.7; Corpus Christi, 75.4; Dallas, 79.7; Houston, 80.5; and Fort Worth, 78 9.

One factor in the relatively low labor force participation in San Antonio, El Paso and Corpus Christi is the annual farm migration, involving substantial numbers of the Mexican-American inhabitants of these cities, which usually begins the latter part of April. Persons not working and expecting to join this migrant trek would tend, at the time of the census enumeration on the first of April not to be seeking employment, particularly those who were convinced no local job would be made available.

Similar relationships between these cities exist regarding female labor force participation, with the exception of El Paso, which has the highest percentage of all, 33.6. In this city, which has a Negro population of less than 6,000 as compared to over 125,000 Mexican-Americans, the women of the latter race have customarily filled the community's demand for private household workers as shown in Table 13.

The unemployment rate for Mexican-Americans is far larger, particularly among males, in the cities with relatively higher representation by this ethnic group. The single apparent deviation from this pattern is the relatively high rate of unemployment among females in Houston. This exception can be at least partially explained by the fact that, at the time of enumeration, nearly half of Houston's total female unemployed were clerical workers and service workers other than private household, two occupations of heavy Mexican-American employment in Houston.

Table 12 presents a picture of labor force participation and unemployment, as percent of the civilian labor force, by ethnic group and sex, for each of six Texas standard metropolitan statistical areas.

In every city, the percentage of males in the labor force was greater for Anglo-Americans than either Mexican-Americans or nonwhites (virtually all Negroes), with the exception of the high rate for nonwhites in El Paso, where the significance is negligible because of the small number of such workers. Further, the participation rate was less for Mexican-Americans in the three cities heavily represented by this ethnic group than were the rates for the nonwhites, with the relationship being reversed for the other three cities.

TABLE 12

SELECTED LABOR FORCE AND EMPLOYMENT DATA
SIX TEXAS SMSA'S, 1960

S M S A	Total All Races	Spanish Surname	Other White	Non-White
Labor Force as Percent of Males, 14 years and over:				
San Antonio	80.5	76.3	82.8	80.2
Dallas	82.5	79.8	83.3	78.3
El Paso	83.8	78.4	86.8	89.1
Houston	82.6	80.5	83.8	78.5
Fort Worth	81.6	79.4	82.3	76.3
Corpus Christi	80.8	76.7	83.2	77.6
Male Unemployed as Percent Civilian Labor Force, Male:				
San Antonio	5.1	7.7	3.1	6.5
Dallas	3.1	5.1	2.6	6.0
El Paso	6.6	9.9	3.6	5.7
Houston	4.2	5.6	3.4	7.3
Fort Worth	3.6	5.2	3.2	6.6
Corpus Christi	6.9	9.9	5.1	10.1
Labor Force as Percent of Females, 14 yrs. and over:				
San Antonio	32.6	26.4	34.4	47.4
Dallas	41.2	32.7	39.7	51.7
El Paso	33.9	33.6	34.4	30.7
Houston	36.4	27.3	34.4	46.6
Fort Worth	35.6	30.0	33.9	51.4
Corpus Christi	31.8	24.4	34.4	49.0
Female Unemployed Percent of Female Labor Force:				
San Antonio	4.7	7.9	3.0	6.1
Dallas	3.4	5.3	2.9	5.4
El Paso	6.4	6.8	5.7	13.0
Houston	4.2	8.1	3.2	6.4

Sources: U.S. Census of Population: 1960. Texas, General Social and Economic Characteristics, pp. 374, 375, 430, 431; Table 11, above. (Computed from enumeration data for total population, Spanish Surname and non-white.)

The same pattern of racial distinction is found in the unemployment rates for males. In every city, the rate for Anglo-Americans is by far the lowest; in the three heavily Mexican-American cities, the rate for Mexican-Americans is highest; in the three other cities the rate of unemployment is highest for nonwhites.

Thus, the above demonstrates not only that the rates of Mexican-American and Negro male employment in these six cities were substantially lower than for Anglo-Americans, both through lower labor force participation and higher rates of unemployment, but that in every city the more numerous subordinate minority was the most disadvantaged. That comparable situations were and are now existent in other Texas cities seems a reasonable assumption.

For each city, the rate of participation in the labor force by women was lower for Mexican-Americans than for Anglo-Americans. In addition to lesser job opportunities, this was due in part to the more prevalent retention by men of Mexican extraction of the cultural taboo on wives working. Conversely, the continuing postslavery custom of Negro women working in private households explains their highest rates of labor force participation in every city except far west El Paso, with its very small Negro population and consequent reliance on Mexican-American women for this type of work.

Data on female unemployment were not available for Fort Worth and Corpus Christi. For the other four cities, the rates for Mexican-Americans and Negroes were, as was true of the men, about twice that of the Anglo-Americans. No other patterns were discernible.

Table 13 presents occupational and industry groups as percents of employed persons of Spanish surname for four Texas standard metropolitan statistical areas.

Among the Spanish surname males, there was found a close similarity in occupational distribution for the four cities, with the professional and white collar occupations - professional and technical, farmers, managers, clerical, and sales workers - a low approximately 20%, blue collar skilled and semiskilled - craftsmen and operatives - about 45%, and service and labor categories about 35%.

The somewhat higher percentages of managers, clerical, and sales workers in San Antonio and El Paso is attributable to the greater consumer demand of the larger Mexican-American population in and near these cities, and consequently more jobs serving their ethnic group. The same is true of women sales workers.

The relatively high percentage of clerical and kindred workers in Houston has been previously noted, as

TABLE 13

OCCUPATIONAL GROUPS AND INDUSTRY AS PERCENTS OF EMPLOYED PERSONS OF SPANISH SURNAME, FOUR TEXAS SMSA'S, 1960

Occupation of Employed	San Antonio	Dallas	El Paso	Houston
Male: Number Employed	48,729	8,017	25,133	16,321
Percent: Total	100.0	100.0	100.0	100.0
Professional, technical and kindred	3.7	5.6	4.1	4.8
Farmers and farm managers	.4	.8	.8	.6
Managers, officials, and proprietors, except farm	4.9	4.6	6.8	4.4
Clerical and kindred workers	7.1	5.6	8.0	6.5
Sales workers	4.4	3.7	5.3	3.7
Craftsmen, foremen, and kindred	22.1	20.0	22.4	19.4
Operatives and kindred workers	24.4	23.5	22.0	24.8
Private household workers	.1	.3	.1	.2
Service workers, except private household	9.8	9.2	8.7	7.3
Farm laborers and foremen	1.6	4.1	2.7	1.5
Laborers, except farm and mine	17.0	17.0	15.7	19.3
Occupation not reported	4.4	5.8	3.5	7.4
Female: Number Employed	19,220	3,422	13,693	5,421
Percent: Total	100.0	100.0	100.0	100.0
Professional, technical and kindred	5.6	5.3	4.7	6.5
Farmers and farm managers	.0	.0	.0	.1
Managers, officials, and proprietors, except farm	2.5	1.9	2.8	2.5
Clerical and kindred workers	21.7	21.9	20.0	24.8
Sales workers	8.6	3.8	10.4	7.9
Craftsmen, foremen and kindred	1.7	1.8	1.2	1.2
Operatives and kindred workers	25.9	41.2	22.3	20.6
Private household workers	9.0	3.2	16.1	5.8
Service workers, except private household	17.2	9.4	16.5	18.0
Farm laborers and foremen	.5	.2	.2	.4
Laborers, except farm and mine	1.0	1.5	.7	1.5
Occupation not reported	6.1	9.8	5.2	10.7
Industry of Employed				
Number Employed	67,949	11,439	38,826	21,742
Percent: Total	100.0	100.0	100.0	100.0
Agriculture, forestry, fisheries	2.4	5.2	3.2	2.6
Mining	.3	.2	.2	.8
Construction	9.8	9.9	10.0	8.8
Durable goods manufacturing	5.2	13.5	5.8	13.6
Non-durable goods manufacturing	10.7	17.9	12.7	10.6
Transportation, communication, and public utilities	4.9	6.5	8.6	10.2
Wholesale and retail trade	24.4	18.9	24.4	22.5
Finance, insurance, real estate	2.5	3.5	2.4	2.2
Business and repair services	3.2	3.4	2.6	4.6
Personal services	9.1	6.2	10.9	7.3
Entertainment and recreational	1.0	.8	.7	1.1
Professional and related services	6.5	5.8	7.5	6.8
Public administration	16.0	2.1	8.3	2.4
Industry not reported	4.1	6.2	2.8	6.5

Source: Computed from numerical data: U.S. Census of Population, 1960, *Persons of Spanish Surname*, p. 164.

well as the high percentage of operatives to serve in the garment and other extensive light industries in Dallas.

The substantially higher percentage of Mexican-Americans employed in manufacturing industries in Dallas and Houston is meaningful only when considered in relation to total manufacturing employment. Comparison of percentages of total manufacturing employment and of Mexican-American employment for each of the metropolitan areas is as follows: San Antonio, 11.2 and 15.7; Dallas, 22.1 and 31.4; El Paso, 16.2 and 18.5; Houston, 21.7 and 24.2. In each city, the proportion of Mexican-Americans employed in manufacturing is greater than the proportion of all workers, and this is most evident in San Antonio and Dallas.

The exceptionally high percentage of employment in public administration in San Antonio is primarily at the large military installations in and surrounding the city. This is of so great importance to the study of the Mexican-American workers of San Antonio that the next chapter will be devoted to the nature, scope and influence of such employment.

The relatively low Mexican-American employment in transportation, communications, and other public utilities in San Antonio will be given special attention in view of widespread charges of racial discrimination in employment by the telephone company and the publicly owned city utilities.

Table 14 shows the nonfarm employment by industry group, in San Antonio and Bexar County in May, 1962.

The most distinctive characteristic of employment distribution in Bexar County is the extraordinarily high government employment, primarily military, which constitutes more than one-fourth of all employment; by contrast, government employment is only 3.6 percent of total employment in Dallas. Another one-fourth of San Antonio's employment is in wholesale and retail trades.

Another unusual characteristic of San Antonio employment is the small size of its manufacturing sector, only 11.2 percent as compared to twice that proportion in both Houston and Dallas. Manufacturing establishments are for the most part quite small, with only 54 employing as many as 100 workers, and average size of work force is only 27 employees.

It is also significant that three-fourths of the manufacturing establishments and two-thirds of manufacturing employment is in nondurable manufacturing, characterized by a predominance of lesser skilled and lower paid occupations. Ninety percent of all nondurable

TABLE 14

NON-FARM EMPLOYMENT
SAN ANTONIO - BEXAR COUNTY LABOR MARKET
MAY 1962

Industry Groups	Number of Establishments Total	Number of Establishments 100 Employees	Total Employment
TOTAL, All Industries	11,910		208,000
Manufacturing - Total	879		24,035
Durable Goods	228		8,225
Lumber & Wood Prods.	18	1	690
Furniture & Fixtures	69	0	620
Stone, Clay & Glass	36	5	1,590
Primary Metals	5	1	300
Fabricated Metal Prods.	19	4	1,745
Machinery	37	2	1,615
Transportation Equip.	7	1	290
Other Durable Goods	37		1,375
Nondurable Goods	651		15,810
Food & Kindred Prods.	389	24	8,360
Apparel & Allied	83	7	3,445
Paper & Allied Prods.	14	1	325
Printing & Publishing	57	4	2,345
Chemicals & Allied Prods.	35	1	490
Prods. of Petroleum & Coal	8	1	235
Leather & Leather Prods.	19	1	285
Other Nondurable Goods	46	1	325
Nonmanufacturing - Total	11,031		183,965
Agri. Serv., For., Fish.	52	0	310
Mining	72	1	2,080
Construction & Allied	603	8	14,070
Transportation	179	10	7,030
Communications	10	4	2,775
Utilities	5	1	375
Wholesale Trade	315	17	11,415
Retail Trade	3,955	47	41,360
Finance, Ins. & Real Est.	1,504	11	12,130
Bus. & Pers. Services	2,251	27	18,020
Medical & Prof. Services	2,006	3	13,715
Private Households	---		7,600
Government	79		53,085

Source: Texas Employment Commission

manufacturing employment is in the three industry categories of food products, apparel, and printing and publishing.

Comparison of 1960 and 1950 data on labor force and employment, by ethnic group and sex, for the San Antonio Standard Metropolitan Statistical Area is shown in Table 15.

Some indications of progress for Mexican-American workers are noted. The small increase in Spanish surname male labor force participation in 1960 over 1950 is more than that for Anglo-Americans, and a slight decrease in Mexican-American unemployment compares favorably with the nearly 50 percent increase in the Anglo-American unemployment rate; however, the Mexican-American unemployment rate in 1960 was still two and one-half times that for Anglo-Americans.

The substantial rates of increase in female labor force participation were almost identical for Mexican-Americans and Anglo-Americans and represents the normal expansion of female employment due to technological reduction of arduous jobs and broader social acceptance of employment for women. Rates of unemployment increase for females were approximately the same for both ethnic groups, with the 1960 rate for Mexican-Americans remaining

TABLE 15

EMPLOYMENT STATUS BY ETHNIC GROUP AND SEX
San Antonio SMSA, 1960 and 1950

1960	Total Population	Spanish Surname	Other White	Non-White
Male: 14 years and over	226,431	71,467	139,124	15,840
Labor Force	182,366	54,517	115,143	12,706
Percent of Total	80.5	76.3	82.8	80.2
Armed Forces	40,354	1,699	35,321	3,334
Civilian Labor Force	142,012	52,818	79,822	9,372
Employed	134,827	48,729	77,332	8,766
Unemployed	7,185	4,089	2,490	606
Percent Civilian Labor Force	5.1	7.7	3.1	6.5
Not in Labor Force	44,065	16,950	23,981	3,134
Inmate of Institution	3,009	1,211	1,716	82
Enrolled in School	17,522	7,404	8,912	1,206
Other, Under 65 years old	10,973	4,875	5,179	919
Other, 65 years and over	12,561	3,460	8,174	927
Female: 14 years and over	233,006	79,327	137,163	16,516
Labor Force	75,987	20,947	47,217	7,823
Percent of Total	32.6	26.4	34.4	47.4
Employed	70,549	19,220	44,180	7,149
Unemployed	3,571	1,665	1,430	476
Percent of Labor Force	4.7	7.9	3.0	6.1
Not in Labor Force	157,019	58,380	89,946	8,693
Inmate of Institution	2,593	704	1,812	77
Enrolled in School	19,509	8,033	10,177	1,299
Other, Under 65 years old	112,444	44,250	62,197	5,997
Other, 65 years and over	22,473	5,393	15,760	1,320
1950				
Male: 14 years and over	180,787	53,238	114,586	12,963
Labor Force	145,460	40,171	94,650	10,639
Percent of Total	80.5	75.5	82.6	82.1
Armed Forces	29,645	925	26,520	2,200
Civilian Labor Force	115,815	39,246	68,130	8,439
Employed	110,884	36,185	66,665	8,034
Unemployed	4,931	3,061	1,465	405
Percent Civilian Labor Force	4.3	7.8	2.2	4.8
Not in Labor Force	35,327	13,066	19,937	2,324
Female: 14 years and over	181,715	57,558	111,020	13,137
Labor Force	52,039	13,095	32,828	6,116
Percent of Total	28.7	22.8	29.6	46.6
Employed	49,082	12,328	30,912	5,842
Unemployed	1,595	745	613	237
Percent of Labor Force	3.1	5.7	1.9	3.9
Not in Labor Force	129,676	44,463	78,192	7,021

Sources: U.S. Census of Population: 1960, *Texas, General Social and Economic Characteristics*, pp. 375, 431. Table 11, above.

U.S. Census of Population: 1950, Vol. II, *Characteristics of the Population, Part 43, Texas*, pp. 106, 116, 119, 124.

well over two and one-half times that of Anglo-American women.

The nonwhite male rate of labor force participation in 1960 was slightly lower than in 1950. Otherwise, labor force and employment of nonwhites followed pretty much the same patterns as those for Anglo-Americans.

An unexpected condition revealed in Table 15 is the higher proportion of civilian Mexican-Americans 14 years of age and over who were regularly enrolled in school in 1960. Percentages enrolled in school for each racial group, male and female, was as follows: Spanish surname, 10 6 and 10.1; Anglo-American, 8.6 and 7.4; nonwhite, 9.6 and 7.9. In the enumeration for the U.S. Census for 1960, the category "enrolled in school" was limited to schooling which "may advance a person toward an elementary school certificate or high school diploma, or a college, university, or professional degree," and specifically excluded schooling which is given "in specialized vocational, trade, or business schools, in on-the-job training, and through correspondence courses."[1]

---

[1]U.S. Census of Population: 1960, _Texas, General Social and Economic Characteristics_, p. xiv.

While the significance of this proportionately higher Mexican-American school enrollment is lessened with recognition of the differences in age distribution (median age for Mexican-American: males, 17.9 and females 19.6; total white population: males 22.8, females 26.1), the matter will be considered further in the chapter on education.

Examination of the data on persons not in the labor force, other than inmates of institutions and enrolled in school, revealed that a much larger proportion of Mexican-Americans, male and female, of this classification were under 65 years of age. Percentages of those under 65 years of age, for each racial group, male and female, were as follows: Spanish surname, 58.5 and 89.1; Anglo-American, 38.8 and 81.9; nonwhite, 49.8 and 82.0. The explanation for this disparity is partially found in the relatively larger proportion of Anglo-Americans over 65 years of age. Percentages of all persons over 65 who were not in the work force and not institutionalized, by racial group, male and female, were as follows: Mexican-American, 67.1 and 92.7; Anglo-American, 60.8 and 81.5; nonwhite, 67.6 and 75.4.

Occupation and industry group distribution of employed persons by ethnic group and sex, in the San

Antonio Standard Metropolitan Statistical Area in 1960, is provided in Table 16.

By subsuming the occupational groups into three categories, (1) professional and white collar - professional and technical, farmers, managers, clerical, and sales workers, (2) skilled and semiskilled - craftsmen and operatives, and (3) service workers and laborers, the sharp ethnic distinctions in employment are highlighted. The following shows, for all occupational groups and for each of these categories, the percentage of total male employment by race:

	Spanish Surname	Other White	Non-White	All Races
All occupations	36.1	57.4	6.5	100.0
Professional and white collar	18.7	78.7	2.6	"
Skilled and semiskilled	44.3	50.0	5.7	"
Service and laborer	58.5	25.6	15.9	"

The percentage by categories of the total male employment within each ethnic group is shown below:

	Spanish Surname	Other White	Non-White
Professional and white collar	20.5	54.5	15.7
Skilled and semiskilled	46.5	32.9	33.4
Service and laborer	28.6	7.9	43.2
Occupation not reported	4.4	4.7	7.7
Total employment	100.0	100.0	100.0

TABLE 16-A

OCCUPATION AND INDUSTRY OF EMPLOYED PERSONS, BY ETHNIC GROUP
SAN ANTONIO SMSA, 1960

Occupation of Employed	Total Population	Spanish Speaking	Other White	Non-White
Male: Total	134,827	48,729	77,332	8,766
Professional, technical and kindred	12,652	1,817	10,543	292
Farmers and farm managers	1,398	194	1,175	29
Managers, officials, and proprietors except farm	16,486	2,387	13,723	376
Clerical and kindred workers	12,368	3,457	8,294	617
Sales workers	10,598	2,138	8,394	66
Craftsmen, foremen and kindred	28,618	10,760	16,702	1,156
Operatives and kindred workers	22,442	11,899	8,773	1,770
Private household workers	249	66	49	134
Service workers, except private household	10,484	4,777	3,204	2,503
Farm laborers and foremen	1,274	797	458	19
Laborers, except farm and mine	11,791	8,281	2,380	1,130
Occupation not reported	6,467	2,156	3,637	674
Female: Total	70,549	19,220	44,180	7,149
Professional, technical and kindred	9,496	1,079	8,046	371
Farmers and farm managers	145	9	136	0
Managers, officials, and proprietors except farm	3,357	487	2,747	123
Clerical and kindred workers	23,423	4,168	18,800	455
Sales workers	6,135	1,653	4,371	111
Craftsmen, foremen, and kindred	919	334	522	63
Operatives and kindred workers	6,984	4,982	1,736	266
Private household workers	6,488	1,739	1,303	3.446
Service workers, except private household	9,381	3,306	4,215	1,860
Farm laborers and foremen	205	94	107	4
Laborers, except farm and mine	314	191	82	41
Occupation not reported	3,702	1,178	2,115	409
Industry of Employed				
Total Employed	205,376	67,949	121,512	15,915
Agriculture, forestry and fisheries	4,067	1,618	2,298	151
Mining	1,260	190	1,061	9
Construction	15,278	6,648	8,114	516
Durable goods manufacturing	7,795	3,543	4,071	181
Nondurable goods manufacturing	14,850	7,280	7,289	281
Transportation, communication, other public utilities	13,159	3,348	9,080	731
Wholesale and retail trade	48,460	16,578	28,620	3,262
Finance, insurance and real estate	10,975	1,679	9,018	278
Business and repair services	6,967	2,150	4,509	308
Personal services	16,409	6,208	5,332	4,869
Entertainment and recreational services	1,684	651	862	171
Professional and related services	23,383	4,424	17,217	1,742
Public administration	32,485	10,860	19,223	2,402
Industry not reported	8,604	2,772	4,818	1,014

Sources: U.S. Census of Population: 1960, Texas, General Social and Economic Characteristics, pp. 389, 403, 440; Persons of Spanish Surname, p. 164.

TABLE 16-B

OCCUPATION AND INDUSTRY OF EMPLOYED PERSONS
PERCENTAGE PARTICIPATION BY ETHNIC GROUP
SAN ANTONIO SMSA, 1960

Occupation of Employed	Spanish Speaking	Other White	Non-White
Male: Total	36.1	57.4	6.5
Professional, technical and kindred	14.4	83.3	2.3
Farmers and farm managers	13.9	84.0	2.1
Managers, officials, and proprietors except farm	14.5	83.2	2.3
Clerical and kindred workers	28.0	67.0	5.0
Sales workers	20.2	79.2	.6
Craftsmen, foremen and kindred	37.6	58.4	4.0
Operatives and kindred workers	53.0	39.1	7.9
Private household workers	26.5	19.8	53.7
Service workers, except private household	45.6	30.6	23.8
Farm laborers and foremen	62.5	36.0	1.5
Laborers, except farm and mine	70.2	20.2	9.6
Occupation not reported	33.3	56.2	10.5
Female: Total	27.2	62.6	10.2
Professional, technical and kindred	11.4	84.7	3.9
Farmers and farm managers	6.2	93.8	.0
Managers, officials, and proprietors, except farm	14.5	81.8	3.7
Clerical and kindred workers	17.8	80.3	1.9
Sales workers	26.9	71.3	1.8
Craftsmen, foremen and kindred	36.3	56.8	6.9
Operatives and kindred workers	71.3	24.9	3.8
Private household workers	26.8	20.1	53.1
Service workers, except private household	35.2	44.9	19.9
Farm laborers and foremen	45.9	52.2	1.9
Laborers, except farm and mine	60.9	26.1	13.0
Occupation not reported	31.8	57.1	11.1
Industry of Employed			
Total Employed	33.1	59.2	7.7
Agriculture, forestry and fisheries	39.8	56.5	3.7
Mining	15.1	84.2	.7
Construction	43.5	53.1	3.4
Durable goods manufacturing	45.5	52.2	2.3
Non-durable goods manufacturing	49.0	49.1	1.9
Transportation, communication, other public utilities	25.4	69.0	5.6
Wholesale and retail trade	34.2	59.1	6.7
Finance, insurance and real estate	15.3	82.2	2.5
Business and repair services	30.9	64.7	4.4
Personal services	37.8	32.5	29.7
Entertainment and recreational service	38.7	51.2	10.1
Professional and related services	18.9	73.6	7.5
Public administration	33.4	59.2	7.4
Industry not reported	32.2	56.0	11.8

Source: Table 16-A

The above schedules point up clearly the domination of the professional, technical, managerial, clerical and sales occupations by Anglo-Americans in San Antonio. This information on quantitative data, however, tells only part of the story. Qualitative differences in rank and renumeration are skewed strongly in favor of Anglo-Americans.

Conversely, Mexican-Americans and Negroes fill the bulk of the labor and service work, with Negroes employed relatively heavily in service occupations. While Mexican-Americans hold more than their representative share of craftsman and operative employment, information to be presented in succeeding chapters will also show their generally inferior qualitative position here.

Strong domination of professional and white collar occupations by Anglo-Americans is also found in female employment. Mexican-American women hold more than 70 percent of female operative jobs, mainly in the apparel and foods industries. Negro women hold more than half of all private household work and are relatively heavily employed in other service occupations.

Substantial Mexican-American employment is found in most industries. Among major industries, underrepresentation exists in communications and public utilities, where charges of gross discrimination are widely heard, and in finance, insurance, and real estate, in which approximately one-third of all Mexican-Americans work for one giant firm.

Public administration, principally military establishments, provides about one-sixth of all employment in each of the three ethnic groups.

Income Distribution By Ethnic Group

Table 17-A shows median family income in 1959, for the three major racial groups in each of six Texas metropolitan areas. Table 17-B gives the family incomes in 1959, by ethnic group and levels of income, for the San Antonio Standard Metropolitan Statistical Area.

These figures are from information gathered in the 1960 U.S. Census from all persons 14 years old and over. The combined incomes of all members of each family are included in the statistics on family income. Since money income only is included, and since incomes reported were frequently based on memory rather than records, and thus subject to omission of minor or irregular incomes, some understatements of income undoubtedly occurred. It is recognized that such understatements of

TABLE 17-A

MEDIAN FAMILY INCOME IN 1959 BY ETHNIC GROUP
SIX TEXAS SMSAs

S M S A	All Families	Spanish Surname	Other White	Non-White
San Antonio	$4,766	$3,446	$5,828	$3,222
Dallas	5,925	4.378	6,494	3,039
El Paso	5,157	3,857	6,227	3,975
Houston	6,040	4,339	6,827	3,386
Fort Worth	5,617	4,679	5,929	3,008
Corpus Christi	4,908	2,974	6,290	3,041

TABLE 17-B

FAMILY INCOME IN 1959, BY ETHNIC GROUP
SAN ANTONIO SMSA

	All Families	Spanish Surname	Other White	Non-White
Totals	156,630	50,579	95,345	10,706
Under $1,000	9,360	4,918	3,419	1,023
$1,000 to 1,999	14,611	7,434	5,322	1,855
2,000 to 2,999	18,576	9,106	7,402	2,068
3,000 to 3,999	20,409	8,595	9,984	1,830
4,000 to 4,999	20,040	7,377	11,121	1,542
5,000 to 5,999	19,052	5,466	12,582	1,004
6,000 to 6,999	13,677	2,817	10,299	561
7,000 to 7,999	9,902	1,668	7,971	263
8,000 to 8,999	8,105	1,210	6,701	194
9,000 to 9,999	5,635	609	4,891	135
10,000 and over	17,263	1,379	15,653	231

Sources, Tables 17-A and 17-B: U.S. Censuses of Population and Housing: 1960, Census Tracts, respective cities, Tables P-1, P-4, P-5.

incomes are more likely to have been made by persons in the lower income levels; however, the validity of these data in comparing incomes of Mexican-Americans with other whites (Anglo-Americans) and nonwhites (virtually all Negroes) is not considered as materially impaired.

It is significant that in comparing the six cities shown in Table 17-A, the median incomes in the three cities with high concentrations of Mexican-Americans were far lower for all families as well as for those with Spanish surnames. In each city there was wide disparity between median incomes of Mexican-Americans and Anglo-Americans, with Corpus Christi, where Spanish surname incomes were only 47.3% of that of other whites, having the greatest gap. San Antonio was next with only 59.1%, followed by El Paso 61.9%, Houston 63.6%, Dallas 67.4% and Fort Worth 78.9%.

Compared to their median incomes for all families, those cities with more Negroes than Mexican-Americans showed the lowest median incomes for nonwhites.

The above information provides further indication that the most numerous subordinate ethnic minority in Texas cities is, on the average, economically disadvantaged to a marked degree.

Distinctions in family incomes among ethnic groups in San Antonio, as provided in Table 17-B, are easily seen when incomes of all employed in each ethnic group are distributed as percentages within broad income ranges, as shown below:

	Spanish Surname	Other White	Non-White
Under $3000	42.4	16.9	46.2
$3000 to 6999	48.0	46.2	46.1
7000 to 9999	6.9	20.5	5.5
Over 10000	2.7	16.4	2.2
Total employed	100.0	100.0	100.0

Thus, nearly half of all Mexican-American and Negro families living in Bexar County had incomes less than the $3000 considered by many economists as the income level below which families suffer poverty. Less than one out of ten families in these two racial groups earned $7000 annually, as compared to 37 percent of Anglo-Americans earning in excess of this amount.

In the nine San Antonio census tracts in which the residents consisted of at least 90 percent Mexican-Americans (refer to map inside back cover), median incomes of all families ranged from $1729 in tract 44 to $3376 in tract 22, with the average of the nine median incomes amounting to $2702, below the arbitrary poverty level.

Summary

The purpose of this chapter has been primarily one of presentation and examination of general information on labor force, employment and incomes in the San Antonio and other Texas metropolitan areas. This information was used as a foundation and guide for field research and for study of socioeconomic relationships.

Among the points noted in the data under examination was that those Texas cities with proportionately high Mexican-American populations had the lowest percentage of male Mexican-Americans in the labor force. The same was true regarding female labor force participation except in a city where the Negro population was very small and it was customary for Mexican-American women to work in household service jobs. The rate of unemployment of Mexican-Americans was also found to be higher in cities with relatively large representation by this ethnic group.

The labor force participation rate for Mexican-Americans was found in each city to be less than that of Anglo-Americans, and the unemployment rates, male and female, were found to be much higher for Mexican-Americans than for other whites.

Cultural restraints on Mexican-American wives accepting employment has been a factor in their low labor force participation, whereas the continuing postslavery practice of household work by Negroes has resulted in a relatively high participation rate as well as a high rate of household employment.

The industrial distribution of employment in San Antonio was characterized by an extraordinarily high government employment, primarily at military establishments; a somewhat high proportion of employment in wholesale and retail trades; and an unusually small manufacturing sector, predominantly nondurables, headed by production of foods and apparel, and printing and publishing.

While the relatively very high rate of Mexican-American unemployment as compared to that of Anglo-Americans in San Antonio improved slightly from 1950 to 1960, it still remained a tremendous two and one-half times as large as the Anglo rate in 1960.

It was noted, unexpectedly, that a higher proportion of Mexican-American than Anglo-American civilians over 14 years of age were regularly enrolled in school in 1960. This was considered significant even after taking into account the lower median age of San Antonio's people of Mexican extraction.

The higher proportion of Mexican-Americans not in the labor force who were under 65 was recognized as resulting primarily from the considerably smaller percentage of the Mexican-American population over 65 years of age.

Anglo-Americans heavily dominated the professional and white collar occupations in San Antonio. Anglos and Mexican-Americans shared about equally, numerically though not qualitatively, the skilled and semiskilled classifications, and the great majority of service and labor jobs were held by Mexican-Americans and Negroes.

Substantial Mexican-American employment was found in most industries, with their employment in the key military industry in proportion to their numbers in the labor force.

Among major industries, proportionately small numbers of Mexican-Americans were employed in communications and public utilities, a situation ascribed by many as mainly due to discrimination. Relatively few Mexican-Americans were found in finance, insurance and real estate.

Median incomes of Mexican-Americans and Negroes were found to be far smaller than for Anglo-Americans in each of the six cities studied, with the relative Anglo-Mexican disparity greatest in the three cities with large Mexican-American populations.

Relationships involving Mexican-American and Negro workers - in data on labor force, employment, and income - strongly indicate that the most numerous subordinate ethnic minority in Texas cities, on the average, is economically disadvantaged in comparison with the other racial components.

In San Antonio in 1959, nearly half of the Mexican-Americans and Negroes had family incomes below the poverty level of $3000, as compared to one-sixth of the Anglo-American families. Mexican-American incomes were found to be lowest in those sections of the West Side in which virtually all the residents were of this ethnic extraction.

CHAPTER V

THE MILITARY - KEYSTONE OF SAN ANTONIO'S ECONOMY

San Antonio has been the inspiration of numerous romantic epithets. Among the most justified are "The Military Capital of the United States" and "Mother-in-law of the Air Force," the latter referring to the many marriages of San Antonio girls to military personnel. When Randolph Field was dedicated, it became known as the "West Point of the Air."

Even more appropriately, the collective military establishments in and adjacent to the city might be called the "Breadbasket of Bexar County," for the military has always constituted San Antonio's largest industry, and it continues to form the keystone of the city's economy.

A study by the Federal Reserve Bank of Dallas for the year 1957 revealed that the combined military and civilian payrolls of military installations of metropolitan San Antonio totaled approximately one-fourth of total personal income, more than three times all manufacturing payrolls, more than twice the combined payrolls of trade establishments, and about five times the receipts from tourist expenditures.[1]

---

[1] "San Antonio," Business Review, Federal Reserve Bank of Dallas, Reprint, June, 1959, p. 10.

Fort Sam Houston, the city's oldest military post, dates back to 1879, when the federal quartermaster depot was transferred from the Alamo. It occupies a 3,000 acre tract in northeast San Antonio. Located with Fort Sam Houston are the Headquarters of the Fourth U.S. Army, center of all army operations for the states of Texas, Arkansas, Louisiana, Oklahoma and New Mexico, and the Brooke Army Medical Center, established in 1946.

The large contribution of the U.S. Army to the economy of San Antonio is overshadowed by that of the U.S. Air Force installations which border the city. Kelly Air Force Base, adjoining the southwestern city limits and founded in 1917, was merged in 1943 with Duncan Field to become the largest aircraft repair center in the United States. Lackland Air Force Base, adjoining Kelly on the west, is the Air Force training and indoctrination center. Randolph Air Base, started in 1928, to the northeast of San Antonio, is the famous Advanced Training School and headquarters for the Air Training Command. Brooks Air Force Base is adjacent to the southeastern city limits and in 1961 was made headquarters of the newly created Aerospace Medical Division of the Air Force Systems Command.

Parlaying a mild and sunny climate, availability of large expanses of land, and astute politics, San Antonio was able to beat out competition from other cities for these outstanding U.S. Air Force bases. It was chosen as the site for Randolph Field with an outlay by the city of only $500,000 to pay for land against offers of $10,000,000 from Oakland, California, and $5,000,000 each from Dallas and Fort Worth.[2]

The Medina Facility of the U.S. Atomic Energy Commission is located just west and southwest of Lackland.

The statistics of military and civilian personnel, their respective payrolls, and the value of local purchases by San Antonio military establishments, shown in Table 18, give a picture of the magnitude of the economic significance of the military to the city.

The aggregate civilian employment for the year ending June 30, 1963, was 37 percent greater than metropolitan San Antonio's total manufacturing employment in 1962.

The $168,266,933 civilian payroll for the year ending June 30, 1961, is 91 percent greater than the $88,000,000 total manufacturing payroll figures provided by the Texas Employment Commission for 1961.

---

[2]Albert Curtis, Military San Antonio, Standard Printing Company, San Antonio, 1943, p. 35.

TABLE 18

SAN ANTONIO MILITARY STATISTICS FOR FISCAL YEAR ENDING JUNE 30, 1963

Installation	Military Personnel	Annual Military Pay	Civilian Personnel	Annual Civilian Pay	Total Annual Pay	Local Purchases
U.S. AIR FORCE						
Aerospace Med. Div.						
Brooke AFB	1,234	$ 6,675,000	885	$ 6,184,000	$ 12,859,000	$ 2,071,234
Kelly AFB	6,781	24,118,608	20,244	126,171,835	150,290,443	17,652,208
Lackland AFB	25,429	52,336,052	2,628	13,779,148	66,115,200	17,549,773
Randolph AFB	4,693	21,365,303	2,147	12,512,426	33,877,729	4,928,820
Wilford Hall USAF Hospital	1,845	8,891,000	527	3,164,000	12,055,000	*
Air Force Totals	39,982	113,385,963	26,431	161,811,409	275,197,372	42,202,035
U.S. ARMY						
Brooke Army Med. Center	4,700	25,200,000	1,059	5,926,000	31,126,000	425,000
Hq. Ft. Sam Houston	6,000	14,524,000	1,900	10,500,000	25,024,000	10,000,000
Hq. Fourth U.S. Army	1,805	6,476,000	838	5,561,000	12,037,000	* *
Army Totals	12,505	46,200,000	3,797	21,987,000	68,187,000	10,425,000
RECRUITING STATIONS PERSONNEL (USA,USAF, USCC, USMC, USN)	124	784,800	9	38,000	822,800	- - -
U.S. Atomic Energy Medina Facility	- - -	- - -	661	4,095,947	4,095,947	228,000
JUNE, 1963 GRAND TOTALS	52,611	160,370,763	30,898	187,932,356	348,303,119	52,855,035
June, 1962	53,449		31,191		338,609,362	52,142,944
June, 1961	55,913		31,125	168,266,933	342,210,209	40,317,000
June, 1960	51,164		30,339		298,946,720	
June, 1959	49,441		32,758		291,204,214	
June, 1958	51,620		35,774		289,727,606	

Source: Public Information Officers' at the above installations
Compiled by: Research & Statistics Department - San Antonio Chamber of Commerce
* Included in Lackland AFB
** Included in Ft. Sam Houston

Of increasing importance to San Antonio's economy has been the "payroll" of pension payments received by retired military personnel who have chosen to live in San Antonio after retirement. In the Spring of 1964 there were 8,589 of these retired Army and Air Force officers (including 125 generals) and enlisted men, who received total annual pensions of $29,411,290.[3] An indication of the rate of growth and increased significance of military pensions is seen by comparing this with a report that in 1945, San Antonio had about 300 retired officers, 18 of whom were generals, who, together with enlisted men, received about $1,250,000.[4]

Leading reasons given as explanation of this preference for San Antonio as a retirement home were availability of fine military hospitals, relatively low living costs, including access to commissaries, use of recreational facilities at military installations, pleasant climate, and the fact that friends also retire in San Antonio.

---

[3]Ben Siegal, "Retired Persons Add Heavily to Economy," San Antonio Light, June 1964.

[4]Green Peyton Wertenbaker, San Antonio, City in the Sun, McGraw-Hill Book Co., New York, 1946, p. 101.

The total annual military and civilian payrolls, plus local military purchases and the pensions of retired military personnel in San Antonio aggregate a whopping $430,569,444 entering the San Antonio economy in a single year.

The military has been chosen for first consideration among the writer's personally conducted surveys of Mexican-American employment for the significant reasons discussed below, in addition to its dominant position as San Antonio's largest employer.

First, while there were widely divergent opinions among workers, union representatives, employers, government officials, social workers and others as to the prevalence and degree of currently existing racial discrimination in San Antonio, there was virtual agreement that least evidence of such practices in the employment and advancement of Mexican-Americans was to be found in Federal government agencies in general, and at military installations in particular. Consequently, military employment may serve to some extent as a standard for comparison with employment practices of other employers.

Secondly, military and other Federal employment has not always enjoyed its present reputation for substantially equal employment opportunity for Mexican-Americans.

Dr. Carlos E. Castaneda, professor of history at The University of Texas, testified at Fair Employment Practices Act hearings before a Congressional subcommittee in March 1945 that less than 5 percent of the total number of persons of Mexican extraction in Texas at that time were employed in war and essential industries, adding that in military installations their employment had been limited and their opportunities for advancement restricted.[5] More specifically, Alonza A. Perales, testifying at the same hearings, asserted:

> At Kelly Field, for example, where our Federal government employs 10,000, approximately, on three shifts, our men of Mexican descent never could hold a position of higher category than that of laborer or mechanic's helper.

He presented as supporting evidence the following statement, dated March 20, 1943, of one Roman Alvarado:

> I have been employed at the San Antonio Air Depot, Kelly Field, Texas, since October 5, 1942, as a classified laborer. During this time, I have had occasion to observe that the American citizens of Mexican descent do not have the same opportunity to advance that is given to citizens of other extractions. He is always given rough, hard work, and, to

---

[5]Alonza Perales, Are We Good Neighbors?, Artes Graficas, San Antonio, 1948, p. 95.

> make matters worse, placed under Negro foremen. There is only one foreman of Mexican descent, while in the section where I am working, there are about 8 or 9 Negro foremen.[6]

In view of these and similar assertions, military employment has presented possibilities for study of the changes that have taken place during the past quarter century in policies and practices involving the employment of Mexican-Americans.

Thirdly, the generally high level of confidence in the equality of employment opportunity at the military establishments and the relatively higher pay and job permanence have combined to make working at these installations especially desirable to the average Mexican-American. Indeed, the attainment of one of the more highly skilled classifications has constituted something of a status symbol serving as an incentive for young Mexican-Americans to obtain better educations and to seek other ways to improve their employment qualifications. A common San Antonio anecdote is told of two young men of Mexican ethnic extraction who were passing the Alamo when one began to sob. "Why are you crying?" asked the other. "The Gringos have

---

[6]Ibid., p. 117.

retaken the Alamo," the first moaned. "Never mind," consoled number two, "we got Kelly Field." This identification by Mexican-Americans of military employment with prospects for higher realization of their productive potential gives additional value to the analysis of employment at these installations, for insights may be gained regarding the extent to which the members of this ethnic group have upgraded their work qualifications in response to better employment opportunities.

Finally, a detailed survey of full-time civilian employment of selected minority groups by all Federal Government agencies was prepared as of June 30, 1962, at the direction of the Civil Service Commission upon request from the then Vice-President Johnson, as Chairman of the President's Committee on Equal Employment Opportunity. The first such survey ever made, it called for totals, by salary and wage classification, for all employees, for Negroes and for Spanish-speaking employees. Persons of Mexican origin were also separately designated for Arizona, California, Colorado, New Mexico and Texas. First line supervisors were ordered to distinguish each individual employee on the basis of the group in "which he considers himself to be, or which he is regarded to be by others in the work environment or the community." The writer was in San Antonio at the time of the survey and, through the cooperation of the military personnel officers and civilian chiefs of personnel at Kelly Air Force Base, Brooke Army Medical Center, and Randolph Field, obtained these detailed data from each of these installations.

Kelly Air Force Base

Table 19 shows the data on civilian employment of selected minority groups at Kelly Air Force Base.[7] Since the data for Negroes were available, it is included even though this paper is not directly concerned with Negroes. For each GS salary classification, only the beginning rate is shown as of June 30, 1962. Starting January 1, 1964, a new salary schedule with increases ranging from $60.00 in GS-1 through GS-3 to $1,100 for GS-15 became effective.

Wage Board income categories are simply extensions of hourly wages for 40 hours per week for 52 weeks. Rates of pay for wage board employees are established by the Army-Air Force Wage Board in Washington, using data collected on wage surveys in the locality. The Wage Board

---

[7]Data were obtained from the Chief of Personnel at Kelly Air Force Base. Additional information reported was secured through personal interviews with personnel division heads and other workers.

TABLE 19

FULL-TIME CIVILIAN EMPLOYMENT OF SELECTED MINORITY GROUPS
KELLY AIR FORCE BASE, JUNE 30, 1962

Pay Category		All Employees	Negro	Mexican Origin	Percent Mex. Or.
GS Class	Starting Salary				
1	$ 3245	25	1	18	72.0
2	3560	88	11	38	43.2
3	3820	1,089	83	550	50.5
4	4110	1,279	93	515	40.3
5	4565	1,028	39	318	30.9
6	5035	148	1	40	27.0
7	5540	697	23	123	17.6
8	6090	42	0	6	14.3
9	6675	1,584	19	237	15.0
10	7290	23	0	1	4.3
11	8045	932	5	91	9.8
12	9475	370	1	25	6.8
13	11150	171	0	6	3.5
14	12845	50	0	0	0.0
15	14565	17	0	0	0.0
16	16000	1	0	0	0.0
Misc. Command GS		300	9	87	29.0
GS Totals		7,844	285	2,055	26.2
Wage Board:					
Under	$ 2000	0	0	0	
$2000 -	2499	0	0	0	
2500 -	2999	0	0	0	
3000 -	3499	408	42	218	53.4
3500 -	3999	2,305	321	1,291	56.0
4000 -	4499	1,147	184	926	80.7
4500 -	4999	2,219	252	1,232	55.5
5000 -	5499	4,524	206	2,483	54.9
5500 -	5999	875	23	287	32.8
6000 -	6499	430	13	116	27.0
6500 -	6999	66	0	9	13.6
7000 -	7999	143	2	12	8.4
8000 -	8999	20	2	1	5.0
9000 -	9999	19	0	0	0.0
10000 -	over	4	0	0	0.0
Misc. Command WB		194	10	110	56.7
Wage Bd. Totals		12,354	1,055	6,685	54.1
Grand Totals		20,198	1,340	8,740	43.3

Source: Kelly Air Force Bace Survey report.

granted hourly increases, effective August 7, 1963, at San Antonio installations, averaging 9.54 cents for foremen, 6.31 cents for leadermen, and 5.92 cents for other workers.

For a schedule of the revised minimum and maximum salaries and basic wage board rates, refer to Appendix B.

Examination of Table 19 shows that the percentage of Mexican-American employees decreased steadily for those classifications above GS-4 and in wage board pay above $5500 per year. On the other hand, except for the few employed in GS-1 and GS-2, Mexican-American salaries compared favorably with the average manufacturing earnings in San Antonio of $3728.40. Seven-eighths of Mexican-American wage board workers at Kelly received more than this average of manufacturing earnings.

Further analysis of Table 19 reveals the following approximate mean annual salaries and wages by ethnic groups:

	GS Classification		Wage Board
	Class	Amount	Amount
Median:			
All Employees	7	$5700	$5000
Anglo-Americans	9	6700	5200
Mexican-Americans	4	4500	4850
Negroes	4	4300	4450

Significantly, in the professional, technical and clerical occupations included in the GS classifications, the level of attainment of Anglo-Americans remained far superior to that of Mexican-Americans, with median salary almost fifty percent greater. In contrast, the average attainment of Mexican-Americans in the skilled and semi-skilled wage categories was not appreciably inferior to Anglos; yet, it is notable that very few Mexican-Americans were found in the incomes above $6500.

Comparison of Mexican-American civilian employment at Kelly Air Force Base with data on total Spanish-speaking civilian workers for the Department of the Air Force, as shown in Table 20, reveals the remarkable fact that this one installation employed more than one-half of all Spanish-speaking in the Air Force, 8740 of a total of 16,496. Actually the proportion was even higher, since the designation Spanish-speaking in the June 30, 1962, Federal survey included people of Spanish, Puerto Rican, and other South and Central American origins as well as Mexican-Americans.[7]

---

[7] Texas Labor Market, Texas Employment Commission, Austin, June 1962, p. 3.

TABLE 20

DEPARTMENT OF THE AIR FORCE, SPANISH-SPEAKING AND TOTAL EMPLOYMENT AND KELLY AIR FORCE BASE, MEXICAN ORIGIN AND TOTAL EMPLOYMENT BY GRADE AND SALARY GROUPS, JUNE 30, 1962

	Dept. of the Air Force				Kelly Air Force Base			
		Spanish-Speaking			Total	Mexican-Origin		
	Total		Percent of		Employ-		Percent of	
	Employees	Number	Total	Sp.-Sp.	ees	Number	Total	Mex.Or.
Total	276,373	16,496	6.0	100.0	20,198	8,740	43.3	100.0
Total Class. Act or Similar	152,715	4,589	3.0	27.8	7,844	2,055	26.2	23.5
GS-1 through 4	52,162	2,532	4.9	15.3	2,481	1,121	45.2	12.8
GS-5 through 11	79,432	1,941	2.4	11.8	4,454	816	18.3	9.3
GS-12 through 18	21,121	116	.5	.7	609	31	5.1	.4
Misc. Undesignated					300	87	29.0	1.0
Total Wage Board and Other	123,658	11,907	9.6	72.2	12,354	6,685	54.1	76.5
Up to $4,499	14,321	3,352	23.4	20.3	3,860	2,435	63.1	27.9
$4,500 to $7,999	106,104	8,531	8.0	51.7	8,257	4,139	50.1	47.4
$8000 and over	3,233	24	.7	.2	43	1	2.3	.0
Misc. Undesignated					194	110	56.7	1.2

Source: Dept. of Air Force data: President's Committee on Equal Employment Opportunity, Statistical Summary, Minority Groups in Federal Employment, June 1962, Spanish-Speaking and total Employment by Grade and Salary Groups.

Kelly Air Force Base data: Table 19.

Distribution of workers of this ethnic group among the different classification levels showed no significant variation (percent of Spanish-speaking column and percent of Mexican origin column.) The higher proportion of wage board workers earning less than $4,500 at Kelly is at least partially explained by the fact that San Antonio wage board rates were among the lowest in the country because of the city's low general wage level.

Table 21 gives an inventory of wage board employees by occupational group classification, showing wage rates in effect October 31, 1961. It will be noted that, even without the two wage increases since that date, the wage in every category, except manual labor and food preparation and service, was in excess of $2.00 per hour.

The following information was distilled from numerous candid discussions at Kelly Air Force Base, including interviews with the heads of the divisions of personnel measurement and evaluation (testing); training; and of placement, respectively, of office personnel, maintenance (planes and equipment), and supply. Nearly all conversations were with persons who had been at Kelly for more than ten years, and several had been employed there since before Pearl Harbor.

TABLE 21

OCCUPATIONAL INVENTORY
Kelly Air Force Base, San Antonio, Texas
October 31, 1961

Occupation	Number of Employees	Wage Rate (Per Hour) Minimum	Maximum	Current Average
Wire Communications Equipment Installation and Maintenance	38	$ 2.47	$ 2.73	$ 2.60
Electronic Equipment Installation and Maintenance	1,120	2.35	2.73	2.47
Electrical Equipment Installation and Maintenance	1,191	2.35	2.59	2.47
Textile and Leather Work	62	2.21	2.45	2.33
Instrument Overhaul	184	2.35	2.59	2.47
Machine Tool Work	889	2.35	2.73	2.47
Manual Labor	458	1.55	1.71	1.55
Masonary and Plastering	10	2.21	2.59	2.35
Metal Processing	205	2.35	2.59	2.47
Metal Work	1,169	2.35	2.59	2.47
Painting and Paperhanging	256	2.21	2.45	2.33
Pipefitting	112	2.21	2.59	2.35
Plastic Work	79	2.21	2.45	2.33
Lithographic, Printing and Reproduction	86	2.21	2.59	2.35
Rubber Work	43	2.09	2.31	2.20
Woodworking	340	2.21	2.59	2.35
Construction and Maintenance	10	2.21	2.59	2.35
General Equipment Maintenance	9	2.21	2.45	2.33
Fixed and/or Industrial Equipment Maintenance	217	2.35	2.59	2.47
Fixed and/or Industrial Equipment Operation	304	2.21	2.45	2.33
Mobile Equipment Operation	547	1.96	2.31	2.09
Mobile Maintenance	35	2.21	2.45	2.33
Railroad Operation	7	1.96	2.16	2.06
Railroad Maintenance	4	1.70	1.88	1.79
Armament Work	126	2.35	2.59	2.47
Warehouse Work	2,169	1.96	2.16	2.06
Packing and Processing	248	1.70	2.03	2.01
Food Preparation and Serving	97	1.62	1.80	1.71
Merchandising and Personal Services	4	1.83	2.03	1.93
Reclamation Work	36	2.09	2.31	2.20
Aircraft Propeller Overhaul	16	2.21	2.45	2.33
Aircraft Engine Overhaul	947	2.21	2.59	2.35
Manufacture Repair, & Industrial Support Supervising	22	Information not available		
Aircraft Overhaul	1,167	2.21	2.59	2.35
Administrative, Clerical, & Technical White Collar Employees	7,308	Information not available		
TOTAL	19,514			

Source: Public Information Office, Kelly Field Air Force Base.

At the time of United States entrance into World War II, Kelly and Duncan civilian employment was approximately 10,000; by 1944, the number at the merged installation had increased to about 26,000, reached a peak of 30,000 at the end of the war, dropped back to about 10,000 in 1947, rose above 20,000 during the Korean War, and has since remained at around 20,000.

While discrimination had never been the overt policy of Kelly, it was acknowledged that before World War II and in the early expansion during the war, considerable discrimination existed in employment practices of individual administrative and supervisory personnel. In 1940, about 10 percent of civilian employment was Mexican-American, almost all working in lower level jobs, and the rate of progress was slow due to educational limitations. Since at that time very few applicants of Mexican extraction were sufficiently educated to pass a qualifying examination even as an apprentice, some who had power of decision over employment assumed the race as a whole to be inferior. On the other hand, no known instance was recalled, even as far back as 1940, in which ethnic distinction in hiring was shown where the applicant had established civil service qualifications and was referred to the base.

World War II materially affected employment practices. The trebling of civilian employment during the war-time worker shortage necessitated the hiring of all qualified persons and their advancement as rapidly as possible; employment requirements were lowered; the employment of Mexican-Americans was accelerated and spread over all departments. Supervisors who before had considered them inferior gained new respect and confidence in their capabilities. Stimulated by the Fair Employment Practices Committee, policy directives against discrimination were made much more explicit. Returning Mexican-Americans from military service were more aggressive as to their rights in employment, and, more importantly, they took advantage of GI educational benefits to improve their employability by qualifying for better jobs and faster advancement at Kelly. By 1950, Mexican-Americans had begun to move into a goodly number of supervisory and technical positions.

Discrimination in both hiring and advancement at the time of the survey was reported as limited to covert actions of a very few supervisors who still seemed to prefer Anglos. While racial discrimination had been nearly eliminated, numerous complaints were still filed, frequently with the intervention of Mexican-American political office holders. Personnel officers reported that some Anglo workers complained that certain supervisors had become so sensitive to Mexican-Americans' claims of discrimination that they were prone to be discriminatory against Anglos.

The prospect of merit promotions stimulated many Mexican-Americans to get further schooling to overcome educational deficiencies. Members of this group have been accepted as qualified in all areas of employment, and many have been notably successful in electronics, which requires considerable mathematics as well as manual dexterity. Among those attaining high level positions was a GS-13 who was named to represent the base in the Mexican Chamber of Commerce. Another, who started as an apprentice, attained the executive level position of planning and management supervisor.

Greatest continuing barriers to employment and advancement for many Mexican-Americans have been the related problems of deficiency in education and lack of facility with the English language. Rapid technological developments in the aircraft industry point up the increasing need in this area. High school graduation became a general requirement for employment, plus satisfactory grades on one or more written tests; tests are also required of those considered for advancement. The psychologist in charge of testing, noting that many Mexican-Americans failed to pass tests for employment, observed a fairly high correlation between language deficiency and test grades. The habit of continuing to think in Spanish and then to translate into English impairs both the speed and the clarity of understanding needed to cope with a timed test.

Other weaknesses noted most frequently among Mexican-Americans were the difficulties many have through getting into the clutches of "loan sharks," and the tendency of some to get into trouble with the police--most often for drunkenness, fighting, or both. Kelly is fairly liberal about police records. Although a person under present sentence, even suspended, will not be accepted, he is likely to be hired if his recent record is satisfactory and he tells the truth.

U.S. Army Installations

In addition to data received on civilian employment of minority groups at Fort Sam Houston, which included the civilian personnel of U.S. Fourth Army Headquarters, and from the Brooke Army Medical Center, the information and insights below were gained through very helpful discussions with the civilian chiefs of staffs Jehl and Hoiriis, respectively, and members of their staffs.

1. <u>Fort Sam Houston</u>

Distribution of employment by selected minority groups and pay categories at Fort Sam Houston as of June 30, 1962, is shown in Table 22. Unfortunately, detailed wage distributions of hourly wage board workers was not made available.

The proportion of Mexican-Americans to total employed was smaller at Fort Sam Houston than at Kelly Air Force Base--respectively 18.3% and 26.2% in GS classifications, 35.0% and 54% in wage board occupations, and 24.9% and 43.3% in total work force.

A factor influencing the relatively fewer Mexican-Americans at Fort Sam Houston was the length of service of employees in general, and particularly in administrative and upper supervisory capacities at this older installation. Two-thirds of all employees had been at Fort Sam Houston for ten years or more. Since Mexican-Americans had begun to make the educational progress required for higher level jobs only during the past decade, it could be expected that other long-tenure employees would continue

TABLE 22

FULL-TIME CIVILIAN EMPLOYMENT OF SELECTED MINORITY GROUPS
FORT SAM HOUSTON, JUNE 30, 1962

Pay Category: GS Class	Pay Category: Starting Salary	All Employees	Negro	Mexican Origin	Percent Mex. Or.
1	$3245	0	0	0	
2	3560	25	3	20	80.0
3	3820	323	15	57	17.6
4	4110	395	4	86	21.8
5	4565	282	1	47	16.7
6	5035	170	1	48	28.2
7	5540	167	1	39	23.4
8	6090	25	0	0	0.0
9	6675	128	0	19	14.8
10	7290	32	0	0	0.0
11	8045	101	0	5	5.0
12	9475	67	0	0	0.0
13	11150	30	0	0	0.0
14	12845	5	0	0	0.0
15	14565	3	0	0	0.0
GS Totals		1,753	25	321	18.3
Wage Bd. Totals		1,137	164	398	35.0
Grand Totals		2,890	189	719	24.9

Note: Data includes employment for Headquarters, Fourth Army.

Distribution of wage board employees by level of wages was not made available.

Source: Fort Sam Houston survey report.

for some years to dominate these positions. Furthermore, while this personnel stability was commendable, the probability cannot be ignored that some of these long-time supervisors retained, consciously or unconsciously, concepts of employment preference developed when substantially all Mexican-Americans were qualified only for unskilled jobs at Fort Sam Houston. The personnel staff members stated, on the other hand, that they found no evidence of deviation from the definite policy of equality of employment opportunity.

Examination of the data in Table 22 reveals the following median salary distribution by race:

	GS Classification	
	Class	Amount
Median of:		
All employees	5	$4800
Anglo-Americans	5	4900
Mexican-Americans	4	4500
Negroes	3	4000

Due to the high numerical concentration of all ethnic groups in the lower paid clerical and other office jobs, it is observed that the median pay of Mexican-Americans was not significantly inferior to that of Anglos, and proportionate representation by classification was quite satisfactory through GS-9, above which employment is substantially all Anglo.

Since the end of World War II, a shift in the proportionate employment among the different salary levels has resulted in relatively increased employment of about 15 percent in classifications GS-3 through GS-6.

Of particular interest has been the experience in employment of Mexican-Americans by the U.S. Army Map Service at Fort Sam Houston. Responsible for map making, involving drafting, engraving, etc., this unit employed in 1950 only 75 workers, of which about 40 percent were of Mexican extraction, employed with a few exceptions in lower level jobs. Since that time, employment jumped to 285, divided as shown below:

Level of employment	Total Employed	Mexican-American	Percent Mex.-Am.
Supervisors	36	2	5.6
Journeymen	94	57	60.6
Others	155	104	67.1
Totals	285	163	57.2

In the early stages of expansion, the head of this unit employed a Mexican-American whose work proved so outstanding that he was asked to help recruit others of his ethnic stock. New workers thus secured were encouraged to recommend friends, and the cumulative employment of Mexican-Americans resulted. The head of the map service group is thoroughly convinced that Mexican-Americans are especially suited, from the standpoint of manual dexterity and temperament, for drafting and related skills. While a widespread belief that Mexican-Americans are superior in manual dexterity was encountered in San Antonio, one wonders what might have been the present ethnic makeup of this unit if the key employee involved had proven to be a dud. The foregoing leads to the conjecture that some mild elements of discrimination in reverse may exist here.

Wage board occupations are made principally of skilled and semiskilled workers in various trades and crafts, truck drivers, laborers, and laundry employees. The number of Mexican-American journeyman craftsmen had increased an estimated 25% since 1946, and an increase of about 35% is noted in truck driver jobs. The majority in labor classifications were of Mexican descent, with the remainder mostly Negroes, and relatively few Anglos. Custodial workers were predominantly Negroes.

The distribution among the approximately 200 laundry workers had always been about the same, 90 percent Mexican-American and the remainder nearly all Negro. With the exception of one Mexican-American and two Negroes, the supervisors were Anglo.

Veterans' preference and improved education and training were noted as major factors in the postwar increase in Mexican-American employment.

2. <u>Brooke Army Medical Center</u>

Table 23 shows the distribution of employment by selected minority groups and pay categories at Brooke Army Medical Center as of June 30, 1962.

The 17.5% of Mexican-American GS salary workers was nearly identical to that of Fort Sam Houston; however, the 50.4% of wage board employees in this ethnic group considerably exceeded the 35.0% at Fort Sam Houston.

The following approximate median salaries and wage board earnings by ethnic groups are derived from Table 23:

	GS Classification		Wage Board
	Class	Amount	Amount
Median for:			
All employees	4	$4500	$3800
Anglo-Americans	5	4700	4350
Mexican-Americans	4	4200	3750
Negroes	3	3800	3750

Brooke Army Medical Center is a complex of medical organizations engaged in medical education, training, treatment and research. More than 80% of their professional staff and workers are military personnel.

TABLE 23

FULL-TIME CIVILIAN EMPLOYMENT OF SELECTED MINORITY GROUPS
BROOKE ARMY MEDICAL CENTER, JUNE 30, 1962

Pay Category: GS Class	Pay Category: Starting Salary	All Employees	Negro	Mexican Origin	Percent Mex. Or.
1	$3245	0	0	0	
2	3560	23	4	10	43.5
3	3820	183	29	42	23.0
4	4110	193	17	41	21.2
5	4565	103	1	13	12.6
6	5035	109	4	17	16.0
7	5540	81	3	6	7.4
8	6090	6	0	0	0.0
9	6675	39	2	6	16.0
10	7290	2	0	0	0.0
11	8045	17	1	0	0.0
12	9475	10	0	0	0.0
13	11150	4	0	0	0.0
14	12845	2	0	0	0.0
GS Totals		772	61	135	17.5
Wage Board:					
Under $3000		0	0	0	
$3000 - 3499		113	36	68	60.2
3500 - 3999		136	51	68	50.0
4000 - 4499		67	17	35	52.2
4500 - 4999		38	15	16	42.1
5000 - 5499		28	4	11	39.3
5500 - 5999		9	0	1	11.1
6000 - 6499		4	0	0	0.0
6500 & over		0	0	0	
Wage Bd. Totals		395	123	199	50.4
Grand Totals		1,167	184	334	28.6

Source: Brooke Army Medical Center survey report.

In June 1962, there were 8 civilian medical officers, none of whom was a Mexican-American; however, it was stated that this was true simply because no qualified Mexican-American had sought appointment. Among the 62 civilian nurses, classified in GS-6 and GS-7, there were eight of Mexican descent.

The bulk of GS rated jobs were in low level clerical occupations, hence the relatively low median salaries of all ethnic groups. Within the past year, one Mexican-American girl had been given a top level secretarial position, the first such attainment.

Here, as at the other military installations, inadequate education and language deficiencies constituted the major obstacles to higher level work, together with the relatively small number of upper level civilian positions available at Brooke Army Medical Center. A personnel staff member reported it was his observation that Mexican-Americans in lower level jobs tend more than ever before to put other things before responsibility to their work. Absenteeism was considered more of a problem at lower levels among Mexican-Americans than it was among Negroes.

The vast majority of wage board employees were laborers, truck drivers, ambulance drivers, mess attendants, elevator operators, and similar unskilled and semiskilled workers. The preponderance of these types of jobs was reflected in the median earnings by all ethnic groups.

Summary

San Antonio has always been a military town, and, particularly since World War I, the economics of the city and Bexar County have been singularly affected by the scope of operations of the military installations within their borders.

From the U.S. Census of 1920 to that of 1940, San Antonio had the lowest rate of population increase of the four major Texas cities. With the armed services build-up largely retained at the close of World War II, the Alamo City enjoyed the highest rate of growth of the four between the 1940 and 1950 censuses. During the next decade, she slipped again to the lowest percentage increase, with the exception of Fort Worth, which had been heavily affected in reductions in its big military aircraft manufacturing contracts.

Military operations have always been the greatest industry of San Antonio, with aggregate civilian employment of 31,000 in 1962 being more than one-third larger than the work forces of all manufacturing establishments, and with a total civilian payroll nearly twice that of all manufacturing firms. Moreover, the 1964 total of $430 million inflow of Federal funds for civilian and military payrolls, pensions for retired military personnel living in the city, and local military purchases, demonstrates the degree to which military establishments provide the life blood of San Antonio as a first-class city. Truly, the military forms the keystone of the city's economy.

Possible abandonment or severe curtailment of the operations of any of the major military installations, either because of marked success in efforts for world peace or because of radical changes in military dependence on aircraft, were considered highly improbable by both the military and civilian leaders in San Antonio. In fact, the military bases were considered as strong stabilizing influences in the economy.

Corroboration of the stability of San Antonio's military bases was indicated by authoritative statements issued the day following Secretary of Defense McNamara's November 19, 1964, announcement of the closing of ninety-five military installations. Representative Henry B. Gonzalez and Major General William T. Hudnell of Kelly Air

Force Base revealed that realignment of activities of five of the bases to be closed would result in expansion of San Antonio's bases, principally at Kelly, including increase of civilian employment of approximately 5,000 persons, a $31 million boost in annual military and military-affiliated payrolls, and $21 million additional construction at Kelly Air Force Base.[8]

It is generally conceded, nevertheless, by local leaders that in the future the military installations cannot be expected to provide as strong growth stimulants as in the past.

Military employment has been of special significance to the Mexican-American segment of San Antonio's population, and this significance has been particularly evident at the giant aircraft maintenance and repair center, Kelly Air Force Base.

Approximately two-thirds of the 31,000 civilian employees of U.S. military establishments at San Antonio work at Kelly, and Mexican-Americans in 1962 comprised 43.3% of the work force at this base, as compared to about 10% of the 10,000 workers in 1940, at which time substantially all were employed in unskilled jobs. The Mexican-American civilians at Kelly made up more than half of all Spanish-speaking employees of the entire U.S. Air Force.

---

[8] San Antonio Express, November 20, 1964.

While Anglos still dominated the highest levels of GS salary classifications and wage board incomes, Mexican-Americans have been hired in all areas of work at the base; six had reached GS-13 with the then starting rate of $11,150, and 13 working at wage board occupations were earning in excess of $7,000. That Anglos occupy the very top positions is due primarily to the continued deficiencies in education of a large proportion of the Mexican-Americans, plus the fact that most of those who have overcome this barrier have done so only within the past few years and have not yet acquired the experience and seniority necessary for the more advanced ratings.

Although 1,053 Mexican-Americans, making up 23 percent of the work force, were civilian employees of San Antonio's two U.S. Army installations, Fort Sam Houston and Brooke Army Medical Center, jobs at these army establishments are not, in general, as attractive to Mexican-Americans as those at Kelly Air Force Base.

One reason for the greater appeal of Kelly is the larger percentage of higher level jobs and advancement possibilities, although Mexican-Americans were employed in proportion to their number at both army installations in classifications with salary and wage levels up to $5500.

Other reasons for preference of Kelly are the elusive status position and the very large proportion of Mexican-American employees; proximity to the West Side residential section; and, more implicit than explicit, the relatively fewer Negroes--13 Mexican-Americans to every two Negroes at Kelly Air Force Base as compared to a ratio of less than three to one at Fort Sam Houston and Brooke Army Medical Center.

Discrimination in any form against Mexican-Americans has never been officially sanctioned at any of the military bases, and since the Fair Employment Practices Committee pressures during World War II, the explicit policy of strict equality of opportunity has been zealously followed. The small amount of covert Anglo preference by a few supervisors is continuing to decline. There are, however, still numerous complaints of discrimination, particularly on questions of advancement, lodged by Mexican-Americans, and frequently these complaints are filed with the aid of Mexican-American officials.

Since Congressman Gonzalez was elected, the number of complaints involving that office has substantially increased. Anglo-American workers are in increasing numbers claiming that personnel staff members and supervisors are becoming so sensitive to Mexican-American claims of discrimination that they are prone to discriminate in favor of Mexican-Americans.

Actually, even those officials that zealously press claims of Mexican-Americans agree that discrimination at the present time is least prevalent in military employment, but they insist that each claim must be investigated to keep discrimination to a minimum. Furthermore, Federal agencies are about the only employers where they feel that impartial investigation of such complaints is assured.

The prospect of merit promotions has been a stimulant to present workers and to Mexican-American youth to continue to improve their qualifications, and as persons of this ethnic group overcome their deficiencies in education and the English language, they tend to become less susceptible to the two other oft-mentioned weaknesses of the ignorant and poor--petty crime, and "loan shark" and other debt problems. The military establishments are fairly liberal on police records, provided the individual's recent record is clear and he is truthful.

On the whole, civilian employment at San Antonio's military installations provides both economic opportunity and challenge for Mexican-Americans, and it also provides standards for comparison of employment practices of other public agencies and private firms, and for judging the degree to which continuing retardation of this ethnic group may be due to other social causes.

CHAPTER VI

ORGANIZED LABOR AND THE CONSTRUCTION INDUSTRY

The work force of San Antonio is the least organized of all the major cities of the "right to work" state of Texas. Less than ten percent of the total persons employed belong to unions, and only slightly over one-fourth of construction workers are members of the locals of the San Antonio Building and Construction Trades Council.

History of Organized Labor in San Antonio

The labor movement has been weak throughout the present century, with the exception of brief upsurges during and immediately after World War I, and in the decade between the Supreme Court's affirmation of the constitutionality of the Wagner Act and the passage of Taft-Hartley. Such was not the case in San Antonio in the latter part of the nineteenth century.

Characteristically, it was the German element, with its liberal sprinkling of socialist-oriented idealists, that took the lead in San Antonio's labor movement.

The Lassallean influence seems to have been strongest. On the other hand, Dr. Adolf Douai, who escaped from a German prison in 1852 and became the founder and editor of the German language newspaper, the San Antonio Zeitung, the following year, has been described by J. B. Andrews as "the most interesting person in the American Marxian Socialist movement."[1]

The first local labor organization was the Arbeiter Verein (Association of Laborers), in 1865. Although primarily a fraternal and benevolent organization, this group became the forerunner of a strong labor movement involving the establishment by 1900 of more than thirty-five local unions, most of which secured national affiliation.[2]

The oldest local still in existence is that of the Typographical Union, founded in 1875. Ten years later, the German carpenters union (later merged with the other carpenters local established in 1888) and the painters union became the first building trades organizations in the city.

---

[1]Ruth Allen, The Great Southwest Strike, The University of Texas Publications, Austin, 1942, p. 21.

[2]For a list of the San Antonio unions in 1900, see H. A. Shapiro, The Workers of San Antonio, Texas, 1900-1940, PhD Dissertation, University of Texas, 1952, p. 260.

That social supernova, the Knights of Labor, having much in common with Lassallean tenets, burned brightly in San Antonio during the middle 1880's. At its height, there were six local assemblies, five for whites and one for Negroes.

The stature of the Knights of Labor is indicated by the following excerpts from the July 22 and July 23, 1886, issues of the young newspaper, the San Antonio Light,[3] upon the occasion of the meeting in San Antonio of District Assembly No. 78:

> It was perhaps the most unique gathering ever seen in the city, white ladies and gentlemen sitting at the same table and eating with their colored and Mexican brethren . . . . These men are sober, industrious, peaceful, law-abiding citizens . . . . The Light recognizes the loftiness of their aims and the necessity of many of the reforms advocated by them, and wishes them every success in their honorable endeavor.

Even as the members and their cause were being thus praised, the catastrophe that was to bring the death knell of the Knights of Labor, the great Southwest strike against the Gould railroad combine, was under way. Within five years, the last assembly in San Antonio had dissolved.

---

[3]Founded in 1881 and given its present name in 1883. The San Antonio Express was founded in 1865, and the Spanish language La Prensa began publication in 1913.

Craft unionism took over from the expiring Knights of Labor. In 1891, the carpenters, trainmen, and typographical locals organized the San Antonio Trades Council. The new association prospered, gained additional representation, and was the first city trades council in Texas to be chartered by the American Federation of Labor, in 1895. During the 1890's, fairly substantial wage increases and some shorter work hours were won by the street railway employees, electricians at the local light company, typographical unions, bakers, barbers, and retail clerks.

But, with the turn of the century, an inexorable opposition to unionism rapidly halted the expansion of the labor movement in San Antonio and threatened to wipe it out completely. Spurred on by the relentless open shop campaign of the National Association of Manufacturers, the local fight against the unions was ably carried out by the Citizens' Alliance.

A strike by the carpenters, electricians, painters, and plumbers to enforce their demands for a closed shop with the general contractors, organized as the Builders' Exchange, was completely lost in 1901. By the end of 1903, a succession of strikes was broken, including those by telephone workers, railway express employees, and street railway employees. Taking the offensive, some employers refused to renew contracts and others discharged their union members and replaced them with nonunion workers.

Within a few years, San Antonio's labor climate changed sharply, and the city was well on its way to becoming an open shop city, or, as organized labor views it, an antiunion city.

While the factors involved in bringing about this change varied with the individual labor disputes, several were fairly common to all.

In the first place, union leadership was generally inept in bargaining, which frequently resulted in unnecessary strikes and ill-advised strong-arm tactics.

Secondly, the National Association of Manufacturers' aggressive and convincing advocacy of the open shop as an employer's patriotic duty to uphold the American "right of freedom of contract" persuaded leading businessmen to hire and arm strikebreakers and to take whatever measures were deemed necessary to break a strike.

Third, due partly to the inarticulate presentation of organized labor's cause, the whole labor movement generally lost social respect, with consequent reaction by civic leaders, politicians, and law enforcement officers.

Finally, San Antonio employers had at their disposal an unlimited supply of labor from Mexico, and they did not hesitate to bring in Mexicans both as strikebreakers and as strike deterrents.

Laborers from Mexico were willing to work for low wages, because the lowest wage in San Antonio was far greater than they were able to get in Mexico. They were generally docile and easy to control. Barriers of language and customs kept them from mixing with others and they, therefore, rarely joined labor unions.

When unions began to regain power during and immediately following World War I, they were just as effectively checked as before by the reorganization of opposition under the name of the Open Shop Association of San Antonio. With the passage of the Wagner Act, this title became untenable; it was changed in 1936 to the less obvious Associated Employers, Inc., and it is so called today. The purpose of the organization is essentially that of its predecessors--the pooling of resources to combat union representation in the members' plants and business establishments.

While the writer does not agree with either their premises or their actions, he is convinced that for the most part the business and industrial leaders who make up the Associated Employers are honorable men who sincerely believe that union representation is not in the best interests of their workers or the community, and that strong preventive measures are justified.

Since the oversupply of workers of Mexican descent, who are willing to work for low wages, tends to keep down the general wage level and inhibits the expansion of union membership and contracts, since Mexicans have many times in the past been used as strikebreakers, and since their language barrier and lack of education made the great majority of them unable to serve a formal apprenticeship, it is not surprising that, prior to World War II, few Mexican-Americans were on the rolls of building trades unions, with the exception of the members of the hod carriers and common labor local.

Local Craft Unions, 1963

Table 24 shows the total active membership and journeyman base pay scale, as of July, 1963, for the local unions affiliated with the San Antonio Building and Construction Trades Council.

Ethnic composition of apprenticeship programs provides an excellent indication of current practices in

TABLE 24

NUMBER OF MEMBERS AND JOURNEYMAN BASE WAGE SCALE AS OF JULY 1963

ORGANIZATIONS AFFILIATED WITH THE

SAN ANTONIO BUILDING AND CONSTRUCTION TRADES COUNCIL

	Members		Wage Scale
	Date	Number	
Asbestos Workers, No. 887	7/63	100*	$4.15
Boilermakers, No. 577	6/62	20*	4.10
Bricklayers, No. 2	6/62	200*	4.08
Bridge and Structural Iron Workers, No. 66	6/62	200	4.00
Carpenters, No. 14	6/62	1,104	3.625
Electrical Workers, No. 60	8/63	354	3.925
Hod Carriers and Common Laborers, No. 93	7/63	316	
Hod Car. and Mortar Mixers			2.125
Common Laborers			1.75
Millwrights, No. 2219	6/62	120*	3.80
Operating Engineers, No. 450	6/62	100*	
Heavy Equipment			3.875
Light Equipment			3.475
Painters, No. 172	7/63	327	3.25
Plasterers and Cement Masons, No. 178	7/63		
Plasterers		120*	4.125
Cement Masons		80*	3.625
Plumbers and Pipefitters, No. 142	8/63	490*	4.15
Sheet Metal Workers, No. 67	6/62	288	4.00

Source: Local Unions
* Union representative estimates
All other data on membership taken from records of the local unions.

employment and union affiliation. Mr. A. W. Helmke, representative in San Antonio for the Bureau of Apprenticeship and Training of the U.S. Department of Labor, graciously made available the records of his office for determination of Mexican-American participation in current apprenticeship programs as of July, 1963, and in those completed during the years 1948 to 1963.

Based on the criterion of Spanish surname, the results of the examination of active apprenticeship records are shown in Table 25. Indications of patterns of single ethnic representation, Anglo-American as well as Mexican-American, are observed. While no Mexican-Americans are found in the active apprenticeship programs for lather, pipefitter, plasterer, machinist, and newspaper pressman, this ethnic group makes up the entire enrollment in the skilled classification of cabinetmaker as well as the semiskilled millman and cement mason classifications. It is interesting to note the Mexican-Americans dominate the program for commercial pressman. In the remainder of the apprenticeships, both ethnic groups are found, and, although the Mexican-Americans are not represented in the larger classes in proportion to their relative numbers in the work force, the broad participation is not unsatisfactory.

TABLE 25

APPRENTICES ENROLLED IN APPRENTICESHIP PROGRAMS
BUREAU OF APPRENTICESHIP AND TRAINING, U.S. DEPT. OF LABOR
SAN ANTONIO, TEXAS, JULY 1963

Program	Total Enrolled	Spanish Surname
Building Trades		
Bricklayer	18	3
Cabinetmaker	2	2
Carpenter	55	13
Cement Mason	7	7
Electrician	71	6
Iron Worker	7	1
Lather	9	0
Painter	36	21
Pipefitter	21	0
Plumber	39	6
Plasterer	5	0
Sheet Metal Worker	25	2
Terrazzo Worker	2	1
Tile Layer	2	1
Other		
Auto Mechanic	18	6
Machinist	6	0
Millman	3	3
Newspaper Pressman	6	0
Commercial Pressman	5	4
Printer	22	5
Stereotyper	3	1
Tool and Die Maker	1	1

Source: Apprenticeship files, Bureau of Apprenticeship and Training, San Antonio.

In an effort to discover the possible existence of ethnic distinctions as to completions of apprenticeship programs, data were collected from all apprenticeship classes held during the 15-year period from 1948 to 1963, in each of six crafts, by total enrollment and Spanish surnames, and by number of persons completing apprenticeship requirements and those who dropped out or were suspended. The findings are shown below:

	Program Completions		Cancellations and Suspensions	
	Total	Spanish Surname	Total	Spanish Surname
Bricklayer	59	12	39	8
Carpenter	120	28	445	96
Cement Finisher	16	10	8	2
Electrician	178	11	270	11
Pipefitter	38	2	23	0
Plumber	126	13	100	10

The proportion of Mexican-American completions follows very closely the patterns for all enrollees, with two minor variations--a somewhat larger percentage of Mexican-Americans completed apprenticeship for cement finisher, and a higher percentage of Anglo-Americans completed electrician training. These mild exceptions were not unexpected, since cement finishers in San Antonio are predominantly Mexican-American and the great majority of electricians are Anglo-American.

The apparently high ratio of total cancellations and suspensions to total completions was considered by Mr. Helmke to be about normal as compared to experiences in other cities. Few enrollees dropped out because of inability to complete the requirements. Most left to accept job offers; no information was available as to what proportion of these remained in the trade for which they were training.

As might be expected, the ratios of completions to cancellations and suspensions were highest for the two occupations requiring only three years of apprenticeship, bricklayers and cement finishers; however, pipefitters and plumbers, with five-year apprenticeships were next high in the relative number of completions, with the four-year apprentice crafts of electricians and carpenters having the relatively poorest ratio.

Some Mexican-Americans fail to qualify for apprenticeships because they do not meet the now general requirements of citizenship and either high school graduation or passing of an appropriate G.E.D. test. However, at the present time, substantially all Mexican-Americans of apprenticeship age (which varies with the craft, lowest minimum being 17 years and highest maximum being 30 years) are citizens, since the great majority were born in the

United States. The problem of educational deficiency is a more common but decreasing deterrent, as more Mexican-Americans are completing high school.

Data on Mexican-American memberships were obtained from nine unions, representing nearly 90 percent of the memberships of all the local organizations affiliated with the San Antonio Building and Construction Trades Council. This information is shown in Table 26.

Where union records were available, they were checked for comparable membership information for previous years, in order to find indications of change in Mexican-American membership practices. Other information was gained from conversations with union representatives.

Asbestos Workers, No. 887. Only about two-thirds of the members of this local worked in the immediate San Antonio area. The union representative stated that he has no recollection of any Mexican-American member. He maintains that there have been no applications from persons in this ethnic group. A large portion of the membership have belonged to the local many years, and in a number of cases their sons have become members.

Carpenters, No. 14. This is one of the oldest, and by far the largest, of the local unions.

TABLE 26

UNION MEMBERSHIP, TOTAL AND MEXICAN-AMERICAN, SELECTED TRADES, SAN ANTONIO, TEXAS, 1962 AND 1963

Classification	Journeymen		Apprentices	
	Total	Mexican-American	Total	Mexican-American
Asbestos Worker	80	0	20	0
Carpenter	1,090	140	74	16
Cement Mason	80	72	*	*
Electrical Worker	300	19	54	6
Hod Carrier & Laborer	316	270	*	*
Iron Worker	192	38	8	1
Painter	312	119	15	6
Plasterer	120	15	*	*
Plumber & Pipefitter	438	42	52	7
Sheet Metal Worker	250	29	38	3

*Not separately reported.

Sources: Records of respective unions.

Union contractors dominated commercial and industrial work, although there was heavy competition from two very large open-shop contractors, one local and the other based in Houston.

On the other hand, there were only three union contractors in residence construction, handling less than five percent of work in this area. There was wide disparity in wage scales, with the union industrial scale being $3.50 as compared to the usual rate of $2.00 for non-union carpenters. The carpenters union recently made a bid for additional residential contracts by setting a rate of $3.00 for such work and providing training and refresher courses for journeymen and apprentices of contractors that sign new union contracts. It was too early to assess the probable success of this program. A number of other unions protested that this concession to home builders threatens union wage scales.

From the excellent membership records of the carpenters union, data for the years 1940, 1950, 1961, and 1962 were secured in order to observe the changes in Mexican-American membership. Spanish surname was the criterion for distinguishing this ethnic group.

It is observed that, in the 45 percent membership increase in the 1940's, Mexican-American membership rose to nearly six times the small 1940 representation, and the increase in apprentices was even higher. Furthermore, in the postwar membership decline, the number of Mexican-American journeymen has continued gradually to increase.

		Journeymen		Apprentices	
Year	Totals Members	Total	Mexican-American	Total	Mexican-American
1940	866	784	20	82	2
1950	1,258	1,124	118	134	26
1961	1,180	1,110	137	70	15
1962	1,164	1,090	140	74	16

Union representatives stated that all local union contractors use Mexican-Americans; however, some contractors would not accept referral of Mexican-Americans they did not know. The main problem was that some members still did not speak and understand English.

Electrical Workers, No. 60. The 19 Mexican-American journeymen constituted only six percent of the 300 union electricians in August, 1963; however, the six Mexican-American apprentices were almost double this ratio among the 54 apprentices.

A union official contended that the LULACS (League of United Latin-American Citizens) were trying to take advantage of the nondiscriminatory apprenticeship program to get more Mexican-Americans in the program than their qualifications justified.

On the other hand he noted that, while Mexican-American members were small in number, they included some of the best workers, and that they "give less trouble than Anglos."

With most open shops having a top scale of $3.25 as compared to the union scale of $3.925, the nonunion contractors had more than 90 percent of home construction. Union officials pointed out that the mass of Mexican-Americans who will work for lower pay hurts the union in two ways: it keeps down all wage scales, union and non-union, and the resultant lower purchasing power causes resort to cheaper nonunion construction.

The secretary-receptionist of the electrical workers union, at the time of the interviews with union representatives, was Mexican-American.

<u>Hod Carriers and Common Laborers, No. 93</u>. This local union has always been predominantly Mexican-American. The 46 members not in this ethnic group were virtually all Negroes. Very few Anglos applied for membership.

While ten different occupational classifications were covered by this union, the great majority of work was for hod carriers and plaster tenders at $2.125 per hour, mason tender at $1.875, and common laborer at $1.75. Workers qualified for the higher classifications accepted employment as common laborers when the other jobs were not available.

Bridge and Structural Iron Workers, No. 66. Data on total membership and persons with Spanish surname, journeymen and apprentices, were secured for the years 1943, 1950, and 1961, to ascertain changes in employment of Mexican-Americans. Apprentices were not separately designated in 1943.

		Journeymen		Apprentices	
Year	Total Members	Total	Mexican-American	Total	Mexican-American
1943	127	127	9		
1950	136	133	17	3	1
1961	200	192	38	8	1

Although the proportion of the membership which was Mexican-American was quite small, the number of members of this ethnic extraction in 1961 was more than quadruple that of 1943, compared to a total membership of one and one-half times that of the earlier date.

The ratio of apprentices to journeymen was exceptionally small in this trade; however, the combination of worker shortage and two-year apprenticeships contributed toward the wartime and early postwar increase in

Mexican-American journeymen. Apprenticeships now require three years.

There was no observable status distinction of Mexican-Americans in this union, whose business representative was president of the San Antonio Building and Construction Trades Council. During the writer's interview at the local office, the Mexican-American chairman of a committee to secure membership contributions to aid striking members of another union came in to confer with the business representative. There seemed to be no ethnic consciousness on the part of either during their discussion of progress of the solicitation.

Painters, No. 172. More than one-third of the membership of the local was Mexican-American, second highest representation by this ethnic group among the skilled trades in San Antonio. There were no Negro members.

Three of the union contractors were reported to prefer Mexican-Americans, approximately 10 others preferred Anglos, and the remaining 15 contractors showed no ethnic distinction.

Union officials noted that Mexican-American members tend to be either among the best and most loyal in the organization, or to be among the most prone to accept nonunion work during slack times.

The painters local tried out an arrangement for supplemental agreements on residential construction at a lower wage scale, but found the plan unsatisfactory.

Plasterers and Cement Masons, No. 178. Mexican-Americans constitute 90% of the cement masons but only slightly over 10% of the plasterers in this union local. The union representative stated there has been "some" increase in Mexican-American representation in both occupational classifications during recent years, but records were not available and the official said he could not accurately estimate the extent of the increase.

Plumbers and Pipefitters, No. 142. Total membership in selected years since 1940 is shown below. The ratio of apprentices to journeymen is roughly one to five.

Year	Membership	Year	Membership
1940	127	1954	594
1945	256	1960	484
1950	528	1963	490

The postwar construction boom brought about the local union's highest membership of 594 in the year 1954.

The major portion of Mexican-Americans that comprised the approximately 10 percent of the journeymen and apprentices of this local in 1963, were new members brought in by the worker shortage during and immediately after World War II.

The present apprenticeship program, in cooperation with the U.S. Department of Labor, Bureau of Apprenticeship and Training, was noted by union officials as more conducive to increase in Mexican-American membership than the old "father-son, word of mouth" sources of apprentices.

The major criticism of Mexican-Americans was that they were more prone to take nonunion jobs when work got slack and less likely to pay fines for reinstatement.

Archbishop Lucey, of the Catholic Archdiocese with headquarters in San Antonio, is strongly prounion, and his Church is also committed to raising the economic standards of Mexican-Americans, who are about 95 percent Catholics. Union workers and their officials tend to be more favorable toward Mexican-Americans as members because of the strong support of the labor movement by Archbishop Lucey, according to a pipefitter union representative.

The secretary-receptionist of the plumbers and pipefitters local was a charming young Mexican-American woman whose husband was enrolled in the law school of St. Mary's University. This seemed significant, both as an indication of the union's views on Mexican-American employment and the acceptance by members of this ethnic group of the current Anglo practice of wives working while their husbands further their educations.

Sheet Metal Workers, No. 67. Mexican-American representation in this local union's membership in June, 1962, was as follows: journeymen, 29 out of a total of 250; apprentices, 3 out of a total of 38.

A Large Nonunion Contractor

This firm, with headquarters in San Antonio and branches in other cities including several in foreign countries, was significant to this study for a number of reasons. It was by far the largest construction company in the city, no union had won representation for any employees, and it was by far the large company most often mentioned by Mexican-Americans interviewed as practicing no discrimination against persons of this ethnic group either in hiring or advancement.

A breakdown of all regular, full-time company personnel stationed in San Antonio by broad occupational categories, total and Mexican-American, is shown on the following page.

While pay scales were not made available, union officials agreed that the company's rates compared favorably with union scales.

Classification	Total Employees	Mexican-American Total	Mexican-American Percent
Top Executives	14	2	14.3
Administrators	18	1	5.5
Engineers and Estimators	40	8	20.0
Electronic Data Process.	14	1	7.1
Office	57	20	35.1
Superintendents	5	0	0.0
Foremen	11	0	0.0
Construction Equip. Oper.	26	9	34.6
Truck Drivers	10	3	30.0
Skilled Workers	35	18	54.3
Laborers and Helpers	54	44	81.1
Totals	284	106	37.3

Source: Company payroll records.

The two Mexican-American top executives were the vice-president and treasurer and the secretary, both of whom were members of the board of directors of the firm.

The writer interviewed the vice-president and treasurer, and he was most cooperative. He had been employed by the company as a clerk in the accounting department immediately after graduation from high school. While continuing to work full-time, he had since earned both the bachelor of arts and master of arts degrees from St. Mary's University and had qualified as a certified public accountant.

The Mexican-American in the key administrative group was field office manager. While the three

Mexican-American top executives and administrators constituted less than ten percent of the total in these positions, it was quite unusual to find any Mexican-American at these management levels in a large San Antonio firm with an Anglo chief executive.

The 20 percent participation of this ethnic group among the engineers and estimators was considered quite high in view of the high level of education required for such positions.

The 20 Mexican-American office personnel, comprising 35.1 percent of the total, included: 1 accounting supervisor, 4 accountants, 4 records supervisors, 1 bookkeeper, 2 secretaries, and 8 miscellaneous clerical workers. The high percentage in the better office positions was admittedly attributable partially to the fact that the vice-president and treasurer of the company had line authority over the office force. The executive maintained that hiring and advancement was without racial bias, explaining that the company's reputation for nondiscrimination against Mexican-Americans in the higher white collar jobs made the cream of this ethnic group available for employment by his firm.

As an example of the prevalence of discrimination in office employment in San Antonio, this officer stated that his daughter had been referred to an employer by the local employment service for a secretarial opening, and she was rejected without an interview when her name was found to be Spanish.

The high proportion of Mexican-Americans among the skilled occupations as well as in unskilled jobs was expected as consistent with the reputation of this firm for hiring persons of this racial extraction.

On the other hand, the fact that none of the 16 superintendents and foremen was Mexican-American tends to give some credibility to the assertion of some San Antonio employers that they are less likely than Anglos both to aspire to such responsible positions and to perform satisfactorily in such capacities.

Unions and Civil Rights Act of 1964

Congressman Henry B. Gonzalez of San Antonio, a strong supporter of the U.S. civil rights law passed in 1964, has maintained that Mexican-Americans will benefit materially from the fight by Negroes and their civil rights advocates. He pointed out that it was a suit in behalf of a Negro against a racially restrictive covenant in real estate which, when it was ruled on favorably by the U.S.

Supreme Court, became the basis for the invalidation of such covenants in use against Mexican-Americans in San Antonio and throughout the Southwest.

Prior to 1963, the only union affiliated with the San Antonio Building and Construction Trades Council found to have Negro members was the Hod Carriers and Common Laborers, Local No. 93, although such data were not specifically requested.

The strong support of the civil rights bill by the AFL-CIO at both the national and state levels, and especially the pressures by the international offices of the various building trades unions, has begun to show some small but definite results in the acceptance of Negroes to membership in San Antonio locals.

The San Antonio Building and Construction Trades Council, in July, 1963, adopted a resolution expressing its full support for policies of nondiscrimination and equal job opportunity for all qualified workers without regard for race.[4]

The first specific breakthrough was the Electrical Workers union's acceptance of its first Negro apprentice in August, 1963.[5] The plumbers and pipefitters local

---

[4]<u>AFL-CIO Weekly Dispatch</u>, July 12, 1963.

[5]<u>Ibid.</u>, August 16, 1963.

made a change in its collective bargaining agreement clause on referral and hiring by providing that "no person will be discriminated against because of age, race, creed, or national origin," in June, 1963.

The passage of the 1964 federal civil rights law will certainly accelerate the penetration of the labor unions by Negroes and, to a lesser extent, open the way to increased Mexican-American membership. As noted in the discussion on claims of racial discrimination in military employment, the Mexican-Americans are as vigorous as Negroes in asserting their rights, once they have a firm legal platform from which to launch their demands.

While the officials of most of the local unions participated in the strong national and state labor movement advocacy of the civil rights law, it is unlikely that the barriers of traditional clannish resistance to change, which characterizes the relatively small union locals, in San Antonio as well as in other cities, would have soon been overcome without actual passage of the civil rights law.

A situation which may well lead to expansion of both Mexican-American and Negro membership in local labor organizations has been the recent political alliance of the three groups in the organization of the Bexar County

Democratic Coalition. Under the leadership of the Political Association for Spanish-speaking Organizations (PASO), the AFL-CIO Committee on Political Education (COPE), and Negro representatives, the coalition merged the mutual liberal objectives of the three groups and was quite successful in the 1964 Democratic primary, getting nominations for five of the six men it endorsed for the State legislature, and winning nominations or large pluralities for its choices for all the major county offices.

Albert Pena, Jr., county commissioner in the Mexican-American West Side precinct, was both state chairman of the Political Association for Spanish-speaking Organizations and chairman of the Bexar County Democratic Coalition. He also writes a regular column in the San Antonio AFL-CIO newspaper, the Weekly Dispatch. Further consideration of the effects of the activities of PASO and the BCDC will be given in the chapter on Politics and Public Employment.

Summary

The San Antonio Chamber of Commerce, in its handsome brochure entitled San Antonio Plant Location Facts, quite accurately states that this city experiences far fewer work stoppages than do most cities of comparable size, and it quotes data from Analysis of Work Stoppages, 1956-1960 by the U.S. Department of Labor, part of which is shown below, as confirmation.[6]

Metropolitan Area	1960 Population	Work Stoppages No.	Work Stoppages Workers	Man Days Idle
Dallas	1,083,601	54	16,020	193,200
Fort Worth	573,215	24	7,430	48,100
Houston	1,243,158	88	39,150	1,054,200
San Antonio	687,151	10	2,260	43,750

What the Chamber of Commerce does not explicitly say is that, even among other large cities in the "right-to-work" State of Texas, the work force of San Antonio is the least organized. Neither does it point out that San Antonio's "exceptionally stable workers" and "quite tranquil relations between labor and management" has not stemmed entirely from a strong mutuality of understanding, respect, and concern.

Motivated by fear and distrust, characterized by intransigence, and buttressed by a sense of mission to protect the sacred rights of private property and individual freedom, the business and industrial leadership of

[6]San Antonio, Plant Location Facts, San Antonio Chamber of Commerce, San Antonio, 1962, p. 49.

San Antonio since the beginning of the present century has waged a successful battle against any substantial advancements of organized labor. Inspired by the zealous doctrines of the National Association of Manufacturers, the concerted campaign was first known shortly after the turn of the century as the Citizens' Alliance. Reconstituted at the close of World War I as the Open Shop Association of San Antonio, to combat the fresh inroads of unionism, the name was necessarily changed after passage of the Wagner Act to the present title of Associated Employers, Inc. Both the purpose and the aggressiveness of the organization remain essentially unchanged.

By contrast, San Antonio was in the forefront of the labor movement in the latter part of the nineteenth century, led by the socialist-oriented Germans. In the middle 1880's, the Knights of Labor were strong, had gained wide public acceptance, and were supported by the press. The San Antonio Trades Council was the first in Texas to be chartered by the American Federation of Labor, in 1895, and union workers secured significant gains during the next five years. However, most of the advancements of labor were quickly lost in the unrelenting assault for the open shop that followed.

There seems to have been little interest by unions in Mexican-American membership, except in common labor classifications, in San Antonio or Texas as a whole prior to World War II, and apparently there was no appreciable effort on the part of members of this ethnic group for union affiliation.

Mullennix, in his history of the Texas State Federation of Labor, devoted substantial sections of each chapter, covering the half century from 1903 to 1953, to the "Negro problem," yet this writer could find not a single mention of a "Mexican problem."[7]

The ever abundant supply of Mexican labor since the beginning of World War I has been a continuing major factor in the notoriously low wage level of San Antonio. Furthermore, the availability of workers of Mexican extraction to serve as strikebreakers has served as an effective deterrent to aggressive union demands. When cultural barriers, language differences, and educational deficiencies are added to the above two factors, it is not surprising that very few Mexican-Americans were accepted as members of the unions affiliated with the San Antonio Building and Construction Trades Council prior to World War II.

---

[7]Grady Lee Mullennix, _A History of the Texas State Federation of Labor_, unpublished Ph.D. dissertation, University of Texas, 1955.

During and after the war, Mexican-American memberships in the building trades locals have shown a steady though gradual increase, relative to total memberships as well as numerically, in all the affiliated unions, with the exception of the asbestos workers local, which still had no member of this ethnic group in the summer of 1963.

The main impetus to the breakthrough in Mexican-American union membership during World War II was the great shortage of construction workers on war related construction, plus the pressures brought to bear through President Roosevelt's Fair Employment Practice Committee to get better jobs and advancement for Mexican-Americans as well as Negroes and other minority groups. The generally successful experiences of San Antonio unions with Mexican-Americans, and the substantial lessening of educational and language deficiences, have contributed to continuing postwar increase in Mexican-American memberships.

An examination of apprenticeship training in the various trades in San Antonio revealed that the percentage of Mexican-American apprentices who completed their apprenticeship programs compared satisfactorily with the records of Anglo-American apprentices.

As of the summer of 1963, a few contractors were reported as preferring Mexican-Americans, a larger number gave preference to Anglo-Americans; most showed no apparent preference between the two racial groups. Some contractors would accept only those Mexican-Americans they knew, but the main problem here seemed to be that some union members still did not speak English well.

For the most part, union representatives appeared sincere in their statements that Mexican-Americans were among their most able and loyal members. On the other hand, several union officials reported that, on the whole, Mexican-Americans were more likely to accept nonunion jobs during slack times, and that they were less likely to pay the required penalty for reinstatement.

The fact that the office secretaries of several local unions, including the relatively large locals of the electricians and the plumbers and pipefitters, were Mexican-American women, was an indication of nondiscrimination by these organizations.

Doubtless, the passage of the 1964 federal civil rights law will prove a stimulant to Mexican-American as well as Negro membership in the construction trades unions. The San Antonio Building and Construction Trades Council has gone on record as concurring with national and state officers of the AFL-CIO in full support of the equal membership and employment opportunity for all races.

An important new factor which should facilitate the attainment of union memberships by Mexican-Americans and Negroes is the recent political alliance of organized labor, the Mexican-American organization, PASO, and the leadership of the Negro community, in the formation of the Bexar County Democratic Coalition, which has been generally successful since 1958 in getting its choices elected for the state legislature and for county offices.

CHAPTER VII

MANUFACTURING INDUSTRIES

Study of San Antonio's manufacturing industries is considered far more important than their 11.2 percent of the city's 1960 employment might seem to justify.

The ratio of Mexican-Americans to total employment was higher in manufacturing, 48.2 percent, than in any other broad industrial group. Persons of this ethnic extraction constituted only 33.1 percent of San Antonio's total employment in 1960.[1] When one also considers that the rate of Mexican-American unemployment was well over two and one-half times that of Anglo-Americans, the nature, scope, vitality, and employment practices of this major source of Mexican-American employment gains further significance.

The above raises additional questions. Why does this seventeenth largest city in the United States have such a puny industrialization? More specifically, what causal relationship may exist between the small manufacturing sector and Mexican-American exployment? To what

---

[1]See Table 16-B, page 66.

extent may the business leadership's relentless opposition to expansion of the local labor movement have been a factor in holding back the development of manufacturing industries?[2] What efforts are being made to build up the manufacturing sector, and what promises of success are evident?

In seeking light on these and related questions, the writer used available written sources, conferred with scores of knowledgeable San Antonians, and interviewed executives of eighteen manufacturing establishments concerning their employment practices. Contacts were also made, where possible, with unions representing the workers of organized plants.

Without exception, the writer was cordially received by the executives visited, though the amount and value of the information obtained varied. Some were gratifyingly frank and specific in answering questions and volunteered important facts and insights. Others were reluctant to reveal precise data and full information on employment practices, although assurance was always given

---

[2]Frederic Meyers, after an unpublished study of manufacturing industry unionization in Texas in 1953, estimated the proportion of eligible jobs unionized in Bexar County as 20-25%, as compared to Tarrant County (Fort Worth) 55-60% McLennan (Waco) and Harris (Houston) Counties 45-50% and Dallas County 40-45%.

that neither the name of the executive or his firm would be mentioned in connection with the material obtained.

To gain perspective in the study of the manufacturing industries in San Antonio, general data on manufacturing employment and earnings will be considered before presenting the findings on individual firms.

Table 27 provides a comparison of manufacturing employment, average weekly earnings, and average hourly earnings for San Antonio, Dallas, Houston, and Fort Worth in 1962.

Manufacturing employee earnings, as well as the number of workers, were found to be far smaller in San Antonio than in any of the other three major Texas cities, with average weekly earnings $14.46 less than the next lowest, Dallas. The disparity was especially great in earnings in durable goods industries, where the average weekly earnings in San Antonio was $25.47 less than in Dallas, and $40.48 less than in Houston.

Houston owes much of its relatively high level of earnings in durable goods to the higher pay in the manufacture of oil production and refining equipment and to the nondurable petroleum refining industry. The nearly 60 percent of employment in durable goods manufacture utilized by the aircraft industry in Fort Worth, with

TABLE 27

MANUFACTURING EMPLOYMENT AND AVERAGE EARNINGS

SELECTED TEXAS STANDARD METROPOLITAN STATISTICAL AREAS, 1962

	San Antonio	Dallas	Houston	Fort Worth
Total manufacturing:				
Number of employees	23,500	103,700	93,300	49,300
Average weekly earnings	$ 71.86	$ 86.32	$ 113.10	$ 99.48
Average hourly earnings	1.77	2.09	2.68	2.38
Nondurable goods:				
Number of employees	15,100	43,200	45,000	16,600
Average weekly earnings	$ 73.75	$ 77.16	$ 117.04	$ 88.78
Average hourly earnings	1.83	1.91	2.78	2.16
Durable goods:				
Number of employees	8,400	60,500	48,300	32,700
Average weekly earnings	$ 67.97	$ 93.44	$ 108.45	$ 105.08
Average hourly earnings	1.67	2.23	2.57	2.49

Source: U. S. Department of Labor, Bureau of Labor Statistics, Employment and Earnings Statistics for States and Areas, 1939-1962, 1963, pp. 551-554.

average weekly earnings of $122.93, explains the high level of earnings in that city. Dallas' manufacturing employment is highly diversified and comprised more than 22 percent of total employment, twice the proportion of San Antonio workers in manufacturing.

The $71.86 average weekly earnings from manufacturing employment placed San Antonio 125th among the 134 cities reported by the U.S. Bureau of Labor Statistics for 1962, and none of the nine cities with lower earnings had a population as high as 120,000 in the 1960 census.[3]

Changes in employment within the various manufacturing industries since 1940 can be seen in the data in Table 28, taken from the records of the San Antonio district office of the Texas Employment Commission.

The proportion of nonagricultural workers employed in manufacturing was actually slightly greater in 1940 than in 1962. A small decline in total manufacturing employment is recorded from 1960 to 1962.

While most industries showed small but steady gains in employment during the past quarter century, some notable exceptions are observed. The apparel industry has

---

[3]1962 Statistical Supplement, Monthly Labor Review, U.S. Department of Labor, Bureau of Labor Statistics, Washington, 1963, pp. 48-50.

TABLE 28

MANUFACTURING EMPLOYMENT, SAN ANTONIO METROPOLITAN AREA

APRIL, SELECTED YEARS, 1940-1962

	1940	1950	1953	1956	1960	1962
Total nonagricultural	94,701	155,363	186,438	184,497	204,402	208,435
Total manufacturing	11,909	17,602	19,840	21,558	23,379	22,775
Total nondurable goods	7,694	12,450	13,375	14,696	15,177	14,830
Food and kindred products	3,929	5,347	5,859	6,731	7,754	7,930
Textile mill products	53	330	327	419	485	510
Apparel and kindred prod.	1,222	3,072	3,405	3,267	2,983	2,720
Paper and allied products	99	210	234	289	419	300
Printing and publishing	1,587	2,266	2,600	2,425	2,145	2,210
Chemicals and allied prod.	338	372	433	509	419	455
Petroleum and coal prod.	364	185	190	315	282	220
Leather and leather goods	102	228	267	307	338	240
Other nondurable goods	0	440	460	434	352	245
Total durable goods	4,215	5,152	6,065	6,862	8,202	7,945
Lumber and wood products	464	439	535	416	581	620
Furniture and fixtures	438	487	553	583	800	525
Stone, clay and glass	682	1,493	1,601	1,694	1,580	1,530
Primary metals	840	117	223	217	269	290
Fabricated metals		872	985	1,158	1,623	1,650
Machinery	763	1,386	1,732	1,889	1,635	1,500
Transportation equipment	223	225	300	711	885	575
Other durable goods	805	133	136	194	829	1,245

Source: Records of San Antonio District Office, Texas Employment Commission

suffered a persistent decline from 1953 to 1962. Though the decrease was less pronounced, the same was true of employment in printing and publishing. Next to food production these two industries have been the mainstays of nondurable manufacturing in San Antonio. Since 1953, employment also weakened in two major durables, machinery and stone, clay and glass. Employment in the metals industries was at a virtual standstill during that decade.

In the face of the foregoing, one can but admire the ingenious phraseology of the Chamber of Commerce writer who pointed out quite truthfully that San Antonio "is the leading manufacturing center of Southwest Texas." For his purpose, he had no reason to add that there is no city with one-tenth the population of metropolitan San Antonio south of Austin and west of Corpus Christi. One may question, however, whether the poetic license of the sales pitch may not be strained when he concludes that "San Antonio industry is extremely diversified."[4]

The Federal Reserve Bank of Dallas not only took a more realistic view in referring to "San Antonio's relatively narrow industrial base," but added that "as a result, the labor force is not, as a general rule, broadly skilled."[5]

---

[4]*San Antonio, Plant Location Facts*, p. 51.

[5]"San Antonio," *op. cit.*, p. 6.

Since the great majority of manufacturing employment is in nondurable industries, discussion of employment practices of individual firms will first be presented on establishments in this category.

Nondurable Goods Manufacturing

Food and Kindred Products

This segment of nondurable goods manufacturing provides more than one-third of all manufacturing employment. Firms studied included two bakeries, two breweries, a flour mill, a meat packing company, a Mexican foods manufacturer, and a candy manufacturer. Their combined employments constituted approximately one-third of all persons engaged in manufacture of food and kindred products in San Antonio.

1. Two Bakeries

The two bakeries visited, designated as Bakery A and Bakery B, had several things in common. Both were established during the 1930's, produced pastries exclusively, had a large proportion of Mexican-Americans on their payrolls, and were nonunion. So far as the writer was able to determine, none of the San Antonio bakeries were organized in the summer of 1963.

Bakery "A": This owner-operated business was established in 1938, and had been in continuous operation under the present head of the firm. About 95 percent of production was pastries for a large air force base, with the remainder made up of cakes prepared for other bakeries.

The total payroll consisted of 50 plant workers and 10 administrative and clerical personnel. Plant employment included 45 Mexican-Americans, 3 Negroes, and 2 Anglos. About 40 percent of the plant workers were women--all of Mexican extraction. All office personnel were Anglo. The general superintendent of the plant was a Mexican-American who had been with the company since its inception; the owner volunteered the information that his salary was "over $150.00 a week and worth every cent of it."

All plant workers began as helpers and were trained for one or more advanced jobs. Starting rate was the Fair Labor Standards Act minimum, and merit promotions were made as openings occurred.

The owner combined excellent labor relations with paternalism in its better connotation. He kept in close contact with his employees, and morale was obviously high. He maintained that he practiced no racial distinctions, either in favor of or against Mexican-Americans; more and better workers simply were available from this ethnic group.

In conversations with the owner and the general superintendent, it was revealed that the former had on several occasions employed from Mexico relatives of his employees and provided an average of $150.00 advance to each for the costs necessary for them to enter the country and come to San Antonio. At the time of the interview, the company had in its employ three Mexican-Americans paroled from prison and hired on the recommendation of parole officers. Some employees had been helped in financing the purchase of homes away from the West Side.

<u>Bakery "B"</u>: Part of a regional chain, this plant was established in 1935, and the manager had been with the company since 1953. The plant's pastries were sold exclusively through distributers.

Of the approximately 250 employees, all but fifteen administrative and office personnel were in production. Employees were hired at the legal minimum, and raises were given "strictly on merit." Applicants usually were referrals from the Texas Employment Commission, which administered dexterity tests before making referrals.

From 40% to 45% of plant workers were Mexican-Americans, two-thirds of which were men. Approximately one-third of the supervisors, including a foreman and an assistant foreman, were of Mexican extraction. Administrative and office workers were all Anglos.

Much of the time of the interview was taken up with a harangue by the manager on the racial limitations of Mexican-Americans. He asserted that the great majority of these people available for work in San Antonio were predominantly of "Yaqui" Indian blood. A Yaqui, he added, can handle well a job that is highly repetitive and subject to simple instructions; on the other hand, he is lacking in reasoning power, and therefore cannot serve as a supervisor or even as a truck driver.

The key to the worker's potential, the story continued, is the precise proportions of Yaqui and Spanish or other Anglo strains--if more than one-third Anglo, he is a high type "Spanish" person and can be trained for responsible, decision-making work; if more than two-thirds Yaqui, he can be trusted only with the most routine jobs, and then he is likely to quit to join the migrant agricultural laborers in the northern beet fields. As an illustration of the limitations of such persons, he stated that one man who was two-thirds Yaqui had been with the company for 33 years and had only reached machine operator status.

The manager actually seemed to believe all this genetic hogwash. The temptation was great to break in to inquire how long it would take for a person to become just two-thirds Yaqui under the usual genetic relationship fractions of halves, quarters, and eighths, how he derived his magic formula, and how racial intermixtures could be finely measured.

The manager stated that the proportion of Mexican-American employees and their relative positions within the job structure had not appreciably changed during the past decade, and the writer considered it doubtful that any material improvement in Mexican-American status would be forthcoming so long as management continues to substitute ethnic mythology for responsible evaluation and development of persons as individuals.

2. Two Breweries

It was inevitable that with the coming of the Germans to San Antonio, the establishment of breweries was sure to follow. The two prosperous plants still in operation were founded in the 1880's, although one closed down during prohibition and did not come back into operation until 1940. The production departments of both had long been organized by the Brewery Workers, Local No. 110, and their small crews of maintenance craftsmen were represented by their respective machinist and building trades unions.

Prior to the 1930's, brewery employment was primarily for Germans, and no Mexican-American had ever been hired in San Antonio. Apparently some applications for jobs began then to be made by persons of this ethnic extraction, for a sign was installed at the plant office of the one brewery then in operation, advising that Mexicans need not apply for employment. This enraged the leadership of the League of United Latin American Citizens (LULAC), and the president of the brewery was warned that unless the sign was removed and the company began employing Mexican-Americans, this ethnic group would be encouraged by LULAC to boycott the company's beer. Since about half of the firm's local beer sales were to Mexican-Americans, the brewery head had the offending sign removed and employed several Mexican-American workers.

With the exception of a reported similar action involving exclusion of employment by a bakery, this was the only occasion in which concerted economic pressure had been effectively applied by this ethnic group.

Employment and production work scales for the two firms, designated as Brewery "A" and Brewery "B," are shown in Table 29.

Brewery "A": The reported Mexican-American employed as a plant supervisor was a machinist working foreman. The personnel director explained that the reason no auto mechanics were Mexican-American was due to the bias of a former German foreman in that department. He maintains that there is absolutely no remaining ethnic discrimination in any department.

The company is always on the lookout for educated, bilingual Mexican-Americans qualified for marketing jobs. Some of the otherwise good prospects have neglected their Spanish.

Most plant workers had to be trained on the job, since skilled men rarely applied. High school graduates were sought for plant work, but this requirement was not rigidly adhered to.

The personnel director stated that it was his observation that Mexican-American city driver-salesmen were prone not to hustle for sales after they had earned $90.00 in a week. Otherwise, he found nothing to distinguish the work of this ethnic group.

TABLE 29

BREWERY EMPLOYMENT AND WAGE SCALES
San Antonio, Texas, 1962

	Employees		Weekly Wage Scale
	Total	Mex.-Amer.	
	BREWERY "A"		
Admin. & Supervisory			
Administrative	30	0	
Accounting, clerical	30	0	
Supervisor, clerical	8	0	
Supervisor, plant	35	1	
Driver-Salesmen			
City	43	8	Commission
Long haul	13	0	Commission
Production			
Brew house	60	2	\$117.22 - \$121.52
Bottle shop	262	17	115.22
Utility	10	5	98.57
Firemen	6	1	111.02
Service Sta. Attend.	1	1	96.72
Maintenance (Incl. Helpers)			
Machinists	34	2	Union Scale
Auto mechanics	11	0	"
Electricians	4	2	"
Painters	4	3	"
Totals	551	42	
	BREWERY "B"		
Admin., cler'l, superv'ry	141	7	
Driver-Salesmen			
City	72	5	Commission
Long haul	8	0	Commission
Production			
Brew house	39	2	\$117.22 - \$121.52
Bottle shop	225	4	115.22
Checking	23	1	not reported
Util., porter, yard	21	12	63.40 - 96.72
Maint. (Incl. helpers)	62	5	Union scale
Totals	591	38	

Sources: Driver-salesmen and production workers, Brewery Workers Union seniority roster; other employees, company records.

A few Negroes were employed, including one city driver-salesman.

<u>Brewery "B"</u>: Of the seven persons on the salaried administrative and supervisory payroll, four were territory salesmen in other parts of the state, one was a city driver-salesman, and two worked in the laboratory in quality control.

Almost all new plant workers had been hired at the plant and trained, since the union rarely had qualified skilled referrals.

The personnel director volunteered the statement that the company also had Negroes in every department.

<u>General</u>: Each of the breweries had a contract with a Mexican-American distributor for West Side sales.

Brewery employment was hard hit by automation during the past decade, and very little hiring had been done in recent years. Of the 262 workers in the bottle shop in Brewery "A," 189 (including 12 Mexican-Americans) had ten or more years seniority, and only 24 had been with the company less than five years.

There had been virtually no plant hiring at Brewery "B" during the previous several years; seniority years of persons with least seniority, by departments, were: driver-sales and checking, 1954; brew house, 1957; and bottle shop, 1958.

A representative of the Brewery Workers Union expressed the opinion that both breweries preferred Anglos when they were available, and he felt that, in general, the preference was justified, since Mexican-Americans had a tendency to be satisfied with lower incomes and would not work as hard as Anglos. It was his further opinion that three-fourths of the Mexican-Americans employed at Brewery "A" were not good workers, and that actually Negroes were usually more satisfactory.

The Brewery Workers official asserted many Mexican-Americans had a hostile attitude, and they were very sensitive about discrimination against them but demanded discrimination in their favor. The union was pressured to follow strict seniority when an opening for a driver-salesman occurred in a predominantly Anglo area, but Mexican-Americans demanded, and were likely to get, a Mexican-American driver-salesman when an opening occurred on the West Side, even when an Anglo was next in line for the job.

One can only guess how much the union representative's unfavorable opinion of Mexican-Americans as a group may have been colored by the disagreeable circumstances surrounding a few driver-salesman assignments.

Mexican-American employment in the brewery industry made very little progress during the past twenty-five years. Most of them were found in the lower pay and status jobs of utility workers, porters, and mechanic's helpers, although a few were employed as city driver-salesmen and skilled craftsmen in maintenance. Among driver-salesmen, at least, company and union officials felt that Mexican-Americans were inclined to be satisfied with smaller incomes and did not work as hard as Anglos. One got the impression that there would be even fewer Mexican-Americans in this industry in San Antonio were it not for fear of a recurrence of economic sanctions.

Technological advancements in the industry had been such that very few new workers had been hired in the past decade, and it was unlikely that this industry would provide any significant further employment for Mexican-Americans or anyone else in the foreseeable future.

3. A Flour Mill

Founded in 1851 by one of the early German immigrants, this was the oldest manufacturing establishment still in operation in San Antonio. Of 160 total employees in June, 1962, 100 plant workers, including 43 Mexican-Americans, were covered by a bargaining agreement with the Brewery Workers, Local No. 110. The information below was secured from a representative of the brewery workers union. Unfortunately, the writer was unable to contact the company management for further information.

Pay scales ranged from $1.26 per hour for unskilled laborers to $2.08 per hour for millwrights. Average hourly rate was approximately $1.60.

The relatively larger number of Mexican-Americans employed at the flour mill relative to brewery employment was ascribed by the union representative to the arduous, dusty nature of most of the jobs and the low pay scale, rather than to a company policy of nondiscrimination. Actually, he reported, the flour mill was probably more discriminatory than the breweries; capable applicants for most of the flour mill jobs were usually virtually all Mexican-American. The union contract provided for advancements solely on seniority where the person in line for an opening was qualified. The union official reported that previously the Mexican-Americans had claimed gross discrimination in job advancement.

One of the other three flour milling companies in San Antonio was also represented by the brewery workers union; the other two had no union agreement. All were relatively small mills.

4. A Meat Packing Company

This old, family-owned, packing company was the largest firm in this significant segment of foods manufacture in San Antonio; seven other such firms had 100 or more employees in 1962.[6]

The company had no union agreement; in fact, none of the workers in San Antonio packing houses were represented by unions affiliated with the AFL-CIO, according to officials of that organization.

The president of the firm advised that his personnel director had resigned and had not yet been replaced, and for that reason more specific information than that given below was not available.

This packing house had, in July, 1962, between 450 and 475 employees, about three times the number of workers employed in 1940. Of this total, approximately 400 were in plant jobs.

---

[6]Directory of Texas Manufacturers, 1962, Bureau of Business Research, University of Texas, Austin, 1963, pp. 304-317.

Mexican-Americans comprised 80 to 85 percent of plant employment, with five serving in supervisory capacities. The proportion of Mexican-Americans, production and supervisory, had remained substantially unchanged since 1950.

The company executive maintained that there was no discrimination in regards to Mexican-American employment in his firm and little in the meat packing industry in San Antonio. He pointed out that the large majority of the plants were located in the West Side. Furthermore, since most of the jobs were hard, repetitive, and generally unattractive, it would be foolhardy not to utilize fully this ethnic group which constituted the major source of supply.

While workers were required to be able to speak English, there were no educational requirements for employment. Most employees were hired as unskilled workers and trained to fill skilled openings, since few skilled applicants were available. While substantial technological advancement was noted during the past two decades, the company's employment practices had not been materially changed.

No breakdown of plant employment nor wage scales could be obtained; however, the local office of the Texas

Employment Commission provided the writer the following local wage information on two common meat packing job classifications:

Job Classification	Hourly Wage Minimum	Maximum	Typical
Beef Boner	$1.25	$2.00	$1.72
Butcher	1.65	2.12	1.79

5. Mexican Foods Manufacturer

This firm, founded in 1896, manufactured canned Mexican foods, barbecue and hot dog sauces, and sandwich spreads, in addition to chili powder. Employment information below was received in July, 1963, from the general manager of the plant, an Anglo-American.

The total payroll of 77 persons included 12 administrative and office personnel and 65 plant workers. Sixty-one plant workers, including the assistant superintendent, the kitchen foreman, and the chief clerk, were Mexican-Americans. The remaining four plant employees were Anglo--a quality control man, the maintenance foreman, a maintenance mechanic, and a night cleanup man. Administrative, sales, and office personnel were all Anglo.

A Mexican-American with the proper technical qualifications had been tried out on the quality control job, but he had been unable to adjust psychologically to the work. Another Mexican-American had been tried out as maintenance foreman, but he had proved unreliable. The company preferred Mexican-Americans, since they could be hired for lower wages, and they were not so likely to quit to accept other employment.

Plant workers were represented by the Amalgamated Meat Cutters and Butcher Workmen, Local No. 171. The minimum scale was $1.34 per hour. All except four workers, who were still on probation, belonged to the union.

There was no educational requirement for plant employment; workers were not even required to be able to speak English. Most workers had to be trained for specific jobs, because rarely had skilled workers been found available. While the labor agreement provided for advancement on the basis of seniority, the union permitted considerable leeway to management in judging qualifications for upgrading.

The general manager came originally from East Texas. He preferred Negro workers to Mexican-Americans because "you can tell more what they are thinking." On the other hand, it was his experience that Mexican-Americans and Negroes tended not to get along well, and since available workers were predominantly Mexican-American, these were employed. Anglos were found to be lazy and too much concerned about promotions and higher wages. Apparently the nature of the foods prepared was not a factor in employment.

The general superintendent apparently saw no connection between his inability to understand the Mexican-Americans and the failure of the quality control man and the maintenance foreman to handle their new assignments satisfactorily.

6. A Candy Manufacturer

The only major candy manufacturer in San Antonio in 1963, this establishment was founded in 1899, purchased by the present family in 1914, and it has since been operated as a partnership. Information recorded was received in an interview with the president of the firm, part of which was during a tour of the plant.

The original owner of the plant had employed only Anglos; however, the present management preferred Mexican-Americans because "they are more loyal--won't talk to union representatives," and because they were considered generally more adapted to the rapid, repetitive movements required of most of the jobs of the factory.

The payroll was made up of approximately 200 plant workers (varying from 180 to 220 maximum) and 20 administrative, sales, and office personnel. While everyone in the latter group was Anglo, all except six plant employees were Mexican-American. These six were all long-time employees, three of whom were supervisors. The remaining 10 supervisors were Mexican-American. About two-thirds of the plant workers were women, and the floorlady in charge of their work was Mexican-American.

All new employees started as beginners. For several years, the owners had followed the practice of hiring only persons given dexterity tests and referred by the local office of the Texas Employment Commission; they found such referrals on the whole more satisfactory than persons hired from among plant gate applicants in prior years.

New employees were required to have a health card, an eighth grade education, and be able to speak English fairly well.

The greater part of the company's employees were brought under the coverage of the Fair Labor Standards Act by the 1961 amendments. As a result, a substantial revision of the production setup was initiated. With the exception of one item, the firm had discontinued the production of the high labor cost handmade candies in interstate commerce.

Some items were produced only for intrastate sale. On production of these items, the minimum scale was $1.00 per hour, whereas payment on interstate production would rise to $1.25 per hour. The company used the workers interchangeably on intrastate and interstate production, paying them the applicable rate, with reportedly no protest from the employees.

The president stated that the management was working toward exclusively interstate production and had spent $145,000 on new labor-saving machines in the year 1962. In spite of increased mechanization, the business had continued to expand sufficiently to increase employment the past several years.

The writer had heard frequent references to the unusual dexterity of the Mexican-American women and had witnessed some evidences of their skills in various occupations, but the performance of the women observed in the wrapping and packaging of candies was little short of fantastic. Their amazing speed and precision of hand and finger movements, and their ability to keep up the fast pace tirelessly for hours, seemingly oblivious to the monotony of the repetition, gave their work an appearance of magic.

The head of the firm stated that Mexican-Americans are sensitive people and appreciative of personal respect and kindnesses. That the company had profited by this understanding was exemplified by the unusually high morale that was evidenced by the workers in the plant.

Tobacco--A Cigar Manufacturer

When the sole remaining cigar factory in San Antonio was established in 1898, there were 18 small cigar companies in the city, according to the present head of the company and grandson of the founder of the firm. As the people's smoking habits changed from cigars to cigarettes, the other factories began to fold, and in August, 1963, there had been only the one cigar manufacturer for several decades.

Shapiro, in referring to this company, as of the time of the first of two strikes by its workers in the middle 1930's, stated that "it rivaled the pecan shellers for the dubious distinction of being the least sanitary and of paying the lowest wages of any industry in the city."[7] Then, as thirty years later, the employees were virtually all Mexican-Americans, and predominantly women.

In 1933, some 350 cigar rollers, strippers, and scrappers formed a union and struck for union regognition,

[7]Shapiro, op. cit., p. 310.

better pay and improved working conditions. After three weeks, the mayor interceded and settled the controversy, with the employer agreeing to take back the strikers, and to adopt the NRA cigar industry code, providing a guaranteed minimum pay of $9.00 for a 40-hour week. The company refused to recognize the union and would not rehire 100 of the women, including the strike leader, because they allegedly could not meet the daily quota of 400 good cigars a day. The National Labor Relations Board upheld the Regional Labor Board's order to reinstate the strikers.

When the workers struck again in the spring of 1935, the company continued to operate, with the aid of the police, and the owner refused to talk either with the union leaders or to the U.S. Commissioner of Conciliation, who went to San Antonio to mediate the dispute. The strike was completely lost.[8]

The hard-fought strikes of the cigar workers lends support to Paul S. Taylor's contention in 1931 that "the docility of Mexican laborers, frequently extolled by employers who seem to have believed them racially strike-proof, is not to be taken literally."[9] It is interesting

---

[8] Ibid., pp. 311-313.

[9] Paul S. Taylor, "Mexicans North of the Rio Grande," Survey Graphic, Vol. XIX, No. 2, May 1931, pp. 201-202.

to note that in each of the three industries in which union memberships and strike participation in San Antonio have been predominantly Mexican-American--cigar manufacturing, pecan shelling, and garment making--the great majority of workers and strikers have been women.

The head of the cigar company in 1963, who had just taken over the presidency the previous year, considered his father's militant victory in the 1935 strike a significant factor in San Antonio's remaining a relatively nonunion town.

In 1963, a combination of new management and labor law revision were bringing about notable changes in the operation of the business.

Until that time, the firm had restricted its sales to Texas and had remained outside the purview of the Fair Labor Standards Act. However, early in 1963, it was adjudged as covered under the 1961 amendments of the law. Thus, the company was required to raise its minimum wage, to an initial $1.00 per hour and eventually to $1.25.

The company president had reluctantly dismissed an undisclosed number of the least productive workers, some of whom had been with the company many years. Then it was found to be less costly to buy tobacco already stripped, so stripping was discontinued, causing further reduction in employment. Although the cigar making was still mostly by hand, the factory was being converted to machines on a gradual basis.

Construction had been nearly completed on a new air-conditioned, one-story factory building to replace the antiquated, smelly old factory structure. The new plant was expected to be ready within two months, after which machine manufacturing would be accelerated.

In the past, the company relied heavily on the use of migrant farm workers during the winter off-season months, thus providing a complementary employment for such workers. Henceforth, no more "hand-made" workers would be trained, a relatively stable work force would be maintained, and workers would be told that those who went to the beet fields and other migrant jobs would not be rehired.

While it may well be argued that the economic loss and hardships from displacement of the less productive employees more than offset the benefits resulting from the inclusion of the workers of this factory in the coverage of the FLSA, the writer is convinced that for San Antonio Mexican-Americans in general as well as for the employees of this extraction retained by this company, the results will prove a milestone in the upgrading of the economic and social status of this ethnic group, so necessary to their eventual assimilation. The company president indicated that, although he regretted the necessity of releasing some of the older employees, he was for the first time since his long association with the family factory unashamed of the incomes of the production workers of the plant.

Of the total of approximately 200 on the payroll of the company in August, 1963, there were 25 administrative, office, supervisory, and sales personnel, and the remainder were plant workers.

All of the factory workers were Mexican-Americans, including the foreman, who had been with the company for 45 years. All cigar makers were women. The only men were the supervisors and the haulers.

About half of the office force was Mexican-American, and the remainder were Anglos. There was one Anglo mechanic. With the exception of one Negro, the salesmen were all Anglos. The president pointed out that, in sharp contrast to manufacturing employment, very few Mexican-Americans smoked cigars.

Apparel Industries

The apparel industries and the cigar industry had two important common characteristics--their employees were principally Mexican-American women, and aggressive efforts to unionize the industries were carried out during the depression of the 1930's. The union met utter defeat in the cigar industry; but organizing work of the International Ladies Garment Workers Union met with marked success.

In the summer of 1937, the ILGWU Local No. 180 won a union shop agreement and wage increase from the Shirlee Frocks Company after a three-month strike. The Texas Infant Dress Company signed a similar contract the following spring after a strike by the ILGWU membership and dissolution by the National Labor Relations Board of a company union organized to combat the strike.

Three other companies, including the largest in the infants' and children's wear industry, Juvenile Manufacturing Company, signed virtually identical union shop contracts. A separate local, No. 347, was established for Juvenile employees.

Shapiro, writing in 1952, made the following comment relative to the place of organized labor in the garment industry:

> Locals 180 and 347 have thrived and appear to be a permanent addition to the union movement of the city. Most of the garment manufacturers have come to accept the ILGWU as an inevitable factor

in their operations and since 1938, there has been no apparent open-shop sentiment among them.[10]

As with many confident predictions, this one was short-lived. Culminating a series of setbacks in the late 1950's, the union lost a strike against Tex-Son, Incorporated, called on February 24, 1959, after the company had refused to agree not to contract out work to nonunion plants. After nearly four years of dispute, and after payment by the union of half a million dollars in strike benefits, the ILGWU finally withdrew its financial support to the strikers in October, 1962.[11] Although some of the women continued to picket until the following February, the once flourishing ILGWU had ceased to exist as a factor in San Antonio industry.

Meanwhile, the union had made its final organizational drive and lost. After a determined campaign for the support of the workers at the Bernard Altman International Corporation plant, the ILGWU gained NLRB approval for an election on September 28, 1962.

The company, represented by Theo Weiss, who had earned quite a reputation for leading successful fights

---

[10]Shapiro, op. cit., p. 327.

[11]AFL-CIO Weekly Dispatch, October 19, 1962.

by garment companies and other Associated Employers members against various unions, maneuvered adroitly in garnering votes and won the election. The vote was 185 for the union, 208 votes against, and 39 challenged ballots were impounded and not counted.[12]

Ironically, the Bernard Altman plant was closed down on orders from the company's New York home office on January 4, 1963, without any prior notice to their employees nor any provision for them. San Antonio had lost its second largest apparel plant, with approximately 450 workers thrown out of their jobs. While financial problems were presumed to have caused the shutdown, no explanation was given the workers. Whether the union could have helped the situation for the workers is, of course, a moot question.

Two questions naturally arise. Why was the ILGWU so successful in its organizational efforts in the 1930's, in contrast to the general frustration of other organized labor activities in this period? Further, what caused the precipitous decline of union representation in the garment industry, beginning in the latter part of the 1950's?[13]

---

[12]*Ibid.*, October 5, 1962.

[13]Discussion of the rise and fall of the ILGWU in San Antonio is based largely on information obtained

The success of the ILGWU for more than 20 years was due primarily to the local union policy of "live and let live" maximization of the possible, involving a genuine effort to help the companies to increase productivity and thereby offset the increased labor costs of employee benefits gained under union representation. The ILGWU made separate agreements for hand embroidery workers at piece rates less than those established for machine operators, in order that an orderly transition from hand to machine work could be accomplished, and so that some of this hand work could continue to be produced. The union cooperated with managements in the implementation of technological improvements.

A second, though lesser, factor was the Wagner Act. When legally bound to bargain in good faith with representatives of their workers' choosing, the employers who resisted organization found it less easy to maintain, even with police assistance, the popular fiction that a labor dispute was merely the violent outburst of a disgruntled and radical minority. The removal of the company union as a counter weapon to national union representation

---

from plant executives and from Miss Rebecca Taylor, business representative for the union in San Antonio from 1935 to 1958 and afterwards personnel manager for Tex-Son, Inc.

proved significant in early organizational campaigns. Probably the broad psychological effects of this legislation in bringing a general reassessment of the power relationships between management and labor, though not subject to accurate measurement, were as important as the more specific provisions of the act.

It was a combination of changing union and legal patterns which were also influential in bringing about the demise of organized labor in the garment industry in San Antonio. Again, it was union policy and practices which consitituted the more important factors, but legislative actions were the first to make their effects felt.

The initial impact of the Fair Labor Standards Act was cushioned by the improvements in plant efficiency and wage scales already induced by organization of the local firms in the garment industry. However, as the minimum wage of the FLSA was increased, two outgrowths inimical to the continued power of the ILGWU began to develop. First, and foremost, the new legal minimum wage levels became substantially the same as those gained through the union, and increasing numbers of workers began to feel that union membership no longer provided clearcut advantages. Secondly, encouraged by their friends in the Associated Employers, some garment executives tended to view extended federal control of wages and hours and the federal support for organized labor as components of the same bitter pill, with consequent strains on union-management relations.

The passage of the Taft-Hartley Act and the Texas "Right-to-Work" law in the same year brought about not only a sharp reversal of the psychological change in the labor-management power struggle resulting from the Wagner Act; the outlawing of the union shop constituted a major blow to the ILGWU in San Antonio.[14]

The ILGWU confidence of union shop control of employees' representation was no longer assured, and the workers were constantly reminded by antiunion forces that their jobs no longer were dependent on union membership, with the propaganda couched in such a way as to categorize the law as an emancipation proclamation.

But the cumulative effects of the labor laws were only secondary factors that augmented and accelerated the fundamental problem, a basic labor-management schism induced by a significant change in ILGWU policy. The

---

[14]The writer is in general accord with Meyers' oft-repeated conclusion in his report on the study of the effects of the Texas law that "the Right-to-Work statute, taken by itself and apart from the whole body of state labor legislation, has had a minimal direct effect." (Frederic Meyers, Right to Work in Practice, The Fund for

national headquarters, under new leadership, determined to standardize labor agreements throughout the country. The San Antonio representative of the ILGWU, asserting that the local firms would not and probably could not meet the demands of the proposed standardized contract, refused to go along with the new policy and was forced to resign. Preferring to stay in San Antonio, she accepted the position of personnel manager for Tex-Son, Incorporated, the company against which the local union was to hold its protracted final strike before expiring.

1. A Children's Garments Manufacturer

This second largest manufacturer of children's wear in San Antonio was incorporated in 1935 under the

---

the Republic, New York, 1959, pp. 4, 21, 40.) However, San Antonio's labor environment, and particularly that of its garment industry, was exceptional. Meyers recognized that the "statute carries some weight in developing a social atmosphere, a general attitude against unions in rural areas as well as in the less well-organized cities." (p. 22) He further stated, "the only areas where the law might be a crucial element are those in which there are enough union members who could win a union shop if they were allowed and thus bring a significant minority into the union. But this kind of balance of forces potentially affects only about 6 percent of the eligible employees of the state." (p. 40) By contrast, the union shop was the established pattern in the garment industry in San Antonio at time of the passage of the Texas law.

present, family controlled management. The company produced boys' and girls' western garments and sportswear.

Table 30 presents a distribution of plant employment by sex and ethnic extraction, plus wage range in each of the four plant departments. Actual earnings of the production workers were on a piecework basis, the general practice in San Antonio's garment industry. Data were taken from the company's payroll records.

TABLE 30

DEPARTMENTAL DISTRIBUTION OF EMPLOYMENT BY SEX AND ETHNIC GROUP, A SAN ANTONIO CHILDREN'S GARMENTS MANUFACTURER, AUGUST 1, 1963

Department	Total	Clerical	Cutting	Factory	Shipping
Total Employees	219	15	22	166	16
Male	27	4	9	6	8
Female	192	11	13	160	8
Anglo-American	37	5	6	10	16
Mexican-American	178	10	15	153	0
Negro	4	0	1	3	0
Hourly wage range		$1.35 1.65	$1.25 1.95	$1.15 2.20	$1.20 1.60

Plant employment is seen to have been 81% Mexican-American and 90% female. In the large factory department, Mexican-Americans made up 92% of all employment. In the smaller clerical and cutting room departments, this ethnic group comprised two-thirds of the workers.

The only reason for the shipping department workers being exclusively Anglo was that this was a continuation of a long established practice, presumably through preference by the department head and the other workers in the department. In contrast to the commonly found wage patterns of ethnic and sex distinctions, the wholly Anglo and half male shipping department was found to have the lowest pay schedule.

The head of each of the four departments was an Anglo; however, the immediate supervisor in the cutting room was a Mexican-American, and five of the nine immediate supervisors in the factory were of this ethnic extraction.

The following information was derived from conversations with the president of the company and with the personnel manager.

From the beginning of the plant operation, Mexican-Americans have comprised the bulk of employment, particularly in the main factory department.

Mexican-American women were found characteristically to have the dexterity and temperament for being adept at both hand and machine needlework. Their ability to work well on highly repetitive jobs was attributed to their Indian ancestry. Their particular proficiency in the skills of garment making was attributed to the centuries-old practice of the Catholic nuns of teaching the Mexican and Indian women to sew, and the emphasis on excellence in needlework was handed down from mothers to daughters. This factor was considered the only distinctive characteristic of Mexican-Americans in the industry.

While Polish and German women were reported to be found more often in plants engaged in the manufacture of women's apparel, Mexican-Americans had always been San Antonio's dominant ethnic group in all firms in the needle trades.

A marked improvement in education and language proficiency had been noted over the prior quarter-century. The Mexican-American women were becoming less dominated by their husbands, were becoming more fully assimilated, and were much more interested in the education of their children. On the other hand, while the ability to speak and read English was considered desirable, it was not required for employment.

The writer was informed that no clothing plants in San Antonio required U.S. citizenship as a condition of employment.

This plant, together with the other San Antonio garment factories, was admittedly very inefficient prior to passage of the Fair Labor Standards Act. In the early 1940's, the company became concerned over the need for scientific management and had since maintained a continuing study of measures for increased efficiency, including the employment of a time-study engineer.

The impact of the minimum wage provisions of the FLSA was felt most when the rate was raised from 35 cents to 45 cents per hour. Since that time, management had been able to increase productivity sufficiently to offset the increases in minimum wage scales.

2. A Work Clothing Manufacturer

This old family enterprise, founded in 1897 and still operated as a partnership, was at the time of this study the largest apparel manufacturing concern still operating in San Antonio. The present head of the firm had been with the company for thirty-eight years.

While precise employment data were not made available, the company president provided the following estimates, which he asserted were quite accurate approximations.

Of the total of about 700 employees in July, 1963, 85 percent were women. Approximately 70 percent of both men and women plant workers were Mexican-American.

All of the 15 administrative and office personnel were Anglo. Six of a total of 30 outside sales persons were Mexican-Americans, as were 7 of 27 plant supervisors.

From 1950 to 1963, total employment had increased about 15 percent. The proportion of Mexican-Americans had remained about the same, with probably a slight increase in the proportion of this ethnic group.

Considerable improvement in the educational level of Mexican-Americans had been noted in the previous two decades, and persons of this extraction were used in all plant occupations. The employer insisted that there was absolutely no ethnic distinction in either employment or advancement.

He complained that 30 percent of the Anglos and Mexican-Americans in San Antonio were equally lazy, satisfied with minimum incomes, and more interested in retirement pay than in work. Absenteeism, with no ethnic differences observed, constituted a major problem. It was his belief that the productivity of workers in the clothing industry in North Carolina and South Carolina was higher than in San Antonio.

All production job earnings were on a piece work basis, with minimum standards set to be equivalent to the FLSA minimum hourly rate. The president stated that mechanization of the plant had already gone as far as possible, and that the forthcoming increase in minimum wage to $1.25 per hour in September, 1963, would have to be met by an increase in the prices of the garments produced. During the interview, he volunteered this information to the writer and also to a garment executive in North Carolina in a telephone conversation. The latter indicated that his firm would try to absorb half of the increase in labor costs.

Contrary to the reported experience by the children's wear plant president, the head of this firm found the Texas Employment Commission testing and referrals useless. The vocational educational programs in the public schools were also considered of little if any value. The firm hired primarily from gate applicants and newspaper advertisements, and applicants were tested on the plant machines. He estimated that the company was spending $100,000 per year on employee training.

While apparel manufacturing employment in San Antonio declined 20 percent, from 3,405 to 2,720, in the period from 1953 to 1962, primarily from the closing of plants with headquarters in other cities, Dallas continued to strengthen its position as the leading Texas garment producer. From 1950 to 1960, Dallas' employment in these industries had increased from 6,953 to 10,062, a growth of 45 percent.[15]

While the capable but poorly supported professional staff of the San Antonio Chamber of Commerce was continuing its search for a company to take over the closed Bernard Altman plant, the local press reported a meeting of the chamber's president and industrial development committee chairman with executives of six Dallas clothing manufacturing concerns, who were in San Antonio to promote the sale of their products at a leading department store.[16]

The chamber of commerce representatives sought to sell the Dallas executives, whose companies had recently established branch plants in several East Texas cities, on San Antonio as a site for expansion of their factories. While the visitors naturally promised to consider the request, no tangible progress was observed. The sales pitch of the chamber's president, a telephone executive, and its chairman of industrial development, the scion of an old

---

[15]U.S. Census of Population, 1950: Vol. II, Characteristics of the Population, Part 43, Texas, p. 105; U.S. Census of Population, 1960: Texas, General Social and Economic Characteristics, p. 403.

[16]*San Antonio Express*, July 28, 1963.

banking family, appears to have been ineffective. One can but wonder why no industrialist was brought to the meeting.

An indication of the Dallas apparel men's opinion of San Antonio's industrial promotion was seen in the gently chiding remark of the vice-president of one of the firms represented: "You should publicize the training of your people. You should tell everyone that they are or can become quickly skilled with the needles."

Printing and Publishing

Throughout the twentieth century, the printing and publishing industry had been near the top in providing manufacturing employment in San Antonio. In 1940, its employment was second only to the general group of manufacturers of food and kindred products. However, printing and publishing employment reached a peak of 2,600 in 1953 and then declined to 2,145 in 1960 before showing a slight increase to 2,210 in 1962.

The printing trades have had the distinction of having the oldest active labor organization in San Antonio, Typographical Union No. 172, established in 1875. With the exception of the city's newspapers, however, the industry had been predominantly open shop since the early 1920's, when thirteen printing plants, including three of the leaders in the industry, became employer members of the open shop movement in the city.[17]

The information below was obtained through personal interviews with a representative of the typographical union and with an officer of one of the leading non-union printing companies.

1. Typographical Union No. 172

Mexican-Americans comprised 69 of the total of 278 journeymen members, a 25 percent representation, in July, 1963, as shown below:

Employers	Total	Mexican-American
Journeymen:		
San Antonio *Express & News*	103	26
San Antonio *Light*	104	18
Other Employers	71	25
Apprentices	23	6

It was noted that the ratio of Mexican-American apprentices to the total number of apprentices was almost

[17]Shapiro, *op. cit.*, p. 305.

exactly that of the journeymen. A Mexican-American was composing room foreman for one of the newspapers.

The union representative stated that "World War II opened the gates for Mexican-Americans in this local." This was attributed to the manpower shortage during the war, the better qualified and more aggressive Mexican-American postwar applicants, particularly those who had taken advantage of education and training under the G.I. Bill, and the pressure against discrimination by the international headquarters of the union.

Only applicants who were high school graduates or passed an equivalent level examination were accepted as apprentices. Education and language deficiences still disqualified some Mexican-American applicants, but this was much less of a problem than before the war. The one ethnic characteristic noted by the union official was that Mexican-Americans tended to be very sensitive to imaginary slights and were prone to blame discrimination for actual individual inadequacies.

2. A Commercial Printing Company

This company, organized in 1901, does commercial printing, lithographing, and engraving, and operates a retail outlet.

Of the total of 170 employees in July, 1963, 35 were administrative, sales, and office personnel, and 135 were working in plant jobs. Six Mexican-Americans, comprising 17 percent of the total, were employed in administrative, sales, and office positions. Mexican-Americans, numbering 115, made up 85 percent of plant employment.

All administrative and outside sales personnel were Anglos. Two inside sales persons, a man and a woman, held key customer contact jobs and were considered especially valuable because both spoke excellent English and Spanish. All supervisors, with the exception of one bindery foreman, were Anglos.

The company official stated that the company got the "pick" of the vocational school graduates, even though they were started as rank apprentices. The schools had reportedly weak programs of aptitude testing, due to a shortage of trained guidance personnel. While graduates were not prepared at the vocational schools adequately to take over as operators at the plant, each had important knowledge of a wide range of equipment and some idea as to the part of the plant in which he would like to work.

In selecting applicants for plant training, the company management preferred Mexican-Americans "to the average Anglo, who has too high an opinion of his immediate pay and fringe benefits."

Mexican-Americans were considered as having pronounced artistic ability.

On the other hand, persons of this ethnic extraction were characterized as having certain fairly common limitations. They were considered temperamentally best suited for routine, repetitive work. As an example, the best proofreader for telephone book printing was a Mexican-American girl, but she could not be trusted with proofreading of material not involving simple comparison with the text.

Mexican-Americans, including the bindery foreman, required close supervision for top notch performance. They also were found to lack maturity in supervisory relationships and had to be led carefully rather than pressured, lest they sulk. Persons of this racial stock were prone to be absent whenever any relative was sick, yet on the job the management found it necessary to give greater stress to them on safety precautions. Mexican-Americans were prone to buy irresponsibly on credit; the company had a rule against borrowing from "loan sharks" and had established a credit union to encourage savings and provide for borrowing needs.

The majority of the workers for this company had for many years been Mexican-American--some were second and third generation employees. The management had obviously studied their traits, made efforts to help them overcome their shortcomings, and seemed genuinely interested in the individuals of this ethnic extraction. The writer left with the definite impression, however, that Anglos would have been employed in most occupations if qualified persons had been available at the wages offered. Wage schedule data were not made available.

Durable Goods Manufacturing

While durable goods manufacturing employment, totaling 7,945, constituted only 35 percent of the small manufacturing sector payroll in 1962, some of the oldest and most stable firms were found in this group.

Personal contacts were made with six firms, each representing a major industrial group, namely: stone, clay and glass (a cement factory); primary metals; fabricated metals; machinery other than electrical (a refrigerator and air conditioner manufacturer); electrical equipment; and transportation equipment (a truck body and trailer builder).

Aggregate employment of the six firms studied was 2,107, which was 26 percent of the total durable goods manufacturing employment in 1962.

A Cement Manufacturer

This largest of two cement plants was established in San Antonio in 1908. The total of 250 employees included 40 administrative, sales, and office personnel and 210 plant workers, including supervisors, as of July, 1963. Information was obtained from a plant superintendent; no detailed data were obtainable on nonplant employees.

Eighty percent of the all-male work force were reported as Mexican-Americans. The superintendent stated that persons of this ethnic extraction were working in all plant departments and there was absolutely no discrimination against them, either in hiring or advancement.

Plant openings were mostly filled from applications received at the downtown office. The majority of workers were hired as laborers, at the starting wage of $1.80 per hour. Skilled jobs were usually filled through upgrading of workers taken from the labor crew. It was the general practice of the department foremen to make advancements on the basis of seniority, provided the persons in line for advancement were qualified; this was not, however, an official company policy.

None of the company's workers were represented by a union.

Applicants, in order to qualify for employment, had to have paid their poll tax as well as be U.S. citizens. A police record report was also obtained for each person considered for employment.

The superintendent stated that he saw no differences between Mexican-Americans and Anglos in regards to their competence or dependability. Some workers of both groups were enrolled in welding and other night school classes to qualify for advancement; the company did not provide any financial assistance for such outside training.

A Primary Metals Manufacturer

This steel castings manufacturing plant was founded in 1938. It is located in the heart of the Mexican-American West Side.

Plant employment had always been dominantly Mexican-American, and approximately 90 percent of the 180 plant workers, as well as four of the 11 administrative and office personnel were of this ethnic extraction as of July, 1963.

Mexican-American employees included 75% of the coremakers, 80% of the molders, and 95% of the grinders, plus a laboratory technician and three of the office girls.

Of nine shift foremen, one was Mexican-American and the other eight were Anglos. Approximately one-half of the assistant shift foremen (working leadmen) were Mexican-American.

Applicants were required to read and write English; there was no other educational requirement. All new employees were hired as helpers at the minimum FLSA scale. Workers were trained on the job in the various occupations and advanced in pay in line with their advancement in skill. None of the workers were represented by a union.

Mexican-Americans had advanced as far and as rapidly as Anglos, with the exception of top supervisory jobs. That only one Mexican-American had attained such advancement was attributed to lack of confidence of many in this ethnic group regarding their supervisory abilities, and also to their educational limitations.

Mexican-Americans were found to have less fear of danger. While this caused them to be more willing to work in hazardous jobs, it presented a problem in maintaining safety precautions, requiring more stress on safety measures. Persons of this ethnic extraction tended to be smaller in size on the average, and were consequently somewhat less powerful physically. Otherwise, no distinctively Mexican-American traits were noted.

A Fabricated Metals Products Manufacturer

One of the oldest industrial establishments in San Antonio, founded in 1878, this family controlled company operates a foundry in addition to making fabricated steel products, fabricating equipment, and general industrial supplies. The information below was taken from conversations and data received from the president, vice-president in charge of plant operations, and the personnel director.

Total employment and number of Mexican-Americans, by department in August, 1962, are shown in Table 31.

Mexican-Americans comprised one-fourth of the total plant employment, with greatest concentration found in the structural steel shop, in which this ethnic group constituted one-half of the workers. Largest number, 27, was found in the foundry, where Mexican-Americans made up about one-third of the total. Representatives of this group were found in all except the stores department.

The ratio of total Mexican-Americans employed to total employment was about the same as in 1950; however, the proportion of skilled workers in this group had increased appreciably.

The two Mexican-Americans on the administrative, sales, and engineering payroll were a telephone salesman

TABLE 31

EMPLOYMENT BY DEPARTMENT, TOTAL AND MEXICAN-AMERICAN

A FABRICATED METALS PRODUCTS MANUFACTURER

SAN ANTONIO, TEXAS, AUGUST, 1962

Department	Total	Mexican-American
Machine Shop	39	8
Foundry	89	27
Structural	35	17
Pattern	5	1
Brass	7	1
Maintenance	11	2
Reinforcing	12	2
Pipe and Plate	23	7
East Yard	10	4
Service	12	1
Stores	17	0
Shipping	43	5
Total Hourly Payroll	303	75
Admin., Sales, Engineering	60	2
Accounting and Clerical	94	0
Total Payroll	457	77

Source: Company payroll records.

and a draftsman. The vice-president volunteered the information that the personnel director had come from Louisiana, and that he may have been biased against both Mexican-Americans and Negroes, thus accounting for only Anglos in all nonplant jobs.

The vice-president asserted that there was no discrimination against Mexican-Americans in his domain, plant employment and advancement, even though applicants for plant jobs were first cleared through the personnel office.

Starting wage scale for unskilled workers was the FLSA minimum ($1.15 at that time).

At the time of the writer's visit to the plant, the Steelworkers Union had just won by a single vote margin an election to represent the workers in the plant shops. The company was contesting the election. For some years, the plant had not been organized, although the workers had at one time been represented by the Machinists' Union.

Company executives estimated that about three-fourths of the Mexican-American employees had voted for the union in the recent election. The president of the union was reportedly a Mexican-American, and the son of one of the oldest employees was one of the several union organizers of this ethnic stock in the plant.

No discernible difference in skills and work performance was noted where Mexican-Americans and Anglos had comparable education and training. Most Mexican-Americans at this plant, many of whom were long-time employees, had very limited education and were satisfied to stay in jobs in which there was little possibility of much advancement.

Most of the Anglos who qualified for higher paying jobs with other employers had already left, and since more of the Mexican-Americans were being advanced, there was little difference in labor turnover between the two ethnic groups.

Mexican-Americans were found to have some definite limitations. While they had worked out satisfactorily as crew leaders, they lacked the confidence and leadership to serve as foremen. They proved not to be satisfactory generally in sales, although the one man in this department was doing an excellent job.

A Refrigerator and Air Conditioner Manufacturer

This company, established in 1883, has long been the largest manufacturing employer in San Antonio. All plant production and maintenance workers had been represented by the International Union of Electrical Workers, Local No. 780, since 1957.

Total and Mexican-American production and maintenance employment data by seniority and by wage distribution, shown respectively in Tables 32-A and 32-B, were taken from the records of the union as of March, 1962. Information on employees not represented by the union was obtained from the company personnel director, in July, 1963.

Plant and maintenance personnel, 56% Mexican-American in 1962, were predominantly Anglo-American prior to World War II, with only 34% of the workers with seniority beginning prior to 1943 found to be Mexican-American.

During the wartime worker shortage and afterward through 1957, the ratio of Mexican-American hiring was reversed. Throughout the period 1943-1957, with the exception of the year 1956, Mexican-Americans added each year to the payroll exceeded those of Anglos, with the former representing 64 percent on the seniority roster for those years.

Women workers, mostly Mexican-Americans, were employed for the first time during the war, and at one time they comprised one-fourth of the plant payroll. In 1963, women made up only eight percent of the workers in the plant. They had been found to be less flexible than men in job assignments.

TABLE 32-A

SENIORITY DISTRIBUTION BY TOTALS AND MEXICAN-AMERICANS
PRODUCTION AND MAINTENANCE WORKERS
A REFRIGERATOR AND AIR CONDITIONER MANUFACTURER
SAN ANTONIO, TEXAS, MARCH 1962

Seniority Years	Total	Mexican-American	Percent Mex-Amer
Prior to 1943	29	10	34
1943 - 1957	467	299	64
1958 - 1962	145	48	33
Totals	641	357	56

TABLE 32-B

WAGE DISTRIBUTION BY TOTALS AND MEXICAN-AMERICANS

Hourly Wage Scale	Total	Mexican-American	Percent Mex-Amer.
$1.45	75	28	37
1.52	154	82	53
1.59	222	139	63
1.67	137	85	62
1.80	22	16	73
2.00	23	5	22
2.25	3	1	33
2.55	5	1	20
Totals	641	357	56

Source: Records, the International Union of Electrical Workers, local no. 870.

Union officials, all of whom (other than the chief steward) were Mexican-Americans, had been disturbed that in each year subsequent to the union's gaining representation in the plant, the ratio of hirings of this ethnic group had been less than that of Anglos. This was notably observed in the years 1960-1962, in which only four of 42 employees of this seniority were Mexican-American. The union president stated that a protest charging discrimination against this racial group had been lodged with the company management. The number of 1960-1962 seniority employees was unusually small in March, 1962, because approximately 100 low seniority workers had been temporarily laid off that month.

The labor agreement provided that all plant promotions be on the basis of seniority where the person in line was qualified for the opening and bid for the job. Wage distribution of Mexican-American workers followed closely the seniority pattern, indicating that Mexican-Americans' advancement in plant jobs was commensurate with that of other employees, both before and after union representation.

Whereas more than half of the 641 production and maintenance workers were Mexican-Americans, only six of the remaining 323 administrative, sales, office, and supervisory personnel were of this ethnic extraction.

These included two of the 30 plant foremen, a draftsman, a secretary, an IBM operator, and a print shop helper. Two Mexican-American foremen were reported to have retired in 1962.

The company executive stated that he had observed a significantly higher ratio of Mexican-Americans with police records. A police check was made on all applicants, and those who lied about their records or had serious or continued police backgrounds were not employed. No other distinctively Mexican-American trait was noted.

An Electrical Equipment Manufacturer

This firm had been manufacturing storage batteries since 1918 and had added a fiber glass insulation plant in 1959. Information below was obtained from an interview with the president of the company in July, 1963.

Of the aggregate payroll of 195 employees, 113 or 57 percent, were Mexican-Americans, distributed as follows:

Division	Total	Mexican-American
Fiber Glass Plant	80	56
Battery Plant	75	45
Admin., Sales, Office, Supervisory and Stores	40	12
Totals	195	113

Plant workers were all men with the exception of two Mexican-American women in the fiber glass plant. Eight women had been so employed at one time, but they tended to be chronic complainers and lacking in strength, and no more women were expected to be hired.

The company reportedly employed a "few" Negroes. The president asserted that no distinction was given in employment and that mixing the races on jobs had been no problem.

All new plant workers were employed as trainees at a starting rate of $1.35 per hour. Openings were usually filled with relatives and acquaintances of employees. The company president found that in using this method, employees who recommended applicants would not only feel responsible to recommend only worthy prospects, but they would also feel responsible for helping the new workers master their jobs.

The International Union of Electrical Workers had attempted to organize the fiber glass plant shortly after it was opened, but they had been unsuccessful and no further effort to organize the company's workers had since been noted.

Mexican-Americans were found to be exceptionally good as fiber glass spinners, the most highly skilled production job. Otherwise, no difference was noted between Anglos and Mexican-Americans in competency and dependability.

Mexican-American supervisory and office employees included an assistant manager of the fiber glass plant (a chemical engineer), the superintendent of maintenance, the warehouse foreman, a shipping clerk, and a woman bookkeeper. No member of this ethnic group had been known to aspire to sales work; all employees in this field as well as administrative and other office personnel were Anglos.

The company president stated that, while Mexican-Americans made excellent "straw bosses" (working leaders), they usually performed best under Anglo supervisors.

A Truck Body and Trailer Builder

This was a relatively small, sole proprietorship, which was in operation before World War II, closed down for two years during the war, and reopened in 1946.

Prior to the two-year cessation of operation, the plant employment consisted of 19 Anglos and one Mexican-American. When the company started production again, very few worthwhile Anglos were available, so the owner was forced to employ mostly Mexican-Americans.

Employment in July, 1963, totaled 51, of which six were administrative and office personnel and 45 worked in the plant. All administrative and office workers were Anglos. Plant employees included eight Anglos, four Negroes, and 33 Mexican-Americans.

Among the plant workers, five Mexican-Americans were skilled and 28 were semiskilled trainees; three Anglos were skilled and five were semiskilled trainees; all four Negroes were trainees, having been hired as porters.

All new employees were hired at the minimum legal rate and upgraded solely on merit. No union had made a serious effort to organize the plant.

The owner frankly stated: "With few exceptions, Mexicans are a sorry race; all but five in the plant would quit if unemployment benefits were increased." Mexican-Americans could not be made supervisors; they would not accept responsibility. They were satisfied with low incomes, and they would not work overtime. On the other hand, the owner volunteered that the highest paid plant worker, a Mexican-American body and fender man, had earned $7,800 the previous year.

He expressed a universal disregard for all government training and labor placement agencies. Veterans' on-the-job training had proved unsatisfactory; all of four vocational high school graduates employed "had to be let out"; referrals from the Texas Employment Commission did not really want to work; and he opposed the Manpower Development and Training programs.

Summary and Analysis

Among Texas' four largest cities, manufacturing employment in San Antonio in 1962 was less than one-half that of the next lowest, Fort Worth, and average weekly earnings were only 83 percent that of the next lowest, Dallas. Furthermore, average weekly earnings from manufacturing employment in San Antonio was the lowest among all cities of comparable size in the United States.

Table 33 shows the number of employees, total and Mexican-American, with distribution between plant production and maintenance workers and other employees (including plant supervisors), for the eighteen manufacturing establishments individually surveyed in this study.

The proportion of Mexican-Americans employed by the eighteen firms was virtually the same as that reported for all firms in the San Antonio SMSA in the 1960 U.S. Census (Table 16, page 66), as shown on the following page:

TABLE 33

EMPLOYMENT, TOTAL AND MEXICAN-AMERICAN
EIGHTEEN SELECTED MANUFACTURING ESTABLISHMENTS
SAN ANTONIO, TEXAS, 1962-1963

	Total Employees			Plant			All Other*		
	All	Mex.-Amer.		All	Mex.-Amer.		All	Mex.-Amer.	
	Races	Total	%	Races	Total	%	Races	Total	%
All Establishments	5,772	2,701	47	4,476	2,590	58	1,296	111	9
Nondurable Goods	3,664	1,788	49	2,951	1,702	58	713	86	12
2 Bakeries	310	143	46	285	140	49	25	3	12
2 Breweries	1,142	80	7	762	59	8	380	21	6
4 Other Food Products	907	623	69	747	605	81	160	18	11
1 Cigar Manufacturer	200	184	92	175	175	100	25	9	36
2 Apparel Manufacturers	935	637	68	847	608	72	88	29	33
1 Printing Company	170	121	71	135	115	85	35	6	17
Durable Goods	2,108	913	43	1,525	888	58	583	25	5
1 Cement Manufacturer	250	168	67	210	168	80	40	**	**
1 Primary Metals	191	159	83	171	154	90	.20	5	25
1 Fabricated Metals	457	77	17	303	75	25	154	2	1
1 Machinery (non-elect.)	964	363	38	641	357	56	323	6	2
1 Electrical Equipment	195	113	58	155	101	65	40	12	30
1 Transportation Equipment	51	33	65	45	33	73	6	0	0

* Includes plant supervisors.
** Information not made available; total not included in computing "All Other" percentage.

Sources: Record, and reports form respective manufacturing establishments.

	18 Firms	1960 Census
Total Manufacturing	47%	48%
Nondurable Goods	49%	49%
Durable Goods	43%	45%

For the individual firms, the proportion of Mexican-American employment varied widely--from 92 percent at the cigar company, including the entire plant work force, to only six percent at one of the breweries.

Table 34 ranks the 18 establishments by percent of Mexican-Americans, total employees, and recency of the firms' beginning uninterrupted operation. The latter two rankings are made to provide rough tests of the hypotheses that the percentages of Mexican-American workers were directly related to (1) size of work force, on the assumption of more objective and impersonal personnel practices in larger plants, and (2) recentness of establishment of the firm, on the assumption of less retardation among newer companies of expansion of Mexican-American utilization due to resistance to change in established patterns of employment policies and practices.

The hypothesis that direct relationship existed between percent of Mexican-Americans and size of total employment was found to be refuted. In fact, six of the nine firms with 70 percent or more Mexican-Americans were

TABLE 34

RANKING BY PERCENT MEXICAN-AMERICAN EMPLOYMENT
TOTAL EMPLOYMENT, AND NUMBER OF YEARS IN BUSINESS
EIGHTEEN SELECTED MANUFACTURING ESTABLISHMENTS
SAN ANTONIO, TEXAS, 1962-1963

Employer	Percent Mexican-American	Ranking By: Percent Mexican-American	Ranking By: Total Number Employed	Ranking By: Number Years in Business
Cigar Manufacturer	92	1	11	12
Candy Manufacturer	88	2	10	11
Primary Metals	83	3	13	3
Children's Garments	81	4	9	5
Mexican Foods	79	5	16	14
Bakery "A"	75	6	17	4
Meat Packer	72	7	6	7
Printing Company	71	8	14	8
Work Clothing	70	9	2	13
Cement Manufacturer	67	10	7	9
Transportation Equip.	65	11	18	1
Electrical Equipment	58	12	12	10
Bakery "B"	40	13	8	6
Machinery (nonelect.)	38	14	1	16
Flour Mill	27	15	15	18
Fabricated Metals	14	16	5	17
Brewery "A"	8	17	4	15
Brewery "B"	6	18	3	2

Source: Employer data, pp. 137-194.

among the nine establishments with 200 or fewer total employees. An inference of inverse relationship could not, however, be accepted since further examination of the data revealed that both proportion of Mexican-Americans and total employment were significantly related to a third factor, the nature of products manufactured.

Of the nine firms with largest proportions of Mexican-Americans, eight were producers of nondurable goods. Moreover, strong indications of Anglo-American preference was found in each of the other four manufacturers of nondurables.

Some support was found for the hypothesis that the proportion of Mexican-American workers would vary inversely with the length of time of company operation. Four of the five companies employing the smallest percentages of Mexican-Americans were also the four oldest establishments, and the fifth company was one of the breweries that was founded in 1880 and discontinued operation after the Eighteenth Amendment became effective.

On the other hand, the companies with the first, second, and fifth highest percentages of Mexican-Americans had all been operating since the 1890's; each had employed Mexican-Americans predominantly for a half century or more.

It is concluded, from the data obtained and from conversations with industrial leaders, that prior to World War II, individual firms established and tended to maintain patterns of "Anglo" jobs and "Mexican" jobs.

The distinction was generally based primarily on the availability of qualified Anglo workers at or near the wage acceptable to Mexican-Americans. A secondary factor was the degree of ethnic preference and language difficulty by the preponderantly Anglo employers and supervisors and by Anglo production workers.

Consequently, prior to 1940, Mexican-Americans were employed almost exclusively in unskilled and low wage semiskilled jobs. Where Anglos were also employed in such occupations, they were usually placed in separate crews.

Because of their reputed manual dexterity and capacity for repetitive labor and their willingness to work for meager wages, Mexican-American women dominated employment in the cigar, candy, and apparel industries when production was largely handwork, and they were retained when the plants were mechanized.

The shortage of skilled workers during World War II is generally recognized as by far the greatest single factor in opening this level of employment to

Mexican-Americans. Employers, who reluctantly turned to persons of this ethnic group, found them quite capable of mastering skilled jobs, and they also found that they could be worked satisfactorily alongside Anglos. By 1963, Mexican-Americans were commonly found throughout plant departments and engaged in substantially all types of skilled occupations.

The survey information belies the misconception that Mexican-Americans are unresponsive to participation in labor organizations. Persons of this ethnic group held all major offices in the International Union of Electrical Workers local, which represented the plant workers of San Antonio's largest manufacturing employer.

In the city's oldest and second largest durable goods employer's plant, company officials stated that a key factor in the Steelworkers Union victory in a recent representation election was the overwhelming union support of the Mexican-American workers, although persons of this descent constituted only 25 percent of the plant work force. The chief organizer was Mexican-American, and company executives estimated that three-fourths of this ethnic group voted for the union.

Fifty-eight of the 60 plant employees of the Mexican foods company, represented by the Amalgamated

Meat Cutters, were Mexican-American. All except four new employees, who were still on probation, were union members.

The workers in the remaining three organized plants in the survey--the two breweries and the flour mill--were represented by the Brewery Workers Union. While no information was secured concerning union activity by Mexican-Americans at these plants, indications of strong preferences for Anglos were noted. This was particularly true of the breweries, where Mexican-Americans constituted only eight percent of the plant force, and both company and union officials felt that a major proportion of this racial stock were lacking in motivation. A union representative observed that they were prone to make false claims of discrimination and made demands for discrimination in their own favor.

The union shop contracts won by the ILGWU in the 1930's and 1940's in the garment industry, in which plant workers were predominantly Mexican-American women, together with the aggressive efforts of the women cigar workers to organize that plant, were clear indications of the responsiveness of female Mexican-Americans to organized labor.

The writer is convinced that San Antonio's Mexican-American manufacturing workers during the past three decades have been at least as receptive as Anglos to unionization.

Ironically, after the predominantly Mexican-American workers at the big refrigerator and air conditioner plant had gained higher wages and other benefits following the IUE election victory in 1957, the proportion of Mexican-American employees began to decline. Only one-third of those hired from 1958 to 1962 were Mexican-American, compared to nearly two-thirds of this racial extraction in prior years. Whether or not the local union officials' charge of unfair employment practices was true, it was obvious that the increased desirability of jobs at this plant had effectively stimulated Anglo competition.

While beginning wage rates at all five plants under union contracts were well above the $1.15 FLSA hourly minimum at the time, ten of the twelve nonunion plants and the one for which union representation had just been won commonly hired new employees at the legal minimum. All eighteen companies found it necessary to train virtually all their own workers.

The significant expansion and broadening of Mexican-American plant employment since World War II was not matched by increased participation in other manufacturing occupations. Whereas 58 percent of plant production and maintenance jobs at the eighteen firms studied were held by Mexican-Americans, they only constituted nine percent of other personnel.

Examination of the nature of Mexican-American employment in such occupations revealed a comparable qualitative disparity. No Mexican-American was found in an administrative level position at any of the eighteen companies surveyed. All except three of the total of 45 Mexican-American supervisory personnel--two general foremen and an assistant general foreman--were first line supervisors. Twenty-eight of the total worked for four of the firms. Four firms employed no Mexican-American supervisor, and four others employed only one each. Officials at eight of the companies volunteered their convictions that Mexican-Americans were generally lacking in one or more of the following supervisory qualifications: mental capacity, judgment, emotional stability, ambition, and worker acceptance.

Mexican-Americans were generally regarded as lacking in both desire and ability for sales work. Eighteen of the 27 in sales positions among the firms surveyed were employed by the two breweries, where company officials reported that several were outstanding but most lacked aggressiveness and were satisfied with relatively low earnings. Six of the remaining nine sales workers were employed by one of the apparel manufacturers.

Of the 28 Mexican-American clerical workers, 10 were employed at an apparel firm and six worked for the cigar company, where they constituted the majority employed in such jobs. Eleven of the 18 companies employed no Mexican-American clerical workers.

The remaining 11 nonplant Mexican-American employees included three quality control technicians--two at a brewery and one at the primary metals plant, two draftsmen--one each at the fabricated metals plant and the air conditioner and refrigerator factory, and six workers at the electrical equipment company's service store.

The continued retardation of industrial development in San Antonio may be attributed largely to a strong resistance to change, bolstered by four interrelated factors--geographical location, highly elastic supply of Mexican ethnic unskilled labor, aversion to organized labor, and the confident reliance on the military establishments to sustain the city's economy.

San Antonio's business leaders generally ascribe the city's lack of industrialization almost solely to circumstances associated with its geographical location, citing its distance from national markets accentuated by high rail freight rates and absence of available water transportation, limited supplies of raw materials, and lack of industrial water required by some heavy industry.

The competent and dedicated professional staff of the local chamber of commerce has diligently sought to woo light industry to come to San Antonio through extolling the community's excellent climate, recreational facilities, and historical and scenic attractions. This approach, while proving quite effective in enticing tourists, has been singularly ineffective in luring manufacturing establishments.

A recent one-third page advertisement by the chamber's industrial development committee in a leading national magazine was headlined "273 YEAR OLD DISCOVERY ELIMINATES WEARING OVERCOAT," with the bulk of the sales pitch devoted to the city's mild winters and recreational attractions.[18] Only brief mention was made, at the bottom of the page, of the schools, churches, transportation, utilities, tax structure, building sites, and "an amicable, cooperative labor pool (extremely small strike loss)."

---

[18] U.S. News and World Report, January 27, 1964, p. 96.

This writer's research has convinced him that the major effect of geographical location on San Antonio's limited industrialization has been its role in the development of the massive military installations which have made industrialization unnecessary to the city's economic growth.

With no strong economic pressure to expand the city's industrial base, many conservative professional, commercial, and political leaders who have strong fears that substantial expansion of the manufacturing sector, particularly in heavy industry, would result in greatly increased labor union power, give little more than lip service to further industrialization. Coupled with the fear of unions is the concern that wages would increase generally, with resultant increases in prices and cost of living. A sizeable segment of San Antonians are satisfied with little manufacturing because they object to the pollution of the air of their fair city.

The development of a broadly skilled work force, so important to prospective new industry, has been greatly retarded because of the availability of an almost constant inflow of Mexicans willing to work at low wages, with the consequent profitability of delay in implementation of advanced technology.

The various increases in the minimum wages required under the Fair Labor Standards Act have had a net salutary influence on improving this problem in general, and particularly the standard of living of the Mexican-Americans who make up the bulk of the low-paid covered workers in San Antonio. Of the eighteen establishments surveyed, only one--the cigar factory--indicated any substantial reduction in employment in either step of the raise in the minimum wage from $1.00 to $1.25 per hour.

CHAPTER VIII

NONMANUFACTURING EMPLOYMENT

This chapter is devoted to specific areas of private employment in wholesale and retail trade, communications, insurance, services, transportation and the professions.

Information includes data and insights obtained through personal interviews with executives of selected relatively large employers, chosen on the basis of one or more of the following characteristics: large proportion of Mexican-American employees, general recognition as representative of current ethnic employment practices in a major field, or widespread charges of employment discrimination against Mexican-Americans. Knowledge gained in an interview with Raymond C. Shafer, South Texas representative of the Teamsters Union, is presented. Data on Mexican-American participation in each of seven professional categories are compared for the years 1940, 1950, and 1961.

The Pecan Industry - Shelling and Wholesale

The pecan industry was started in San Antonio in 1882, when G. A. Duerler shipped 50 barrels of shelled nuts to eastern cities.[1] Since the pecan is Texas' most valuable native crop, since usually more than half of the seedling (native) yield of the state is within 250 miles of San Antonio, and since transportation costs for shelled nuts is cheaper because the meats make up only 38 percent of the total weight of the pecans, the city became the natural center for shelling and wholesaling pecans.

From the beginning, pecan plant labor has been virtually all performed by workers of Mexican extraction, predominantly women, because of the constant supply of workers of this ethnic group willing to work for small remuneration, the reputed manual dexterity of Mexican women, and the presumption that they were not susceptible to unionization. In addition, San Antonio became a marshalling point for Mexican-American migrant farm labor, and a large proportion of these migrant workers found complementary jobs in the pecan plants, where the highly seasonal employment reached its peak from late in November through March.

---

[1]Texas Writers' Program, San Antonio, A History and Guide, The Clegg Co., San Antonio, 1941, p. 36.

The Duerler Company, which had for nearly half a century been the leading firm in the industry, was by 1928 substantially mechanized, with the nuts cracked and graded by machine.

It was, however, during the depression of the 1930's that the pecan industry surged to its greatest height both in numbers of workers employed and in proportion of local business revenue. Led by a rapidly growing newcomer, the Southern Pecan Shelling Company, the industry took advantage of the vast pool of San Antonio's Mexican-American people, who were willing to work for almost any compensation offered, to revert all shelling operations to hand labor.

In 1936, Southern Pecan Shelling Company's sales rose to more than $3,000,000, constituting in excess of one-fourth of the nation's sale of seedling pecans.[2]

Shelling completely by hand required many more workers and much more space, so the larger operators turned over most of their pecans to contractors, whom they financed and largely controlled. The contractors provided their own crude shelling facilities and/or

---

[2]Seldon Menefee and C. C. Cassmore, The Pecan Shellers of San Antonio, Works Progress Administration, Washington, D. C., 1940, p. 8.

subcontracted the pecans to families, whose members shelled the pecans in the unsanitary conditions of their squalid homes.

The total number of workers thus employed increased tremendously. While the circumstances precluded accurate employment statistics, estimates of maximum numbers of workers in the industry in San Antonio ranged from 12,000 to 20,000. Unfortunately, the workers' incomes, paid on a piecework basis, were pitifully meager Information presented in a 1934 labor board hearing gave the average piecework wage for a 54-hour week as $1.56.[3]

Three major factors combined to bring about the end of the completely handwork shelling through mass employment of woefully ill-paid workers. In 1936, a city health ordinance was passed which outlawed pecan shelling in homes and required contractors to meet prescribed standards for facilities and working conditions, including installation of running water and inside flush toilets. Another significant factor was the increasingly effective unionization of pecan workers, beginning in 1934 and involving a series of major strikes. The final blow came with the decision of the Wage and Hour Division of

---

[3]Texas Writers' Program, op. cit., p. 36.

the U.S. Department of Labor, on January 19, 1939, denying the request of the pecan operators that their plants be exempted from the 25 cents minimum hourly wage of the Fair Labor Standards Act.

Forced to pay the minimum wage, the large operators began to remechanize, with a resultant sharp decline in employment in the industry. In March 1939, the Southern Pecan Shelling Company had reduced its payroll from a peak of approximately 10,000 to some 1,800; the company's labor force continued to decline to a maximum of 350 production workers in 1950.[4] In 1961, this establishment, operated as a division of Standard Brands, had a peak employment of 212 persons.

The following information was secured in an interview with the head of one of the largest of the ten pecan-shelling establishments operating in San Antonio in 1963. This executive had been associated with the family owned business since 1930.

The company began mechanization of its plant immediately following the Wage and Hour Division decision denying exemption for the pecan operators, and production

---

[4]Shapiro, op. cit., p. 141.

had been almost fully mechanized for a number of years at the time of the interview.

Maximum plant employment was reported to be approximately 200, of which about 80 percent were women. It was the current company policy to maintain substantially full production and employment for eight months of the year, in order to retain the more productive and better trained personnel, and in order to get maximum use of the production machinery.

During the slack summer months, employment was reduced to about 50 persons, production cut to a bare minimum, and the period devoted primarily to repairs, maintenance and other preparation for the new season. Most of the workers laid off in the summer were housewives who were satisfied to stay at home and draw their unemployment compensation, although some found temporary employment during the layoff.

With the exception of one of the two supervisors, all plant employees were Mexican-American. Women were used exclusively in the shelling and picking operations, and the men took care of maintenance, materials handling and all other heavy work. Nearly all the men, because of the nature of their work and the competitive demand for their labor, were paid wages above the legal minimum.

While most of the women were paid the minimum wage, a few were paid higher rates.

The company executive stated that no particular stage in the progression of the legal minimum wage rate from 25 cents to $1.25 had presented more of a problem to the success of the business than had the others. Continued improvements in mechanization, increased efficiency of workers, and the fact that all major competitors were required to pay the same scale, made possible continued profitable operation. His labor bill per hundred pounds of pecan meats was reported to be less than when the company was unmechanized, and it was his opinion that probably as many pecans were shelled in the 1960's as in the 1930's, even though the current maximum employment by San Antonio operators totaled considerably less than 2,000 workers.

The role of unionization in the pecan industry is significant in that it demonstrates the responsiveness of Mexican-American workers to unionization, and it indicates that real and suspected Communist leadership of the pecan workers has been a factor in the continued general public rejection of the labor movement in San Antonio.

The first successful organizing of the pecan shellers was in the independent Pecan Shelling Workers' Union, under the leadership of Magdaleno Rodriguez. At its peak the union claimed 10,000 members in 1934-35, but a much smaller number actually paid dues. The organization gradually lost support and had virtually disappeared by 1937, when the remnants of the union reappeared as the Texas Pecan Shelling Workers' Union.[5]

Emma Tenayuca, the fiery young local woman Communist head of the San Antonio chapter of the Workers Alliance of America, although she held no official capacity in either union, became the de facto standard bearer for the struggling pecan workers.[6]

When the Southern Pecan Shelling Company contractors announced on January 21, 1938, that they would lower the pickers' pay from six cents per pound for pieces

---

[5]Menefee and Cassmore, _op. cit._, p. 16.

[6]Local Mexican-Americans remember Emma as a brilliant schoolgirl, especially gifted in public speaking, who bitterly resented discrimination against her and her fellow students of Mexican extraction. According to one informant, she became enraged when she was denied a place on the school's debate team purportedly because her being Mexican would tend to adversely affect the judge's decision. She quit school, embraced communism, married a communist organizer, and became the impassioned spearhead of the movement in San Antonio, gaining the great majority of her followers from the city's multitide of destitute Mexican-Americans.

and seven cents per pound for halves to only five cents and six cents respectively, Emma Tenayuca became the spokesman for the shellers in a "spontaneous" strike that soon involved half of the approximately 12,000 workers in the industry.[7]

The Texas Pecan Workers' Union did not join in the strike, and as the strike gained momentum, the union's members began to defect, and the organization soon folded.

A CIO union, the United Cannery, Agricultural, Packing, and Allied Workers of America (UCAPAWA), which had begun organizing the pecan shellers shortly before the walkout, strongly supported the strike, soon signed up nearly all of the strikers, and thus took over the leadership from Emma Tenayuca.

The strikers, with very few exceptions, were concerned wholly with maintaining their pitiable level of existence, neither understanding nor interested in communist ideology, and there was no evidence that the CIO local union was communist-motivated or controlled. Nevertheless, even though no other significant assistance was offered them. the strikers alienated practically all of San Antonio's influential groups by accepting communist leadership and

---

[7]Even at the old rates, workers were reported to be earning only from five to eight cents per hour.

the transfer of allegiance to the CIO union was considered hardly less reprehensible in view of the highly publicized infiltration of many CIO organizations by communists at that time.[8]

From the outset, the strikers were strongly opposed by Mayor C. K. Quin and Police Chief Owen Kilday. More than 1,000 pickets were arrested, and tear gas was used against the pickets. Even those historical friends of the Mexican ethnic group--the Mexican Chamber of Commerce, the League of United Latin American Citizens (LULAC), and Catholic Archbishop Brossaerts--refused any assistance to the strikers unless they renounced the CIO union's leadership, which they refused to do.

The local press denounced the strike, laying heavy stress on the communist and CIO leadership, and upholding the strong-arm measures of the police. When the union and the operators, after intervention by Governor

---

[8]Texas Congressman Martin Dies, in a San Antonio speech on May 17, 1951, stated "In 1938, under legal process we raided every Communist organization in the U.S., and we got all their records. We discovered twenty-one international unions affiliated with the CIO, representing a majority of the unions affiliated, had entrenched Communist leadership, and that nearly one-half of the members of the executive board were members of the Communist Party."

Allred, agreed to arbitrate the dispute, the San Antonio Express, in an editorial on May 11, 1938, stated,

> After more than a month, San Antonio pecan shellers and their employers are submitting their differences to arbitration. As a strike, the dispute was a failure . . . No plant was forced to shut down. Pecan shelling is piece work and can be done by anybody. Paid agents of the CIO and Communist agitators before them, convinced the pecan shellers that they were being treated unfairly . . . Chief of Police Kilday, knowing the CIO, did well to take firm action to prevent disorders.

The arbitrator compromised, setting the rates one-half cent less than the old rates. On this basis the union negotiated with the larger operators closed-shop contracts which expired on November 1, 1938. An increase to eight cents and seven cents was agreed on as of that date, but this was superseded by the decision of the Wage and Hour Division denying the exemption of the industry from the 25 cent minimum wage.

The union continued to represent the employees of the Southern Pecan Shelling Company until 1947, when the company, under new ownership, refused to renew the contract. The union closed down the following year, and the pecan workers have had no union organization since that time.

While the drastic reduction in employment in the pecan industry following the implementation of the Fair Labor Standard Act minimum wage resulted in a temporary loss of earnings for many families, the effect for a large proportion of them was to have one pecan sheller earning as much or more than the labor of the entire family had previously provided, at the same time freeing the other members to attend school, seek other employment and care for family responsibilities.

Above all, at a time when the future seemed to offer only further degradation for San Antonio's Mexican-Americans, the minimum wage provision brought economic stability and a new-found dignity and self-respect to a large segment and a measure of hope to all the members of this ethnic group. At the same time, the application of the wage and hour law tended to some extent to diminish the heavy inflow of unskilled Mexican labor into San Antonio.

Retail Trade; A Leading Department Store

With the exception of government service, retail operations in San Antonio provide employment for more people than any other industrial classification. In May 1962, according to statistics of the Texas Employment Commission, 41,360 Bexar Countians, constituting 20 percent of all employment, worked for 3,955 retail establishments. Approximately one-third of all retail workers were Mexican-Americans.

The department store company chosen for detailed employment analysis was selected because it was the largest retail employer in San Antonio, it was an old and stable firm with a branch store on the West Side, it had a diversified job structure, and its reputation in the Mexican-American community as to employment of persons of this ethnic extraction was generally considered to be among the less discriminatory of the retail establishments.

The information below was secured in personal interviews with two of the firm's top executives and from a structured payroll listing of employees as of August 1, 1963.

One of San Antonio's oldest mercantile establishments, the company was locally owned until sold to a national chain in 1935. The West Side store was built in 1955. With the exception of the local telephone company and a giant insurance enterprise, it was the largest private employer in San Antonio at the time of this survey, with an average payroll of 1570 during the year ending June 30, 1963.

Table 35 shows employment by departments and the number and percentage Mexican-Americans. The 30.9 percent Mexican-American participation on the payroll is slightly less than for all retail establishments in San Antonio.

No Mexican-Americans were found among the 19 top executives and members of middle management. Most

TABLE 35

EMPLOYMENT BY DEPARTMENTS, TOTAL AND MEXICAN-AMERICAN
A SAN ANTONIO DEPARTMENT STORE COMPANY
AUGUST, 1963

	Total Employees	Mexican-Americans Total	Mexican-Americans Percent
GRAND TOTAL	1442	446	30.9
Executives and Middle Mgt.	19	0	0.0
Top Executives	6	0	0.0
Middle Mgt.	13	0	0.0
Main Store	1321	388	29.4
Dept. Mgrs. & Assts.	168	19	11.3
Dept. Mgrs., Sales Supporting	28	3	10.7
Asst. Mgrs., Sales Supporting	27	4	14.8
Dept. Mgrs., Merchandising	57	2	3.5
Asst. Mgrs., Merchandising	52	10	19.2
Mgrs., Clerical	4	0	0.0
Other Personnel	1153	369	32.0
Control and Credit	129	36	27.9
Sales Promotion and Display	61	16	26.2
Merchandising	581	138	23.8
Sales	369	79	21.4
Clerical	164	28	17.1
Stock	48	31	64.6
Personnel and Operations	240	108	45.0
Store Mgt. Staff	15	2	13.3
Employment and Personnel	7	0	0.0
Customer Service	13	3	23.1
Selling Services	64	43	60.9
Delivery	34	25	73.5
Receiving and Marking	57	33	57.9
Maintenance	48	2	4.2
Power Plant Operation	2	0	0.0
Workrooms	142	71	50.0
Applicance Service	79	38	48.1
Womcn's Tailor Shop	12	1	8.3
Men's Tailor Shop	11	10	90.9
Other Workrooms	40	22	55.0
West Side Store	102	58	56.8
Dept. Mgrs. & Assts.	23	6	26.1
Dept. Mgrs., Sales Supporting	4	1	25.0
Asst. Mgrs., Sales Supporting	2	0	0.0
Dept. Mgrs., Merchandising	17	5	29.4
Other Personnel	79	52	65.8
Sales Supporting	33	17	51.5
Merchandising	46	35	76.1

Source: Company Payroll List

persons in these categories had been brought in from other branches of the chain, and the remainder were long-time employees whose service with the company began many years before Mexican-Americans were employed in any but the more menial jobs.

Whereas virtually all main store department managers and assistant managers had been Anglos prior to World War II, 11.3% were Mexican-American in 1963--including 5.6% of the department managers and 17.7% of the assistants.

Mexican-Americans were working in all except the small personnel and power plant operation departments. A great proportion of this ethnic group were found in stock and warehouse jobs, selling services, delivery, receiving and marking, and in appliance services, men's tailor shop and other workroom classifications.

Of the 36 Mexican-Americans in the control and credit department, 11 worked in the collections section, in which all employees were required to be bilingual. The remainder were in sales audit, accounts receivable, accounts payable, payroll and other accounting jobs.

In the sales promotion and display department, all of the 16 Mexican-Americans were in the display section, making creative displays for windows and store interiors.

The delivery department employees, 73.5 percent of whom were Mexican-Americans, were reported as being among the higher paid workers, averaging $82.00 per week. A company executive frankly attributed this relatively high pay partially to the desire of the company to forestall organization of the employees by the Teamsters Union.

The maintenance department was made up of 11 mechanics and 37 porters, with one Mexican-American employed in each category. The remaining 10 mechanics were Anglos, and the other 36 porters were Negroes.

It is interesting to note that, whereas 10 of the eleven workers in the men's tailor shop were Mexican-American, there was only one among the 12 persons employed in the women's tailor shop.

At the West Side store, located in the heart of the Mexican-American sector of the city, 56.8% of the employees were of Mexican descent, including 26.1% of the department managers and their assistants.

A company executive stated that a survey of sales at the West Side store had revealed that only 43 percent of the customers were of this ethnic group. He interpreted this as meaning the store was not getting enough Mexican-American business but agreed with this writer's observation that it could also be attributed to the inferior purchasing power of these people.

The firm reportedly maintains a strict policy of nondiscrimination between Anglos and Mexican-Americans in all new hirings, pay rates, and advancement opportunities. It was conceded that a few department heads may retain some covert, probably unconscious, Anglo preferences, but top management declared that its close surveillance assured that this was a small and diminishing problem.

More widespread prejudice was found among department managers to the employment of Negroes. When the executives, in implementing a recent new policy of expanding Negro employment, decided to place the first sales person of this race in a particular department chosen because of the stability and open-mindedness of the department head, this long-time supervisor threatened to quit if a Negro were assigned to him.

Adverse customer reaction to Mexican-American sales personnel was reported to be no longer a factor in hiring, although persons of very dark skin or coarse appearance were not assigned to certain departments.

Because of rapidly expanding sales to customers from Mexico as well as increasing Mexican-American business, the company required that all sales departments have persons who speak Spanish fluently, and the great majority of these bilinguals were Mexican-American. The company included members of this ethnic group in the 25 persons chosen each year for management training.

The continuing advancements in education and social assimilation of the Mexican-Americans, together with the relatively smaller supply of qualified Anglo workers available at the pay scales of many beginning retail jobs, indicate a sustained trend toward increased employment and advancement of Mexican-Americans with this company and in the retail trade in general.

Southwestern Bell Telephone Company

The local branch of the Southwestern Bell Telephone Company was considered especially important to this research because it was the largest private employer in San Antonio and because it was the company which Mexican-Americans most frequently charged with discrimination against their group.

Unfortunately, the telephone company was the only San Antonio employer whose management refused to provide any information concerning its employment of Mexican-Americans. Several efforts to secure an interview with the San Antonio division manager to discuss such information in the summers of 1962 and 1963 were fruitless. The employment manager, who provided the limited information on general personnel policies and practices given below, promised to pass on the request to the division manager, but he gave his personal opinion that such data would be and should be considered confidential.

According to the employment manager, total company employment in San Antonio was between 1,800 and 1,900 persons. After World War II, the payroll increased rapidly from less than 1,300 in 1946 to a peak of approximately 2,000 in 1957. Labor turnover was reported as being very low, with almost no new male employees since 1955, and a total of only 32 were hired in the quarter-year preceding the interview.

The only persons considered for employment were those who made application in person at the local company employment office, although staff members worked with counsellors in high schools and took part in career days to stimulate students' interest in working for the company.

Minimum requirements for all new personnel included United States citizenship, at least high school education, satisfactory grade on an aptitude test, and passing of a physical examination by the company doctor. Other important factors were good appearance, pleasing personality, and probable permanency with the company. Clear and distinct speech, without any accent, was necessary for employment as an operator. New hirings were usually limited to persons not over thirty years of age, and only on rare occasions were persons employed older than thirty-five years.

Table 36-A shows data as of August, 1963, provided by the district representative of the Communications Workers of America, covering total and Mexican-American employment of members of the five San Antonio locals of the CWA union, all of which are employed by the telephone company. Table 36-B lists the total membership and percent Mexican-American in each of seven other CWA locals in Southwest Texas.

Weekly wage scales at that time in the occupations covered by union contract were as follows: Operators, \$57.50 to \$76.50; Accounting, \$57.50 to \$83.00; Commercial, \$63.50 to \$87.50; Plant Craft, Installers, Repairmen, and Linemen, \$65.50 to \$128.00.

Local telephone company employment of Mexican-Americans in occupations covered by contract with the CWA was only five percent, compared to representation of 36 percent by this racial group in San Antonio's total employment in 1960. By contrast, 93 of the 95 employees in these categories in Laredo were Mexican-Americans. While it is true that 90 percent of Laredo's total employed in 1960 were Mexican-Americans, the important point is that persons of this ethnic descent have been able to qualify for, and work satisfactorily in, these diverse occupations.

TABLE 36-A

MEMBERSHIPS, TOTAL AND MEXICAN-AMERICAN
FIVE COMMUNICATIONS WORKERS OF AMERICA LOCAL UNIONS
REPRESENTING SAN ANTONIO TELEPHONE WORKERS, AUGUST, 1963

Local No.	Telephone Company Department	Total Members	Mexican-American Number	Mexican-American Percent
6103	Toll Traffic Operators	400	50	12
6104	Local Operators	131	15	11
6142	Accounting & Commercial	267	6	2
6143	Plant craft, Installers, Repairmen, Linemen	600	6	1
6131	Janitors, Garagemen, and Maids	50	0	0
	TOTALS	1448	77	5

TABLE 36-B

MEMBERSHIPS, TOTAL AND PERCENT MEXICAN-AMERICAN
SEVEN COMMUNICATIONS WORKERS OF AMERICA LOCAL UNIONS
IN SOUTHWEST TEXAS, AUGUST, 1963

Local No.	Cities	Total Members	Percent Mexican-American
6108	Brownsville	75	50
6109	Harlingen	143	5
6110	Laredo	95	98
6135	McAllen, Edinburg, Mission	149	10
6137	Corpus Christi	450	8
6176	San Marcos	24	8
6208	Victoria	130	3
	TOTALS	1066	18

Source: District 6, Communications Workers of America

All members of San Antonio Local No. 6143--janitors, garagemen, and maids--were reported to be Negroes. Membership other than Mexican-Americans in the other four locals was reported to be entirely Anglos. There were only 12 Mexican-Americans among the total of 867 in the accounting and commercial division and plant and field operations combined.

The writer observed the employment department, customer services, and other nonunion staff categories without seeing a single person who appeared to be of Mexican extraction. Only in the female operator occupations had the Mexican-Americans made any real penetration of telephone company employment in San Antonio, with a representation of about 12 percent of workers in these jobs.

The foregoing information has convinced this writer that, with the exception of employment of women operators, there existed a continuing practice at the San Antonio office of the Southwestern Bell Telephone Company tacitly to consider jobs as janitors, garagemen, and maids as "Negro" and all other employment as "Anglo."

Data in Table 36-B indicate that similar conditions exist at five of the seven other heavily Mexican-American areas, with Laredo and Brownsville being the only cities in which large proportions of workers were of this racial extraction.

San Antonio's Mexican-Americans appeared frustrated in their efforts to secure increased and more diversified employment, since the telephone company, as a private monopoly, could not be subjected to a consumer boycott nor to voter rejection.

Actually a number of avenues for seeking redress are open. The oldest and probably least promising action would be an appeal to the state regulatory commission to exert pressure on the company. Another alternative is to file charges against the company as a federal contractor with the President's Committee on Equal Employment Opportunity. Charges of unfair labor practice against both the company and the CWA union could be filed with the National Labor Relations Board. The probability of favorable action by the NLRB is much greater since the Board decided in the 1964 Hughes Tool case that violation of the duty of fair representation constitutes an unfair labor practice.[9]
The most recent means of action against discrimination is the utilization of Title VII of the Civil Rights Act of 1964, which became effective for employers of 100 or more workers on July 2, 1965.

---

[9]Ray Marshall, "Equal Employment Opportunity: Problems and Prospects," Unpublished address delivered to the Industrial Relations Research Association, Buffalo, N.Y., May 3, 1965, p. 18.

A Large Insurance Company

This organization is an outstanding example of the indirect influence of the military establishments on the economy of San Antonio. Operated to provide automobile, real and personal property, and personal liability insurance exclusively for commissioned and warrant officers of the U.S. armed services, this mutual type organization was the city's second largest private employer in August, 1963, with a payroll of approximately 1,700 persons.[10]

Approximately 600 employees, 35 percent of the total, were reported as being Mexican-American. Of the 250 supervisory personnel, about 50 were of this racial stock. Ninety percent of the firm's employees were women, who, except for those in supervisory capacities, worked in clerical jobs--secretaries, stenographers, typists, key punch operators, file clerks, general clerical, etc. Men were employed almost exclusively in administrative, technical and maintenance capacities and in claims work. Mexican-Americans constituted about one-fourth of male employment and were working in all the above categories. No breakdown of job classifications or of pay scales was made available.

---

[10]Information reported was obtained in personal interviews with the personnel director and the job analyst except as otherwise noted.

The personnel director stated that the company strictly maintained a long-standing policy of making no distinction between Anglos and Mexican-Americans in filling any job openings. This was generally confirmed by local Mexican-American leaders and representatives of the Texas Employment Commission.

No information was sought or offered concerning employment of Negroes; however, a representative of the Chamber of Commerce told the writer that this firm was among the first to offer its cooperation in a recent movement for voluntary extension of Negro employment.

Virtually all new employees were screened, tested, and referred by the Texas Employment Commission. High school graduation was required of all applicants, and they were required to make satisfactory scores on general clerical and general knowledge tests, as well as in stenographic skills for jobs involving such skills. The management operated a comprehensive training and upgrading program, filling advanced jobs from within whenever possible.

The working environment contrasted sharply with that of the West Side residential areas in which most of the Mexican-American employees lived. The headquarters building, situated in the northeast part of the city, was modern, spacious, and tastefully and efficiently laid out. The dress, grooming, and general appearance of the employees were appropriate to this environment.

The personnel director refuted the contention made by some employers that Mexican-American girls lacked knowledge and sense of taste in American dress and grooming. They tended to assimilate readily with other company personnel. She found that persons of this ethnic group usually had good "ears" for music and sense of rhythm, and they made excellent typists and key punch operators. The management provided counselling, including matters of personal hygiene where needed, to its employees. Visiting nurse service was also provided.

The personnel director and the Texas Employment Commission representative in charge of referrals to this company agreed that the greatest deterrents among Mexican-Americans to qualifying for employment were inadequate education and language deficiencies. The latter problem was most pronounced in writing, including the common error of translating into Spanish idiom.

The personnel director expressed a strong conviction that the local public school system was failing to provide adequately for the education of Mexican-American children, and she stressed the need for language laboratories to aid these students to learn English. She felt the community was lethargic in seeking to supply these needs and decried leaders' unwillingness to use federal funds.

The practice of equal employment opportunity to Mexican-Americans by this large San Antonio employer has been a good example and no doubt has been an influence in lessening local discriminatory employment practices. The new knowledge and understanding which workers in this environment have taken home to their West Side families has been a positive force toward higher motivation and easier assimilation of members of that ethnic group in that blighted area of the city.

Services: A Laundry-Dry Cleaning Company

One of San Antonio's largest laundry-dry cleaning establishments was chosen as representative of the city's service industries, in which the great majority of jobs are characterized by low wages and long hours, minimal mental and educational requirements, little job diversification and quite limited advancement possibilities. As expected, these jobs are filled predominatly with Mexican-Americans.

The laundry-dry cleaning plant chosen for study was founded in 1926 by the father of the present owner. No union had bargaining representation for any of the company's workers, as was true of all other such establishments in San Antonio. The personnel of the firm totaled 316--with 204 employed in plant operations serving the general public,

55 doing cleaning and laundry for an air base under contract with the company, and 57 nonplant employees. A more detailed breakdown of employment, showing Mexican-American participation, as secured in an interview with the owner, is shown in Table 37.

With the exception of an Anglo male supervisor on each shift, the laundry workers were all women. Men were employed in all cleaning and pressing of men's clothing, and women performed all cleaning and pressing of women's clothing. Among plant operative personnel, Negroes made up the majority of the workers not Mexican-American.

Five Mexican-Americans, six Anglos and one Negro held plant supervisory positions. The office and substation workers of this ethnic extraction were women. The Mexican-American maintenance employee was a welding and pipefitting helper.

Payment of plant workers was on individual and group piecework incentive plans. A Christmas bonus arrangement was considered an important factor in reducing turnover during the previous six years. No pay scales were made available. The following information on going wages in the industry in San Antonio was secured from the local office of the Texas Employment Commission on three major job classifications:

TABLE 37

EMPLOYMENT BY DEPARTMENTS,
TOTAL AND MEXICAN-AMERICAN,
A SAN ANTONIO LAUNDRY-DRY CLEANING COMPANY,
AUGUST, 1963

Department	Total Employees	Mexican-American
General Plant:		
Laundry	160	Approximately 90%
Cleaning and Pressing	44	Approximately 90%
Air Base Contract:		
Laundry	50	Approximately 90%
Cleaning and Pressing	5	5
Nonplant:		
Office	7	2
Substation Attendants	20	2
Maintenance	5	1

Job Classification	Hourly Wage Minimum	Maximum	Typical
Shirt Presser	$0.65	$0.85	$0.75
Machine Presser	.65	1.50	1.00
Dry Cleaner	1.00	1.50	1.25

The owner of the company surveyed reported that reliable, qualified applicants for job openings were rarely found, making it necessary to train nearly all new employees. The firm had no stated minimum requirements for employment.

Mexican-Americans were found to be quite capable in hand and machine operations and at least average in willingness to work and loyalty. Particularly the young women of this group have evidenced better education, appearance, and interest in improving their economic conditions; on a number of occasions they had found shortcuts in the use of equipment.

Transportation: Teamster Union Representation

The information below was taken from an interview in August, 1963, with Raymond C. Shafer, South Texas Regional Representative for the Teamsters Union, and from the Southern Conference Local Freight Forwarding Pickup and Delivery Agreement, effective February 1, 1961, to January 31, 1964.

Teamster Union membership of approximately 650 in San Antonio at the time of the interview was reported to be double that of 1953. Specific data on Mexican-American memberships were not made available; however, the union representative stated that well over one-half of the members in San Antonio were of this ethnic group.

Hourly wage rates in effect in August, 1963, were as follows: Checker $3.04, Driver $3.04, and Dockman $2.88. In addition employers contributed $3.50 per week for each employee into a health and welfare fund and $6.00 per week into a pension fund, provided eight paid holidays, and provided seniority-based paid vacations of from one to four weeks.

Local Teamster labor agreements were reported as including all major common carrier motor freight lines, all railroad trucking operations, and truck delivery for most of the meat packers, several biscuit companies, and one dairy.

Shafer, whose dynamic leadership in voter registration and compaign strategy had been largely instrumental in the unprecedented election of an all Mexican-American city council in Crystal City, Texas, in April, 1963, expressed the conviction that it was necessary for Mexican-Americans to organize politically before they could effectively organize economically. He considered the $1.75 Texas poll tax a major deterrent to advancement of this racial group, and he expressed confidence that abolition of the poll tax would accelerate the already rapidly growing Mexican-American vote.

Seven Professions

Decennial comparisons of total number of persons and Mexican-American representation, based on Spanish surnames, in seven leading professional categories in San Antonio are shown in Table 38.

The data revealed a small but persistent increase in Mexican-Americans, both numerically and as a proportion ofthe total, in each of the professions, with the exception of architects, for which none in this ethnic group was found as late as 1950, and in the special borderline category of midwives.

Mexican-Americans in 1961 still represented less than ten percent in each of the major professions--accountants, architects, attorneys, dentists, and physicians--in contrast to their comprising 33 percent of total employment in San Antonio.

Conversations of the writer with numerous professional men in San Antonio revealed general agreement in several areas.

TABLE 38

NUMBER OF PERSONS AND MEXICAN-AMERICAN REPRESENTATION

SEVEN LEADING PROFESSIONS

SAN ANTONIO, TEXAS, 1940-41, 1950, 1961

Profession	1940-41			1950			1961		
		Mexican-American			Mexican-American			Mexican-American	
	Total	Number	Per cent	Total	Number	Per cent	Total	Number	Per cent
Accountants, Public	49	0	0.0	120	3	2.5	145	5	3.4
Architects	39	0	0.0	56	0	0.0	82	4	4.9
Attorneys	528	19	3.6	483	20	4.1	605	46	7.6
Dentists	141	4	2.8	172	6	3.5	235	13	5.5
Physicians and Surgeons	375	24	6.4	506	33	6.5	579	55	9.5
Nurses	326	5	1.5	553	39	7.1	365	44	12.1
Midwives	37	36	97.3	46	43	93.5	34	33	97.0

Sources: San Antonio City Directory, 1940-41.
San Antonio Telephone Directory, January, 1950, and September, 1961.

Medical and legal practitioners from the elite old families of Spanish and Mexican lineage had served San Antonio in these professions since the early history of the city. On the other hand, these aristocrats shunned such business-oriented professions as accounting and architecture.

Increasing numbers of Mexican-Americans from middle and even lower social and economic backgrounds have been graduating from college and training for the professions. This has been most pronounced in the field of law. That few are entering public accounting and architecture may be attributed partially to a general cultural disinterest in these vocations and, to a somewhat greater extent, difficulty of success because of continuing, though diminishing, racial discrimination. The dean of the graduate school of St. Mary's University stated that Mexican-American graduates with master's degrees in accounting virtually all were forced to accept employment in federal service or in other cities because they were unable to compete successfully with Anglos with equal qualifications for private employment or in private practice in San Antonio.

At the time of this survey as well as in the past, Mexican-Americans entering the major professions in San Antonio were, almost without exception, from families who had "escaped" the West Side and were living in neighborhoods with high proportions of Anglos.

The fairly rapid rise in the proportion of Mexican-Americans in nursing to 12.1 percent in 1961 can be attributed, partially, to the growing acceptance by this sector of the population of professionally trained medical care. and partially to the shortage of Anglo girls willing to endure the rigorous training, hard work and relatively low remuneration of nursing.

Midwives in San Antonio are licensed by the city, and may therefore be considered in a very broad sense as professionals. While only 34 midwives, of which 33 were Mexican-Americans, were listed in the 1961 telephone directory, the San Antonio Express in an article on March 2, 1964, quoted W. B. Forster, administrator of the Robert B. Green Memorial Hospital, the Bexar County public hospital, as estimating that several hundred midwives were then practicing home-style obstetrics, mostly on the West Side. He characterized the situation as alarming.

Summary and Analysis

The demechanization of San Antonio's pecan shelling industry during the 1930's was a classic example of the long-range diseconomy of technological inversion not uncommon in that period, plus the ruthless exploitation through meager pay rates of the large, vulnerable Mexican-American segment of the population. Conversely, no better example is found of the salutary effect of the Fair Labor Standards Act than in the pecan industry, in spite of the sharp reduction of employment and dire predictions by the operators of the industry's demise. Shelling operations a quarter of a century after passage of the act were still performed almost exclusively by Mexican-American women at the respectable minimum pay of $1.25 per hour, and the season of substantially full employment had been extended to eight months. Volume of pecans shelled and sold compared favorably with that of the 1930's, and increased productivity had made possible continued profits to employers.

The writer's research, including interviews with San Antonio business, professional and labor leaders, has led him to the conviction that extension of coverage of the Fair Labor Standards Act to include such service industries as laundries and cleaners, hotels and restaurants, and to include smaller retail establishments would provide a stong boost to the economic and social status of the Mexican-American workers making up the employment in most of the lower wage jobs in these industries. The added purchasing power would provide a net benefit to the city's economy in spite of some expected temporary reduction in employment. As was found in the pecan, clothing and cigar industries, workers displaced would be principally from multi-worker familes in which increased earnings of employed members would at least largely offset incomes of those losing jobs. Furthermore, young people released from the necessity of working to help support their families could continue their education and training, with the added incentive of expectations of higher incomes.

On the other hand, it appeared doubtful that early increase of the federal statutory minimum wage, reduction of the forty-hour week before overtime, or the requiring of double time for overtime would be on balance best for the Mexican-Americans. While education, training and other qualifications of this ethnic group were improving, the continued limitations of a large proportion would likely result in widespread loss of employment from such increases in employers' wage bills.

San Antonio businessmen and industrialists had not forgotten after twenty-five years the communist leadership of the pecan workers' union and the suspected, though never proven, communist influence in the subsequent CIO organization of the pecan shellers. The success of foes of organized labor in general and industrial unions in particular has been enhanced by their portraying to employers an identification of aggressive union leadership with radical political ideology.

The broad participation and stubborn persistance of organized pecan shellers against tremendous odds in the 1930's, and the current majority membership of the Teamsters Union in San Antonio provide further evidence of the responsiveness of Mexican-Americans to unionization.

The studies of employment of the retail department store and the large insurance company revealed definite programs by top managements for expanding job opportunities to both Mexican-Americans and Negroes, although the department store executives recognized the necessity to overcome racial bias of some department heads.

Information obtained in the study of employment of the local branch of the telephone company strongly supported the almost universal contention by Mexican-American leaders that racial discrimination was widely practiced. While repeated efforts to obtain information on ethnic distribution of employees from management proved fruitless, data obtained on workers covered by contracts with five local unions of the Communications Workers of America was quite revealing. Of the 1,448 workers covered by contracts of the five locals, only 77, or 5 percent, were Mexican-Americans. Sixty-five of this racial stock were women operators. Only 12 of 867 employees in accounting, commercial, plant craft, installers, repairmen and linemen were Mexican-American. All others in these categories were Anglos. On the other hand, all 50 workers employed as janitors, garagemen and maids were Negroes.

Proof that Mexican-Americans had been found capable of satisfactorily performing the duties of substantially all the above-mentioned jobs is found in the employment of the Laredo branch of the company, where 98% were shown to be Mexican-American, and at the Brownsville office, where 50% of employees were of this racial stock. Further evidence that ethnic discrimination in local branches was, however, widespread was revealed in the employment data of the five other heavily Mexican-American localities in the South Texas district, in which Mexican-American employment ranged from three percent to ten percent of the total payrolls.

Mexican-Americans were frustrated in their efforts to overcome ethnic discrimination by the telephone company mainly because they lacked the capable and agressive leadership needed to utilize the several available avenues for redress.

CHAPTER IX

POLITICS AND PUBLIC EMPLOYMENT

Failure to achieve effective political organization for advancement of their common interests has been a significant factor in the retardation of the economic and social progress of Mexican-Americans in San Antonio and throughout the Southwest.

This chapter will be devoted to a discussion of underlying deterrents to Mexican-American political maturity, an analysis of some of the major political developments in San Antonio during the last twenty-five years, and an examination of municipal employment information, including widespread charges of discrimination in personnel practices at two city-owned public utilities.

Deterrents to Mexican-American Political Maturity

Students of Mexican-American affairs virtually all agreed that the Texas poll tax of $1.75 severely restricted the voting power of this ethnic group. For the great proportion of poor Mexican-Americans, it has been difficult to deny their families the satisfaction of urgent immediate needs during the poll tax payment period, October 1 through

January 31, in order to pay for the privilege of voting in elections the following August and November.

An aggresive campaign to repeal the Texas poll tax through a constitutional amendment was defeated in November, 1963 by a vote 303,763 to 327,524. The Bexar County vote was 18,373 to 15,664 in favor of repeal. After the amendment bid was lost, hope for early abolition of this archaic and discriminatory qualification for voting turned to the federal government.

Until recent years, a large proportion of Mexican-Americans were ineligible to vote bacause they were aliens who, through choice or because of illegal entry, did not meet the citizenship requirement. Menefee and Cassmore reported that in 1939 at least half of the Mexicans of voting age in San Antonio were not citizens.[1] This situation has been improving rapidly, however. Only slightly more than ten percent of San Antonio Mexican-Americans were aliens in 1950 (Tables 6 and 7). While it can be assumed that the majority of these persons were 21 years old or over, this would still place the alien proportion of the voting age in this ethnic group at less than twenty percent. Continued decline in the significance of alien status as a factor in Mexican-American political participation appears certain.

---

[1]Menefee and Cassmore, p. 50.

A large, though diminishing, proportion of Mexican-Americans had moved about so much that they had difficulty in proving legal residence, were away from their legal domiciles at election time, or failed to become interested in elections and other community affairs. This had been particularly true of the more than 12,000 migrant agricultural workers concentrated in and around San Antonio, with the annual exodus of this group well under way in April and many of them not returning until after mid-November. Transiency as a factor in political activity of Mexican-Americans is expected to continue to decline, particularly that due to migrant farm work. Henry LeBlanc, chief of the Farm Placement Service of the Texas Employment Commission predicted in a speech on November 6, 1964, that within three years all crop harvesting would be done by machine, displacing the Texas migrant workers, then numbered at 128,000.[2]

Students of Mexican-American problems have found that the political retardation of people of Mexican descent has been caused in large part by a combination of resistance to cultural change, ignorance, and lack of competent and trustworthy leadership within their own ethnic group.[3]

---

[2]San Antonio Express, Nov. 7, 1965.

[3]John H. Burma, Spanish-speaking Groups in the United States, Duke University Press, Durham, 1954, pp. 104,

The great majority of twentieth century immigrants from Mexico have been of Indian and Spanish-Indian "mestizo" stock. A high proportion of them were illiterate peasants from a semifeudal agricultural background, with a heritage of complacent subservience and dependence on their "patrons." As might be expected, when these people migrated to the United States, with its unfamiliar laws and customs and different language, they voted, if at all, with a poll tax paid by their employers and for candidates favored by their employers.

Even those Mexican-Americans who were more knowledgeable and concerned for their economic and social advancement were commonly ineffectual politically because their exaggerated individualism, manifested by oversensitiveness, jealousies and animosities, prevented them from organizing and cooperating toward common goals. Unfortunately, too often the Mexican-American's mistrust of his ethnic leaders was well founded, for they tended to become self-serving "coyotes" or "exploiters" who exploited the ignorant through providing real or spurious services for

---

123; Pauline R. Kibbe, Latin-Americans in Texas, The University of New Mexico Press, Albuquerque, 1946, pp. 227, 228; Paul S. Taylor, An American-Mexican Frontier, University of North Carolina Press, Chapel Hill, 1934, pp. 236, 285; Ruth D. Tuck, Not with the Fist, Harcourt Brace and Co., New York, 1946, pp. 146-148; Woods, op. cit., pp. 74-81, 97.

exorbitant fees and delivered their votes to Anglo politicians for personal gain.

Recent Political Developments

The Mexican-American West Side had supported Maury Maverick when he ran unsuccessfully for re-election to Congress, and, in his campaign for the office of mayor of San Antonio in 1939, he pledged assistance to this ethnic group. Upon his election, he took immediate steps to improve the city's notoriously poor health program, became a prime mover in getting San Antonio's first federal housing project, Alazan Courts, started on the West Side in 1940, and gave official support to a drive against usurious loan companies which had been victimizing the Mexican ethnic population for years.

Prior to the end of World War II, Mexican-Americans in San Antonio had made little headway toward concerted political action, and no person of this racial extraction had been elected to a city office. The war, however, marked a turning point in the political development of the Mexican-American population. Civilians were encouraged by their successful penetration of job levels previously denied them and the consequent increases in incomes and standards of living. Many rejected their formerly accepted roles as second-class citizens and began to seek political solutions to the many long-standing problems of their ethnic groups. Returning veterans were no longer satisfied to return to slums and pick up again their marginal existence. Many improved their qualifications politically as well as economically through taking advantage of the educational provisions of the G.I. Bill, and they became increasingly active politically.

In 1948, the Mexican-Americans and Negroes combined their voting strengths and elected representatives of both groups to membership on school boards. Ethnic leaders observed that this was the first time that the residents of the West Side had stuck together in supporting a Mexican-American candidate.

Republicans, conservative Democrats, and independents formed in 1950 a local political organization known as the Good Government League. This group, in the following year, spearheaded a successful campaign for a new city charter, replacement of the grossly inefficient mayor-commissioner city government with a council-manager municipal administration and the implementation of an effective civil service system. San Antonians are in virtually complete agreement that the new arrangement has been a long overdue improvement.

The Good Government League has elected its slate of mayor and nine councilmen every two years since 1952. One Mexican-American councilman was elected in 1952, and two were elected in 1954 and in each subsequent election, by tacit agreement of the leadership in the Good Government League, a number of whom are conservative Mexican-Americans. These men pointed out that their moderate approach to serving the city's Mexican-Americans has also resulted in appointments of representatives of this ethnic group to all of the municipal boards: hospital board 2, library board 2, water board 1, police and civil service board 2, urban renewal board 2, and city planning board 2.

Voter turnout at city elections, held in April of odd-numbered years, has always been very small. In the 1963 election, less than 15 percent of those who paid poll taxes voted. In school board elections, less than five percent participation of eligible voters has been the general rule.

Bexar County has the commissioner form of government, with a commissioner elected by the voters of each of four precincts.

Albert Pena, Jr., a Mexican-American lawyer, was first elected in 1956 as County Commissioner for Precinct 1, the southwest quadrant of the county, which includes the greater part of the city's West Side. In November, 1964, he was re-elected for a third four-year term. He has been an articulate spokesman for the liberal wing of the Democratic Party.

In 1964, Pena was state chairman of the Political Association of Spanish-speaking Organizations, PASO. The major objectives of PASO were described by Pena as increasing the voter registration and educating people to participate in politics, and focusing the attention of the public on the problems of the Spanish-speaking people. He asserted that the voter registration drives conducted by PASO chapters throughout Texas had increased the number of Mexican-Americans with poll taxes from 230,000 in 1960 to 450,000 in 1964.

Pena was also chairman of the Bexar County Coalition, a confederation of four broad groups: Mexican-Americans--represented by PASO, Negro organizations, organized labor--represented by COPE of the AFL-CIO, and representatives of a broad spectrum of liberals designated as independent liberals. Since 1958, the coalition had named slates for county office and state legislative seats. Pena boasted of the election of 90 percent of coalition-backed candidates between 1958 and 1964, including two Mexican-American state representatives.

PASO leaders, headed by Pena, shared credit with Ray Shafer and the Teamsters Union for steering the successful campaign of an all Mexican-American city council against a long-entrenched Anglo administration in Crystal City, Texas, in the spring of 1963. Unfortunately, dissension soon broke out among the uneducated and inexperienced councilmen, and trouble developed between the mayor and Ray Shafer. The new administration was defeated by a predominantly Anglo council slate in the spring of 1965. This may well be an indication of doubtful viability of the Bexar County Coalition as well as the long-run effectiveness of joint Mexican ethnic and Teamster union action.

Neither PASO nor the Coalition had sponsored slates of candidates for city offices in San Antonio in opposition to the Good Government League. PASO still lacked the required disciplined solidarity, and the leaderships of the Coalition's component groups had not been able to agree on candidates to oppose the smooth organization of the League. Pena has been outspoken in his criticism of the conservative policies and programs of the city administration, and he has frequently endorsed personally the opposition candidates running as independents.

It may be argued that the political conflict of Pena and at least a large segment of the Mexican-American electorate with the leadership of this ethnic group in the Good Government League has tended to weaken the overall political effectiveness of San Antonio's Mexican-Americans. On the other hand, a key Mexican-American member of the League pointed out that Pena and PASO, by demanding less desirable alternative action, on a number of occasions helped him and his associates to get their programs to improve the status and living conditions of the Mexican-Americans approved by the administration.

The rapid rise in public office of San Antonio's Henry B. Gonzalez has been an outstanding example both to Mexican-Americans and Anglos of the political possibilities of persons of this ethnic extraction. Gonzalez was elected to the city council in San Antonio for the first of two terms in 1953. He was elected state senator in 1956, the first person of Mexican descent to be elected to this office from Bexar County since 1846. After being returned to the senate for a second term, he was elected to Congress from the 20th District of Texas, the first Texan of Mexican descent to be elected to the U.S. House of Representatives. In 1962 and 1964 he was re-elected by large margins.

The congressman remained aloof from the differences among his ethnic group, but he was not unmindful of the Mexican-American population. A personnel officer at

Kelly Field pointed out that claims of discrimination against workers of Mexican descent had multiplied since Gonzalez became congressman, and he added that one could be sure that each claim was carefully investigated. Gonzalez' persuasive opposition to the extension of Public Law 78 was a prime factor in bringing about the termination of the Mexican bracero program. He has been a prime mover in getting approval of federal poverty program projects for San Antonio.

It would be a mistake to assume from the foregoing that in the short period of time since World War II the Mexican-Americans of San Antonio had attained political maturity. The continued long-time practice of Mexican-Americans who have broken through the educational, economic, and social barriers to dissociate themselves from the fight for advancement of their ethnic group has kept the movement short of quality leadership. A large proportion of Mexican-Americans still gave narrow family allegiances, petty jealousies and personal animosities precedence over concerted action toward common goals.

Liberal leaders cited the small vote in municipal elections as substantiation of their charge that the local power structure did not want a politically educated consitituency. They pointed to the persistent squalor and inadequate community facilities on the West Side as evidence both of the low priority given by the city administration to the needs of West Side residents and of the continued political ineffectiveness of these people.

A Calculation of 1960 Voter Participation

In order to obtain an approximation of the relative voter participation of low income Mexican-Americans as compared with that of other Bexar Countians, the writer calculated for the 1960 presidential election the proportion of residents 21 years old and over who cast votes in the economically depressed, predominantly Mexican-American County Commissioner's Precinct No. 1, and corresponding data were derived for the remainder of the county.

The number of persons 21 years old and over residing in County Precinct No. 1 was obtained by taking the sum of the 1960 census tract enumerations of this age group for tracts corresponding to the geographical area of the precinct. Data on numbers of votes cast were taken from the official vote count.

That voter participation among low-income Mexican-Americans was still badly retarded in 1960 is clearly revealed by the barely 30 percent of adults in Precinct 1 who voted, only two-thirds the proportion who voted in the other three precincts. Actually, the disparity between Mexican-American participation and that of citizens of other ethnic groups is probably somewhat greater than that of the precinct distinction, due to inclusion in the data of the Mexican-Americans residing in Precincts 2, 3, and 4, particularly those living immediately north of Precinct 1.

	Persons 21 Years And Over		Percent
	Total	Votes Cast	Voting
Bexar County	377,990	149,969	39.7
Precinct 1	113,960	34,137	30.0
Precincts 2, 3, 4	264,030	115,832	43.9

Sources: U.S. Censuses of Population and Housing: 1960. Census Tracts, San Antonio, Texas, pp. 23-41. Bexar County official election vote count.

Municipal Employment

With the exception of three separate agencies--the City Public Service Board, the City Water Board, and the Transit System--employment for municipal departments was handled through the office of the City Personnel Manager, who referred qualified candidates to 17 departments and 2 special offices for approval.

Table 39 shows municipal employment by department in August, 1962.

TABLE 39

MUNICIPAL EMPLOYMENT BY DEPARTMENTS

CITY OF SAN ANTONIO, TEXAS

AUGUST, 1962

Department	Employees
Office of City Manager	5
City Clerk	3
Legal	40
Finance	198
Police	708
Fire	508
Public Health	202
Public Works	1,037
Parks and Recreation	356
Aviation	64
Personnel	34
Planning	22
Public Library	120
Housing and Inspection	72
Civil Defense	1
Urban Renewal	17
Welfare	24
Traffic and Transportation	53
Tuberculosis Control	7
Total	3,471

Source: City Personnel Records

The personnel manager stated emphatically that he rigidly enforced a policy of equal employment opportunity for Mexican-Americans in his department and that he had no evidence of discrimination by any of his staff or heads of other departments to whom he referred persons for openings. Employment policy relating to Negroes was apparently in a state of change; the personnel manager volunteered the information that the first Negro girl had been recently hired to work in the city hall.

He offered to permit the writer to check a personnel file card arrangement for identification of Spanish surnames, and a tentative acceptance was made; however, a survey of ethnic leadership revealed no charges of discrimination, and the proposed card check was dropped.

The City Public Service Board. The facilities providing electricity and natural gas to San Antonio were bought by the city and put under the management of a City Public Service Board. When the bonded indebtedness of these utilities was refinanced in 1951, the board was made an independent agency, and its membership was made self-perpetuating, reportedly at the insistance of the bondholders to insure against political mismanagement.

The City Public Service Board was denounced almost unanimously by Mexican-Americans for asserted discrimination against persons of Mexican descent in all but laborer and semiskilled jobs.

Table 40 gives data on Mexican-American employment secured from State Representative John C. Alaniz. The information had been prepared for him from the payroll of the City Public Service Board.

Total of all employees as of August 20, 1960, was reported as 2,100, making the proportion of Mexican-Americans about 33 percent.

The multilith operator of Mexican descent was one of two assistants to the head of the printing shop. The cadet engineer was a young college graduate.

The personnel director, when interviewed by the writer in August, 1962, declined to supply any detailed data on employment, although she acknowledged that the 1960 information received from Representative Alaniz was probably essentially correct. She added that total employment as of the time of the interview was around 2,150.

She denied that discrimination was practiced against Mexican-Americans, adding that a much larger proportion of this ethnic extraction did not meet educational requirements, for which high school graduation was the minimum, and many failed the rigid physical examination. Each applicant was thoroughly investigated as to police

TABLE 40

MEXICAN-AMERICAN EMPLOYMENT BY JOB CLASSIFICATION

CITY PUBLIC SERVICE BOARD

SAN ANTONIO, TEXAS, AUGUST 20, 1960

Job Classification	Employees
Multilith Supervisor	1
Cadet Engineer	1
Draftsmen	2
Time and Material Clerk	1
Labor Foreman	1
Pipemen	32
Truck Drivers	23
Car Washers	8
Helpers or Designated Laborers	50
Special Laborers	138
Common Laborers	415
Porters, Maids, and Messengers	16
Total	688

record and credit habits, and Mexican-Americans frequently were disqualified on these counts.

The general procedure followed in filling openings was for the employment division to interview and test applicants and to investigate those otherwise qualified. Three to six applicants were referred to the department manager with the job opening, and the latter made the final selection.

The writer was convinced, after further interviews with Mexican-American leaders and persons who reported having been rejected for employment, that widespread covert discrimination against this ethnic group was practiced by the City Public Service Board in higher level jobs. The failure of Mexican-Americans effectively to penetrate even the middle level jobs in any department indicated the likelihood discrimination was encountered at least partially in the employment division, probably centered in extremely rigid application of disqualifications because of police records and delinquent credit.

That considerably larger proportions of Mexican-Americans were arrested for petty offenses than were Anglos was found to be true. It was widely held by some of San Antonio's most responsible leaders, however, that Mexican-Americans were commonly arrested under circumstances in which Anglos would not be picked up by the police. They were most often arrested for drunkenness, petty larceny, burglary, and disorderly conduct. They were reportedly no more prone than Anglos to commit major crimes.

The Mexican-American's propensity for getting into the clutches of loan sharks and for yielding to persuasion to buy on installments beyond his means has been largely due to his ignorance of credit arrangements and the predatory nature of some creditors. Interested employers had told the writer that they had benefited as well as their employees when they had helped these workers out of credit jams and educated them in good credit habits. Some employers had helped their workers by promoting the establishment of credit unions.

The monopoly nature of the City Public Service Board's services, together with the autonomy of control by its self-perpetuating board, have made it difficult for Mexican-Americans to combat discrimination. It is expected that discrimination may be at least reduced through filing of charges under Title VII of the Civil Rights Law of 1964.

City Water Board. The municipal water system was also under the management of a separate board of trustees, but, unlike the City Public Service Board, the City Water Board trustees were appointed by the city council.

The employment data in Tables 41-A, 41-B, and 42 were provided by the personnel manager at the request of the Mexican-American vice-chairman of the board, Alfred G. Vasquez.

Mexican-Americans comprised 91 percent of 218 workers in various laborer and helper categories. While the beginning pay scales were small, they all were above the FLSA minimum wage and provided for several increases.

All administrative office and skilled personnel were included in the monthly classifications. Commissioner Pena and some others charged discrimination against persons of Mexican descent in employment in these categories. The Mexican-American participation of only 12.4 percent was quite small, and no one of this ethnic group had attained a high level position. On the other hand, distribution was diversified and included fairly high level office, technical, and skilled classifications.

After study of the data, interviews with the vice-chairman of the board, the general manager, and the personnel manager, and discussions with knowledgeable community leaders, the writer concluded that discrimination in employment was probably less than in most private firms, that the relatively small degree of discrimination resulted from retention of ethnic bias among line managers rather than

TABLE 41-A

EMPLOYMENT BY ETHNIC GROUP
CITY WATER BOARD, SAN ANTONIO, TEXAS
JULY 1, 1964

Classification	Total Employed	Mexican-American		Negro	
		Total	Percent	Total	Percent
Monthly	315	39	12.4	8	2.5
Special Monthly	48	39	81.3	9	18.8
Total Monthly	363	78	21.5	17	4.7
Hourly	170	160	94.1	2	1.2
Totals	533	238	44.7	19	3.6

Source: City Water Board Personnel Records

TABLE 41-B

SALARY AND WAGE SCALES
SPECIAL MONTHLY AND HOURLY EMPLOYEES
CITY WATER BOARD, SAN ANTONIO, TEXAS
JULY 1, 1964

Work Classification	Beginning Scale
Special Monthly:	
Janitors	$221
Groundsmen	221
Groundsmen-Drivers	232
Rotation Laborers	256
Rotation Helpers	286
Hourly:	
Laborers	1.31
Helpers	1.47

Note: Janitors, Groundsmen, and Groundsmen-Drivers receive increases of $12 per month after 6, 9, and 12 months.
Rotation Laborers and Helpers receive increases of $10 per month after 6, 9, and 12 months.
Hourly Laborers and Helpers receive increases of $0.05 per hour after 6 months and after 12 months.

Source: City Water Board Personnel Records

TABLE 42

MEXICAN-AMERICAN AND NEGRO MONTHLY EMPLOYEES
CITY WATER BOARD, SAN ANTONIO, TEXAS
JULY 1, 1964

Occupation	Mexican-American	Negro
Main Office:		
Internal Auditor	1	0
Computer Operator	1	0
Reports Control Clerk	2	0
Collection Contact Clerk	1	0
Draftsman, Maps and Rec.	2	0
File Control Clerk	1	0
Customer Records Clerk	0	1
Meter Reader	3	2
PBX - Receptionist	3	0
Printing Machine Operator	1	0
Key Punch Operator	1	0
Mail Cashier	1	0
Final & Del. Bill Clerk	1	0
Skilled and Semiskilled:		
Equipment Operator II	1	0
Foreman, Street Repair	1	0
Auto Body Repairman	1	0
Mechanic	1	0
Foreman, Grounds Maint.	1	0
Apprentice Electrician	1	0
Foreman, Vault and Street	1	0
Field Meter Technician	4	0
Meter Repairman II	1	0
Mechanical Maint. Helper	1	0
Equipment Operator I	2	3
Fire Hydrant Repairman	1	0
Heavy Equipment Serviceman	1	0
Surveyor's Aide	1	0
Meter Repairman I	1	0
Building Maintenance Helper	1	0
Auto Serviceman	1	2
Totals	39	8

Source: City Water Board Personnel Records

from board personnel policy, and that it was probably more pronounced in determining advancement than in new employment.

The very few Negro employees may well have been an indication of racial bias. On the other hand, Negro employment had increased from 14 on January 1, 1963, to 19 on July 1, 1964, and the monthly employment had increased from 4 to 8.

City Transit System. The City Transit System is also operated under the management of a separate board appointed by the city council.

The bus drivers and all shop workers were represented under a working agreement with the Motor Coach Employees Division Local No. 694, affiliated with the Amalgamated Association of Street Electric Railway and Motor Coach Employees. The data on ethnic distribution of employees was taken from the union's payroll roster, and the other information, including wage scales, was obtained from a union official who had been employed by the transit system since 1927.

Total employment and the number and percent of Mexican-Americans employed as bus drivers and in shop classifications in August, 1963, are shown on the following page.

	Total Employed	Mexican-American Total	Mexican-American Percent
Bus Drivers	568	183	32
Shop Workers	108	39	36
Totals	676	222	33

Wage scales in effect in August, 1963, were:

Occupation	Beginning Rate	
Bus Drivers	$ 1.93 Hr.	($2.15 after 18 mo.)
Leadmen	19.64 Day	
Shop Repairmen	18.64 "	
Painters	18.32 "	
Shop Helpers	15.00 "	($17.12 after 18 mo.)
Miscellaneous	12.00 "	to $16.00 Day

Very few Mexican-American bus drivers were employed prior to 1940. The big breakthrough came during the worker shortage of World War II and substantial employment of persons of this ethnic group had continued thereafter. In 1963, the assistant superintendent of the shop and the first vice-president of the union were Mexican-Americans.

The safety records, competence, and general reliability of Mexican-American workers were reported as comparing favorably with those of Anglos. The union official maintained that there was no discrimination against persons of Mexican descent either in employment, advancement, or union status, and the writer found no contrary evidence during the course of his research.

Summary

Political ineffectiveness was found to be a major factor in the retardation of economic and social assimilation of San Antonio's Mexican-American population.

The Texas poll tax constituted a continuing strong deterrent to the expansion of political participation among the masses of low income families of this ethnic group. A proposed state constitutional amendment to repeal the poll tax was defeated in 1963, but it was hoped that federal action would remove this barrier in the near future.

The sharp decline noted in the proportion of aliens in recent years indicated that lack of citizenship as a bar to voting was rapidly losing significance. The acceleration of agricultural technology was expected to curtail drastically the use of migrant farm workers within a few years; this would lessen the problem of transiency of residence as a deterrent to political participation.

Cultural barriers, particularly temperamental individualism, ignorance, and lack of outstanding leadership within their own ethnic group, continue to be much more important and persistent deterrents to Mexican-American political maturity.

Encouraged by the expansion of economic well-being brought about by extension of employment opportunities during

World War II, aggressive participation of returning veterans, and improvement of education of the young people of Mexican descent, this ethnic group has increased its political activity during recent years, and some progress has been made toward unity of action.

The participation of conservative Mexican-American leadership in the Good Government League has resulted in representation in the city council and on community agency boards and a slow but steady improvement in providing for the great needs of San Antonio's squalid West Side. Liberal Mexican-American leaders, headed by County Commissioner Pena and operating through the Political Association of Spanish-speaking Organizations and the Bexar County Coalition, have been instrumental in increasing voter registration and the election of candidates of Mexican descent to county offices and to the state legislature. Henry B. Gonzalez' election to Congress highlighted an evolving reassessment by both the Mexican-Americans and the Anglos of the capacity for advancement of members of this ethnic group, and Gonzalez' influence has been noted in progress toward equality of employment opportunity, especially at military installations, as well as in the implementation of antipoverty programs and other federal assistance.

In spite of significant advances toward political maturity, continuing cultural inhibitions, ignorance, and inadequate leadership had kept the Mexican-Americans of San Antonio at far below their political potential. This was demonstrated by the results of the calculations showing that the proportion of adults voting in the West Side County Precinct No. 1 in the 1960 presidential election was only two-thirds that of the remainder of the county.

The writer found evidence of justification for the widespread charges of discrimination against persons of Mexican descent in employment by the City Public Service Board. They had considered themselves almost powerless to combat this situation due to the seemingly impervious positions of the membership of the self-perpetuating board of this municipal monopoly. It is hoped that this condition may be at least partially rectified through favorable action on complaints which may be filed after July 2, 1965, with the Equal Employment Opportunities Commission. The degree of discrimination against Mexican-Americans at the City Water Board was found to be relatively small, although persons of this ethnic group had not yet penetrated the top level positions and held only 12.4 percent of office, technical, and skilled jobs. Substantial equality of opportunity for Mexican-Americans was found in employment practices of the transit system and the personnel office serving the other municipal departments.

CHAPTER X

EDUCATION AND TRAINING

Employers, professional and civic leaders, and Mexican-Americans of all walks of life were almost unanimously agreed that the greatest limiting factor to the economic advancement of persons of Mexican descent was their inadequate education and training.

The purposes of this chapter are to ascertain basic facts concerning the levels and scope of formal education and training of San Antonio's Mexican-Americans, and to investigate measures implemented and proposed to bring about improvements in these areas.

Census Data on Formal Education

Table 43-A shows data on years of school completed for all persons 25 years old and over in the San Antonio Standard Metropolitan Statistical Area, distinguished as between persons of Spanish surname (Mexican-Americans), other white persons, and nonwhites (97% Negroes), taken from the 1960 U.S. Census. Table 43-B shows the same information for the 1950 census.

TABLE 43-A

YEARS OF SCHOOL COMPLETED, BY ETHNIC GROUP
SAN ANTONIO STANDARD METROPOLITAN STATISTICAL AREA
U.S. CENSUS, 1960

	Total	Non-White	Spanish Surname	Other White
Persons, 25 yrs. old & over	337,315	24,199	106,101	207,015
No School Years Completed	22,557	677	19,742	2,138
Elementary: 1 to 4 yrs.	39,303	2,927	27,268	9,108
5 to 7 yrs.	54,853	4,835	25,282	24,736
8 yrs.	34,293	2,985	9,008	22,300
High School: 1 to 3 yrs.	54,248	5,193	10,757	38,298
4 yrs.	72,890	4,476	9,418	58,996
College: 1 to 3 yrs.	33,727	2,106	3,115	28,506
4 yrs. or more	25,444	1,000	1,511	22,933
Median yrs. completed	10.0	9.4	5.7	11+
Percentage completed:				
Eighth Grade	65.5	65.1	31.9	82.6
High School	38.9	31.3	13.2	54.4
College	7.5	4.1	1.4	11.1

Source: U.S. Census of Population and Housing: 1960, *Census Facts, San Antonio*, pp. 13, 52, 54.

TABLE 43-B

YEARS OF SCHOOL COMPLETED, BY ETHNIC GROUP
SAN ANTONIO STANDARD METROPOLITAN STATISTICAL AREA
U.S. CENSUS, 1950

	Total	Non-White	Spanish Surname	Other White
Persons, 25 yrs. old & over	264,885	19,650	75,625	169,610
No School years completed	17,985	630	15,525	1,830
Elementary: 1 to 4 yrs.	36,335	2,900	24,560	8,875
5 & 6 yrs.	29,630	3,075	13,850	12,705
7 years	16,990	2,075	4,295	10,620
8 years	27,940	2,570	4,610	20,760
High School: 1 to 3 yrs.	41,810	4,070	5,285	32,455
4 years	49,510	2,445	4,590	42,475
College: 1 to 3 years	22,380	925	965	20,490
4 yrs. or more	16,900	625	660	15,615
School years not reported	5,405	335	1,285	3,785
Median years completed	9.1	8.4	4.5	10+
Percentage Completed:				
Eighth Grade	59.8	54.1	21.2	77.7
High School	33.5	20.3	8.2	46.3
College	6.4	3.2	.9	9.2

Sources: U.S. Census of Population, 17 Census: 1950, Vol. II, Characteristics of the Population, Part 43, Texas, pp. 98, 103.
U.S. Census of Population, 17 Census: 1950, Spl. Report: Persons of Spanish Surnames, pp. 55,58.

The data reveal the tragic lack of educational attainment of San Antonio's Mexican-Americans, with 19% of those 25 years old or over in 1960 never having completed the first year of school. The 31.9% who completed the eighth grade was only 40% the proportion of other whites who attained this level and less than half that of the non-whites. For higher levels of education, the inequality increased. The proportion of Mexican-Americans who had graduated from high school, the minimum required for most skilled and office jobs, was only 13.2%, less than one-fourth that for other whites and less than 40% that of nonwhites. The proportion of Mexican-Americans who had completed four years of college was only 1.4% as compared to 11.1% for other whites and 4.1% for nonwhites.

The increase from 1950 to 1960 in the proportion of Mexican-American high school graduates was 61%, an indication of progress in the improvement of educational attainment for this ethnic group. Increase in the proportion of high school graduates during the same period for other whites and for nonwhites was 18% and 54%, respectively.

The almost perfect positive correlation between proportion of high school graduates, median years of school completed, and median family income is revealed in Table 44.

TABLE 44

COMPARISON OF EDUCATIONAL ATTAINMENT AND FAMILY INCOME PERSONS OF SPANISH SURNAMES, SEVEN STANDARD METROPOLITAN STATISTICAL AREAS U.S. CENSUS, 1960

	Persons 25 Years Old & Over		
S M S A	Percent Completed 4 Years High School	Median School Years Completed	Median Family Income 1959
Corpus Christi	11.2	4.5	$2,974
San Antonio	13.2	5.7	3,446
El Paso	16.9	6.5	3,857
Houston	16.9	6.4	4,339
Dallas	18.8	6.5	4,378
Fort Worth	20.8	7.1	4,679
Los Angeles	26.2	8.9	5,564

Sources: U.S. Census of Population: 1960. Persons of Spanish Surnames, pp. 138, 144, 178-181. Data for Median Family Income: Table 17-A.

San Antonio Mexican-Americans ranked fifth among the six major Texas cities in proportion of persons who had completed four years of high school, in median school years completed and in median family income. The percentage of San Antonio's Mexican-Americans who had completed four years of high school was only half that of Los Angeles, the only city in the United States with a larger number of residents of Mexican descent.

Elementary and Secondary Education

Public education at the precollege level in Bexar County was provided by thirteen independent school districts. The area of none of these districts coincided with any political subdivision. Approximately two-thirds of the students enrolled were served by the San Antonio Independent School District. There were also a number of parochial and private schools, but few Mexican-Americans were able to pay the fees charged by these institutions, so virtually all school attendance of their ethnic group was in the public schools.

Although only 41.5% of the population of the city of San Antonio was Mexican-American in 1960, the scholastic population was already 51.5% this ethnic group in 1951, and the proportion had increased to 52.1% in 1960, as shown in the following data taken from scholastic censuses compiled on the basis of Spanish surnames by the San Antonio Independent School District. Enumeration was for children of ages 6 through 17 years.

Ethnic Group	1951 Census Number	1951 Census Percent	1960 Census Number	1960 Census Percent
Mexican-Americans	34,287	51.5	47,246	52.1
Other Whites	27,808	41.8	35,082	38.7
Negroes	4,476	6.7	8,304	9.2
Totals	66,571	100.0	90,632	100.0

The increase of 85% in the relatively small segment of Negro scholastics during the period 1951-1960, raising the proportion of total participation from 6.7% to 9.2%, is noteworthy.

Legal segregation of children of Mexican descent in the public schools has been outlawed since the 1948 court decision in the Delgado case involving the Bastrop, Texas, Independent School District. Nevertheless, the concentration of Mexican-Americans in San Antonio's West Side has resulted in a high degree of de facto segregation.

Analysis of data compiled by the San Antonio Independent School District on the number and proportion of Spanish surname students in each of its schools in 1955-1956 revealed that, out of a total of 76 elementary schools, 100% of the students enrolled in 10 schools were

Mexican-American, and in 13 others the children of this racial extraction comprised more than 90% of the enrollment. At the other extreme, 19 elementary schools had less than 10% students of Mexican descent. Of the seven high schools, enrollment of Mexican-Americans in one was 100% and in another 93.6%. In contrast, enrollment of this ethnic group in three other high schools was 4.0%, 10.4%, and 12.9% respectively.

Enrollment in each of two elementary schools was more than 99% Negro.

School segregation of children of Mexican descent had been defended by some in the past on the grounds that they were severely handicapped by linguistic difficulties and tended to have unhappy experiences in mixed classes with Anglos. San Antonio's educators and sociologists, however, are in agreement with those experts who have found that Spanish-speaking children learn faster and assimilate more readily in mixed classes.

Dr. George I. Sánchez, eminent Texas University authority on Mexican-American educational problems, has been emphatic on this point, stating

> In elementary classes that I have taught, in all the schools of which I have been principal, and in all those which I have supervised, children who did not know a word of English upon first entering a school

> were participating normally with their English-speaking classmates before the second month of school was over.
>
> In all my experience, I have found that Spanish-speaking children learn English best and most quickly when they participate normally in mixed classes with English-speaking students. The initial vocabulary deficiency of the child who comes to school knowing only Spanish is an obstacle that can best and most quickly be overcome in mixed classes . . . . School segregation is pedagogically unsound, socially dangerous, and unquestionably un-American.[1]

Other authorities have pointed out that segregation emphasizes English in the minds of the students as a foreign language, creating a mental block to the attainment of the social integration looked for in learning the national language. Even more important, when Spanish-speaking children are by themselves, they invariably speak Spanish.

A remedial reading program for seventh graders was instituted by the San Antonio Independent School District in the summer of 1962, with an initial class of 85. According to a school official, at least 3,000 children at this grade level, of which more than 70 percent were Mexican-Americans, were in need of remedial reading.

Irregular school attendance and dropping out of school have been outstanding problems in the education of

---

[1]George I. Sánchez, Concerning Segregation of Spanish-Speaking Children in the Public Schools, The University of Texas, Austin, December, 1951, p. 32.

San Antonio's Mexican-American children, particularly those in the families of the approximately 15,000 migrant farm workers, in which the children were customarily taken out of school for the migration before the end of the spring session and did not return until the succeeding fall session was well underway. Lack of parental interest in their children's educations, and the young people's conviction that ethnic discrimination would keep them from securing jobs for which an education would prepare them, have combined to aggravate the problem.

Protestant and Catholic settlement houses, the Bishops' Committee for the Spanish-speaking, the LULACS, and other community agencies have worked hard to combat these problems with some success, and improvement in employment opportunities has increased the incentives for Mexican-American youth to further their education, but the problems of school dropouts and irregular attendance were far from solution. In November, 1964, a Youth Education Service (YES) program, whereby part-time employment was sought through the public employment office for students needing it to remain in school, was established in San Antonio.[2] As of June, 1965, the Texas Employment

---

[2]San Antonio Express, November 8, 1964.

Commission, with one employee assigned full-time to this program, had secured jobs with private employers for 130 students. The TEC representative estimated there had been between 1,200 and 1,500 applicants for such work. Approximately 60 percent of the students employed were Mexican-American. When one considers the small number and proportion of applicants placed, the fact that some of these students would have gotten jobs without YES, and the estimated cost of about $30 per placement in the salary of the TEC worker alone, the value of this program during the first year was subject to question. However, the TEC planned to continue the project in the 1965-66 school year. Increase in the number of job placements was to be sought through better promotion of the program.

The San Antonio Independent School District has developed a comprehensive program of vocational education in six high schools, with the aggregate 1962-1963 enrollments of 1,818 comprising 23 percent of the 7,880 total high school enrollment in the system.[3] Student enrollments by ethnic groups as distributed between the schools

---

[3]Unless otherwise noted, data and information on the vocational educational program were taken from school records and a conversation with George L. Fling, director of vocational education for the school district.

and by course title are shown in Tables 45-A and 45-B, respectively.

During the year 1962-1963, the entire student body at Lanier High School was Mexican-American, and all students attending Wheatley High School were Negroes. Edison High School enrollment was approximately 90% Anglo and 10% Mexican-American. Racial distribution in the total vocational program was Mexican-American 78.9%, Anglo 16.1%, and Negro 5.0%.

The very high proportion of Mexican-Americans was explained as due almost entirely to two factors. First, the increasing number of employment opportunities available to persons of Mexican descent with training in vocational skills made these courses desirable. The second, and probably more generally governing, reason was the practice in the high schools of shifting into vocational subjects those students not able to qualify for the college preparatory curriculum.

The average I.Q. test score of vocational students both at the all Mexican-American Lanier High School and at the all Negro Wheatley High School was 86, whereas the average was 97 at the predominantly Anglo Edison High School. The low average I.Q. scores of Mexican-Americans was attributed largely to English language deficiency.

TABLE 45-A

STUDENT ENROLLMENT BY SCHOOL AND ETHNIC GROUP
HIGH SCHOOL VOCATIONAL EDUCATION COURSES
SAN ANTONIO INDEPENDENT SCHOOL DISTRICT, 1962-1963

High School	Total Enrolled	Anglos	Mexican-Americans	Negroes
Brackenridge	232	25	195	12
Burbank	430	150	279	1
Edison	81	76	5	0
Fox Vocational and Technical	752	41	701	10
Wheatley	68	0	0	68
Lanier	255	0	255	0

TABLE 45-B

STUDENT ENROLLMENT BY COURSE AND ETHNIC GROUP
HIGH SCHOOL VOCATIONAL EDUCATION COURSES
SAN ANTONIO INDEPENDENT SCHOOL DISTRICT, 1962-1963

Course Title	Total Enrolled	Anglos	Mexican-Americans	Negroes
Agriculture	69	57	11	1
Automobile Mechanic	203	57	116	30
Auto Body Repairing	98	7	91	0
Building Trades	38	6	32	0
Commercial Art	126	12	113	1
Commercial Photography	47	0	47	0
Cosmetology	145	3	104	38
Distributive Education	117	53	64	0
Drafting	149	13	136	0
Electrical Trades	49	1	47	1
Machine Shop	52	30	22	1
Metal Trades (Sheet Metal)	43	0	41	2
Metal Trades (Vocational)	96	20	75	1
Metal Trades (Welding)	38	1	37	0
Mill Cabinetmaking	129	7	111	11
Needle Trades	68	0	68	0
Piping Trades	50	3	46	1
Printing	115	2	113	0
Radio and T.V. Service	186	20	161	5
Totals	1,818	292	1,435	91

Source: Vocational Education Records, San Antonio Independent School District

Male students of Mexican descent were found to excel in training for commercial art and drafting, and girls proved especially adept in cosmetology and garment making. Mexican-Americans on the average were observed to have more trouble with the mathematics required in technical areas. No data on the proportion of Mexican-American vocational students dropping out was available, but it was adjudged to be somewhat higher than that of Anglos. On the other hand, those completing their school programs were able to secure local employment in the areas for which they were trained.

Vocational instruction was restricted to students in grades 10, 11, and 12, with the exception of agriculture, in which ninth graders were permitted to enroll. Pointing out that a large proportion of dropouts occur at below the tenth grade, some community leaders have urged that vocational subjects be taught at the junior high level. Authorities did not consider the idea practical because students of junior high school were neither mature enough for training, especially on heavy or dangerous equipment, nor would they be able to secure employment at that age. The cost of the required additional equipment and personnel was also a major deterrent to teaching vocational courses in the junior high schools.

Higher Education

The San Antonio Union Junior College district operates two public two-year colleges, San Antonio College and St. Phillips College.

The San Antonio College is the largest junior college in Texas, with regular session 1962-63 enrollment of 3,713 in the day division and 6,101 in the evening division, a total of 9,814 according to the college bulletin. In the May 1963 graduating class of 380, there were 79 students with Spanish surnames, 21 percent of the total. This was treble the less than seven percent Mexican-Americans among all persons 25 years old and over in 1960 (Table 45-A) with one to three years of college. It indicates an increasing participation of this ethnic group in higher education, even though it is probable that the proportion of San Antonio College graduates who are Mexican-American may be somewhat higher than for all San Antonians at that educational level.

St. Phillips College, formerly a Negro institution, was integrated in 1955. It offers a collegiate program, composed primarily of liberal arts, business, and preprofessional, plus a vocational curriculum. The 1962-1963 aggregate enrollment of 1,196 students included 586 collegiate students and 610 vocational students. No breakdown of ethnic distribution was made available.

St. Mary's University and Trinity University are the two largest private institutions of higher education in San Antonio. A check of the rosters of their graduates for the school years 1961-62 and 1962-63, respectively, revealed the following data:

	St. Mary's		Trinity	
Degree Conferred	Total	Spanish Surname	Total	Spanish Surname
Bachelor of Arts	116	31	67	3
Bachelor of Science	21	2	179	10
Bachelor of Music	5	3	8	2
Bachelor of Bus. Adm.	124	17		
Bachelor of Laws	21	3		
Total Bachelors	287	56	254	15
Master of Arts	11	3	9	
Master of Science	7		32	1
Master of Education			53	3
Total Masters	18	3	94	4
Total Degrees Conferred	305	59	348	19

St. Mary's is a Roman Catholic institution located in the north portion of the West Side, and Trinity is a Presbyterian affiliated university situated in an Anglo area northeast of the business district. A Trinity official confirmed the writer's observation that the small number of Mexican-Americans enrolled there were virtually all from economically advanced and highly assimilated families.

Since a great majority of San Antonio's citizens of Mexican descent are Catholics, it was expected a larger proportion of them would attend St. Mary's. An official of the university pointed out that failure of the masses of young Mexican-Americans to learn to speak, read, and think in English seriously prejudiced their possibilities for success in higher education. They frequently spoke and wrote in a hodgepodge of both languages and were handicapped by retention of the habit of thinking in Spanish terms and translating back and forth into English. At least 60 percent of those who had graduated from St. Mary's still retained strong accents. He added that eighty percent of the lower quarter of St. Mary's graduates were Mexican-Americans, and he attributed this situation primarily to their never having acquired proficiency in the English language.

It would seem reasonable to assume that the average participation of Mexican-Americans in these two institutions would give a rough measure of the proportion of San Antonians graduating from college who were of this ethnic group. Total bachelors degrees conferred by the two schools were 541, with 71 of them, 13.1 percent, Mexican-American. This compared favorably with the 5.7 percent Mexican-Americans among persons 25 years old and over who were college graduates in 1960. The seven Mexican-Americans who received masters degrees from the two institutions constituted 6.2 percent of all persons receiving these degrees.

MDTA Projects

The San Antonio area was not certified for training programs under the Area Redevelopment Act, but a rapidly expanded program of diversified projects under the Manpower Development and Training Act was in progress.[4]

The first training class was started in January, 1963, and during the next eighteen months 293 persons had completed training in sixteen projects, with training ranging from 12 to 52 weeks per program. By May, 1965, the San Antonio MDTA program had organized 49 training projects in seven centers, and 1,354 persons had been trained or were in training. Seventy-five percent of enrollees had completed their courses and obtained employment.

---

[4]Data and related information on local MDTA projects were obtained from John W. Long, MDTA coordinator at the Texas Employment Commission in San Antonio.

Training projects have covered a very broad spectrum of skilled trades, office, sales, and services occupations. A number of the 1964 and 1965 projects involved literacy training for lower level service occupations. The MDTA coordinator told the writer that much more literacy training was planned for the future, and that emphasis would also be placed on the various phases of youth training.

In March, 1964, a check of the project enrollments revealed that 73 percent of all persons in training had Spanish surnames. No later data on ethnic participation were made available; however, in view of the increased emphasis on literacy projects, it is probable that the proportion of Mexican-Americans had somewhat increased.

The MDTA program was of too short duration for any close evaluation; however, interviews with some of San Antonio's more knowledgeable industrial and business leaders and Mexican-American authorities disclosed that they generally considered the training projects well administered, the instruction competent, and the training a valuable means for improving the educational and economic status of the city's marginal Mexican-American masses.

Illiteracy and English Deficiency

The deplorably widespread English language deficiency, nurtured by persistent use of Spanish in the home, at work, and socially, and fostered by de facto segregation in the schools, constitued by far the single greatest barrier to economic and social advancement for that large majority of San Antonio's Mexican-Americans living on the West Side.

At the bottom of the educationally disadvantaged are the functional illiterates--persons who have completed only four years or less of school. Bexar County (same as the San Antonio SMSA) had 61,860 persons 25 years old or over in this category in 1960, of which 47,010 or 76 percent were Mexican-American.

Community efforts to combat illiteracy were focused in the San Antonio Literacy Council since its organization in 1960. The council is a private, nonprofit organization which has depended on sponsoring groups and contributions for its limited financing and has relied heavily on volunteer teachers and other workers. The local United Fund agreed to include the council among its agencies for 1965 in the amount of $10,000.

The literacy council conducted teaching centers from October through May, using the methods developed by

Dr. Frank C. Laubach. In its first year of operation, 1960-1961, the council conducted six teaching centers attended by 150 students. During 1963-64, students totaling 939 were taught at 31 centers served by 183 part-time volunteer

Since the council estimated in 1964 that San Antonio illiterates over 18 years of age totaled 109,000, its leadership was keenly aware of the need to greatly expand the scope of its operations, but this tremendously important effort to combat one of San Antonio's greatest problems continued to suffer from inadequate financial support. It was hoped that the promised backing of the United Fund would provide the impetus for a far more comprehensive program.

The League of United Latin American Citizens, commonly known as LULAC, has done much to promote the education of people of their ethnic group, including generous scholarship and loan assistance, but their most significant contribution to education has been the "Little Schools of 400," initiated in 1958. Under this program, preschool children of Mexican descent, who have never spoken any English, are taught 400 basic words in the English language to prepare them for their first year in public school. This project proved so successful that since 1960 it has been subsidized partially by state government appropriations through the State Department of Education. Approximately 20,000 children, 3,000 of them in San Antonio, were trained in these LULAC schools in 1963, according to an editorial commendation in a local newspaper.[5] The Little Schools of 400, in a manner of speaking, got a head start on the federal government antipoverty program "Project Head Start."

Economic Opportunity Act Projects

The San Antonio Economic Opportunity Development Corporation was organized in the spring of 1965 to coordinate projects authorized under the Economic Opportunity Act of 1964. Policies were determined by a board of 60 citizens. Board officers consisted of a president, two vice-presidents, and a treasurer. A prominent Mexican-American was one of the first vice-presidents. The board employed a professional social worker as full-time executive director and ex-officio secretary.[6]

---

[5] San Antonio Express, July 11, 1963.

[6] General information on the EODC was obtained from executive director Shurman. Additional information on the ACD and NYO projects was secured form Rev. John Wagner and Rev. John Yanta, respectively.

Three projects had been approved and were in operation at the end of June, 1965. These included programs for preschool education, improvements in migrant worker residential areas, and a neighborhood youth corps.

The preschool training involved seven separate projects, each calling for eight weeks of English instruction and social development of children from poverty families who were to enter the first grade of school in September. The combined projects called for enrollment of 7,276 children, at an approved aggregate cost of $662,624, financed 90 percent by federal grants. The first and most comprehensive project was developed under Catholic leadership, with provision for 1,571 children at 16 locations, mostly parochial schools, at a cost of $201,548. The largest project was that of the San Antonio Independent School District, for 3,000 children in schools throughout the city, costing $201,674. Another large project was that of the Edgewood Independent School District, on the West Side, serving 2,100 children, at a cost of $156,642. Four other school districts had projects with aggregate enrollments of 905 children. The projects called for varying degrees of contacts with parents of the children. Mexican-American children comprised more than three-fourths of the total enrollment.

Educators and social scientists applauded the preschool education arrangement as a big step toward overcoming the language and social problems which have severely handicapped the children of low income, unassimilated families. The EODC executive director advised that applications had been made for approval of similar projects extending over the full year.

The project for broad neighborhood development was approved on April 29, 1965, under the sponsorship of Action for Community Development, a nonprofit organization set up for the purpose. The project was to serve the three widely separated areas of Villa Coronado, Linda Vista, and Meadowbrook Acres, with an aggregate population of 7,300 persons. Plans for the project had been developed by the National Council for the Spanish Speaking, a Catholic offshoot of the Bishops' Committee for the Spanish Speaking.

This ACD project, financed 90 percent by federal funds, embraced three programs for the neighborhoods served. The most comprehensive program, with its own professional staff, provided for extensive family and homemaker education, including sanitation, hygiene and child care, at an approved cost of $258,946. The second program provided for technically trained leadership to assist owners of substandard homes to make their own repairs and put in better water and sanitation installations. Substantially all of the materials and much of the equipment to be used were expected to be secured as contributions. Cost approved for this portion of the project was $71,792. The third part of the project provided for prevocational diagnostic evaluation classes. Basic education skills were to be taught those persons in the neighborhood with little or no formal education. Allocation for this work was $61,105. Total anticipated expenditures, as approved, were set at $391,843 for the ACD project.

The neighborhood youth project was sponsored by the San Antonio Neighborhood Youth Organization, Inc., a nonprofit corporation. Executive director of the project was Rev. John Yanta, a Catholic priest who had spent the previous three years in social work in San Antonio's West Side slums. A 12 weeks program was begun on June 2, 1965, in 18 schools, 17 of which were on the West Side. Each center, as well as the central administration, was staffed with professional teachers and social workers who supervised the work-training program of 962 boys and girls aged 16 through 21 who had been screened by the Texas Employment Service to determine their need to have summer incomes in order to go back to school in the fall. An effort was made to secure school dropouts, but only a small proportion were in this category. Approximately 900 were Mexican-Americans and the remainder were Negroes. Each worker-trainee was responsible for a program of citizenship training and recreation of at least 10 younger children, for which he received $1.25 per hour for 25 hours per week. In addition, he attended without pay 5 hours of counseling, including 3 hours of job orientation, 1-1/2 hours in a comprehensive leadership training course, and one-half hour in career guidance. Rev. Yanta reported that the leadership and career guidance counseling was proving the most valuable part of the program, with gratifying results being evidenced in improved citizenship and increased motivation. Including the younger children attending the centers, the program was reaching a total of more than 10,000 young people. Federal grants for the project totaled $575,000, covering 90 percent of the cost. Rev. Yanta stated that application had been made for funds for a similar program during the school year, with the centers operating in school facilities after school hours. The proposed program would provide for slum children's study and recreation, supervised by the worker-trainees employed. Rev. Yanta pointed out that study was virtually impossible in the crowded and poorly lighted homes of children from poverty level families.

San Antonio did not have a Job Corps center, but 110 young people in the age group 16 through 21 had been sent to centers throughout the country from February, 1965 through June, 1965. The local Texas Employment Service distributed information and application blanks, which were filled out by the applicants and sent to the Office of Economic Opportunity in Washington, where they were evaluated and sent back to the local TEC office for screening as to economic circumstances of the applicants. The OEO then made final selections and advised the TEC the names of persons approved, along with instructions for sending those chosen to designated centers. While some of the corpsmen had been sent to the San Marcos, Texas center nearby, most had been sent out of the state with a large proportion being sent to centers in the states of Washington and Oregon. The TEC representative responsible for screening and sending approved applicants to job corps centers pointed out two high cost features of this program. In the first place, all corpsmen were sent to centers and returned on commercial airplanes, usually jets. He stated that even youths sent to the San Marcos center only 50 miles from San Antonio were, by instruction, sent 75 miles to Austin by plane and thence to San Marcos by bus. He also reported that corpsmen could quit the program at any time and demand to be returned to San Antonio. The TEC office had no record of the number of job corps youths from San Antonio who had dropped out of the program, but the TEC representative said he knew of several such persons, and, considering the strong family ties of the Mexican-Americans, the proportion of dropouts of this ethnic group would probably be large. He estimated that 90 percent of young people sent to job corps centers from San Antonio were Mexican-Americans, and virtually all of the remainder were Negroes.

All of the projects developed under the Economic Opportunity Act of 1964 had just gotten under way at the close of this research in June, 1965; consequently, no real evaluation was possible at this stage. Certain observations concerning the three projects in operation can be made. In the first place, each project was focused on the removal of grave, fundamental and pervasive root sources of poverty. Second, selection procedures seemed successful in concentrating the participation in the programs on Mexican-American and Negro slum families. Thirdly, each of the projects showed evidence of perceptive, careful and thorough planning and choice of competent leadership. The writer had brief opportunities to discuss the work with participants in the neighborhood youth corps and the program at Villa Coronado, and he found a high level of enthusiasm and appreciation for the value of the projects.

Several considerations seemed to deserve attention in projecting the expansion of San Antonio's poverty programs. A more comprehensive and thorough study of the poverty problems of the city's residents and a long-range coordinated plan of action was needed. The director of the Economic Opportunity Development Corporation indicated that this would be the central objective of that organization. While the Catholic leaders deserved commendation for their outstanding work in planning, securing approval, and implementing poverty programs, there was need for a broader and more committed participation of top professional and civic leadership in the central planning and project development. A major project which needed to be incorporated in the poverty program was a massive, county-wide attack on adult illiteracy, utilizing the leadership and programs of the Literacy Council and other organizations in a comprehensive drive aimed at elimination of this basic barrier to economic advancement.

Local evidence indicated that expenditures on job corps trainees' travel might be excessive. It also appeared likely that there was overpermissiveness in allowing enrollees to drop out of the program. Early dropouts of Mexican-Americans were considered probable because of their close family ties. The charge might be made that costs of the initial local projects were excessive, but care should be taken not to endanger the quality of programs through inadequate financing.

Summary

The writer's research confirmed the consensus among San Antonio's business, professional, and ethnic leaders that the lack of adequate education constituted the greatest barrier to economic advancement of the city's Mexican-Americans.

The degree of this ethnic group's educational deficiency was indicated by 1960 U.S. Census data, which revealed that the proportion of Mexican-Americans 25 years old and over who had completed four years of high school was only 13.2%, one-fourth that of other whites, and the 1.4% Mexican-Americans who had completed four years of college was only one-eighth that of other whites. Evidence of educational progress was noted, however, in the 61% increase in the proportion of high school graduates of Mexican descent during the period 1950 to 1960.

Data for six Texas cities and Los Angeles, California, for 1960 revealed almost perfect correlation between proportion of high school graduates, median years of school completed, and median family income. The proportion of San Antonio's Mexican-Americans with four years of high school was only half that of Los Angeles.

The San Antonio Independent School District 1960 census showed the scholastic population to be 52.1% Mexican-American, 38.7% Anglo, and 9.2% Negro. The proportion of Mexican-American scholastics was increasing.

Mexican-American students made up four-fifths of the 1,818 total enrollment in vocational education in the high schools of the San Antonio Independent School District. This large ethnic representation was attributed to the increasing job opportunities for Mexican-Americans in these vocational fields, and to the practice in the high schools of shifting students not able to qualify for the college preparatory curriculum into vocational courses. Proposals to offer vocational education in the junior high schools, as a means of discouraging dropouts at that level, was considered by school authorities to be impractical.

Comparison of Mexican-American students' representation in recent junior college and university graduating classes with 1960 census statistics for persons 25 years old and over revealed a fairly substantial increase in the proportion of graduates who were of Mexican descent;

however, this ethnic group constituted only about one-eighth of the 1963 college graduates.

English language deficiency was found to be by far the greatest single deterrent to the advancement of students of Mexican descent at all educational levels. The de facto segregation of the great majority of Mexican-American children attending West Side schools, coupled with the persistent use of Spanish by this ethnic group in and outside the home, made it extremely difficult for children living in this part of San Antonio to attain competency in the English language. The "Little Schools of 400," sponsored by the LULACS and partially supported by state funds, were of significant value in teaching English to preschool children.

The rapidly expanding and diversified training projects implemented since 1963 under the Manpower Training and Development Act were of too short duration for close evaluation, but the evolving program appeared to be well planned and administered, and evidence indicated that MDTA training would be a valuable means for improving the educational and economic status of the Mexican-Americans who comprised about three-fourths of the trainees.

The three local projects just begun in the summer of 1965 under the Economic Opportunity Act of 1964--

preschool education, improvements in migrant worker neighborhoods, and the neighborhood youth corps--were properly focused on the inhabitants of the sity's slums, were well planned programs attacking deep-seated and pervasive sources of poverty, and appeared to be getting enthusiastic response from participants. Further evaluation was not possible due to the newness of the projects. A comprehensive, long-range plan for poverty relief was needed; it was hoped that the newly organized Economic Opportunity Development Corporation would provide such a plan. Catholics had provided most of the top leadership for existing projects; broader participation at this level by the city's professional and civic leaders was needed. Local evidence indicated that travel expenditures for sending trainees to job corps centers and return home were excessive. There were also indications that the overpermissiveness of the job corps encouraged early dropouts, considered an especial problem for Mexican-American youths because of the very strong family ties of this ethnic group.

The most urgent current need under the poverty program was for a massive, county-wide attack on adult illiteracy. This basic barrier continued to bar the advancement of San Antonio's slum residents. In 1960, 19 percent of Mexican-Americans 25 years old and over had not completed one year of school. The San Antonio Literacy Council estimated in 1964 that 109,000 Bexar Countians were functional illiterates, those with four years of schooling or less. Mexican-Americans made up three-fourths of this group. While the literacy council, the settlement houses and other local agencies had been doing a creditable work in this area for a number of years, a massive and well-financed drive was badly needed to combat this persistent economic problem.

C H A P T E R X I

HOUSING AND HEALTH

The acute problems of housing and health have always been closely associated with education as prime factors in the economic retardation of the great majority of San Antonio's Mexican-Americans living on the West Side.

Prior to the close of World War II, unfortunately, the usual focus for concern by the Anglo leadership was the threat posed to the economic and physical well-being of the Anglo sector, rather than the improvement of the lot of the Mexican-Americans. An example of this perspective is shown in an excerpt from an address by the head of the industrial department of the newly created City Public Service Board in 1943, regarding findings in a recently completed survey:

> Problems of housing, sanitation, education, juvenile delinquency, etc., were found to be largely concentrated among the Latin-Americans, whose principal job qualifications are, we believe, preponderantly agricultural and ill-fitted to be useful in the city. We found the Latin-American group was one of the contributing causes retarding the growth of the city and causing a terrific loss of manpower and municipal expense. We found few users of gas and electricity in this group, although service was available in their neighborhoods. We found their residential sections yielding a relatively small tax revenue, but absorbing

> a substantial amount of the City Budget. The purchasing power of this group helped the business of the city only a very small extent, but the groups made a large demand upon relief and charity funds. This group was a menace from a health standpoint to other groups and in particular to the United States military personnel.[1]

The same spokesman had previously stated in the official survey report: "Replacement of 35 percent of the Latin-Americans by an equivalent number of economically independent families would transform San Antonio socially, politically, economically, and in health."[2]

This chapter will be concerned with basic information regarding housing and health conditions among San Antonio's residents of Mexican extraction, and with measures that have been implemented or proposed to improve the standards of this ethnic group.

Housing

T. G. Rogers, in a research study of 1,541 West Side houses in the middle 1920's, noted, in addition to

---

[1]Theo N. Picnot, "Socio-Economic Status of Low Income Groups of San Antonio." Address before the San Antonio Social Workers Association, San Antonio, 1943, pp. 2, 3.

[2]T. N. Picnot, An Economic and Industrial Survey of San Antonio, Texas, Public Service Co., San Antonio, 1942, p. 124.

the generally poor construction and dilapidated condition of the dwellings, the following primitive conditions concerning facilities:

> Water: hydrants inside, 238; hydrants outside, 1,264; houses with barrels, 39.
> Toilets: sewer connected inside houses, 159; sewer connected outside houses, 804; surface toilets, 578.
> Heating and Cooking: gas, 99; kerosene, 207; wood, 1,168; charcoal, 55.
> Light: electric, 394; kerosene, 1,141; none, 6.[3]

While accommodations had improved during the intervening thirty-three years, living conditions for Mexican-Americans in 1960 were still crude and shabby, as revealed in the U.S. Census data in Table 46.

Only 49.7% of Mexican-American residences were in sound condition with all standard plumbing facilities, as compared to 94.0% for other whites, and 59.5% of nonwhites.

At the other extreme, 12.6% of Mexican-American houses were dilapidated, a designation for housing which does not provide safe and adequate shelter. Only 3.7% of other white houses, and 9.5% of nonwhite houses were included in this category.

---

[3]T. G. Rogers, Housing Situation of the Mexicans in San Antonio, Texas, unpublished Master's Thesis, University of Texas, Austin, 1927, p. 41.

TABLE 46

CHARACTERISTICS OF HOUSING UNITS, BY ETHNIC GROUP
SAN ANTONIO STANDARD METROPOLITAN STATISTICAL AREA
1960

	Total	Non-White	Spanish Surname	Other White
All Units	196,783			128,843
All units occupied	181,854	13,218	54,722	113,914
Owner occupied	115,477	7,082	32,272	76,123
Renter occupied	66,377	6,136	22,450	37,791
Vacant	14,929			14,929
Condition and Plumbing				
Sound	154,359	8,851	34,207	111,301
Lacking some or all facil.	12,248	991	7,009	4,248
Deteriorating	30,073	3,117	13,637	13,319
Lacking some or all facil.	13,377	1,247	7,873	4,257
Dilapidated	12,351	1,250	6,878	4,223
Persons per Room				
0.50 or less	62,619	4,853	8,302	49,464
0.51 to 0.75	35,979	2,659	8,235	25,085
0.76 to 1.00	44,869	2,995	13,717	28,157
1.01 or more	38,387	2,711	24,468	11,208
Median value: Owner occupied	9,300	6,500	6,000	
Median rent: Renter occupied	56	46	38	

Note: Data for occupied units only were available for Nonwhite and Spanish Surname.

Source: U.S. Censuses of Population and Housing: 1960. Census Tracts, San Antonio, Texas, pp. 61, 71, 76, 78.

The socially undesirable and unhealthy crowding of residences that has been quite typical of Mexican-American families in San Antonio is confirmed by the data showing that 44.7 percent of the houses of this ethnic group had more than one person per room. By contrast, this level of concentration of persons was found in only 9.8% of the homes of other whites and 20.5% of nonwhite houses.

The writer accompanied a representative of the Bishops' Committee for the Spanish-speaking to a number of slum dwellings to which he was delivering their government surplus food allotments. The abject poverty evidenced by the crudely built hovels and their sparse furnishings was appalling. One place occupied by an aged couple had no floor, and a single small window in the little bedroom, which with the even smaller lean-to kitchen was the entire house. Water had to be brought in from a neighborhood hydrant, and there was no provision whatever for artificial light. Other houses were much the same, except for having floors and kerosene lamps or lanterns.

Of course, families with wage earners were usually somewhat better housed, but many homes were without public utilities, and a common sight was a cluster of a half-dozen little two-room "row-houses" sharing a single outside toilet. Some areas were still without water and sewer connections because city officials considered there were not sufficient customers to justify extension of the mains for these facilities. As a result, people had to carry water from a considerable distance to their homes. Streets were unpaved, dusty, and poorly drained.

Rogers noted in the 1920's that in the districts that had the greatest percent of home owners were found the poorest homes and grounds.[4] To a very large extent this was also true in the 1960's. Mexican-Americans seemed to have an unusually strong desire to own a piece of ground and a house of their own. Furthermore, migrant workers found it convenient to buy a shack for a small sum, live in it during the winter, board it up at the start of the seasonal migration, and have a place to return to for the next winter.

San Antonio's public housing projects constituted by far the most significant program implemented for the improvement of housing conditions of the city's economically deprived Mexican-Americans at the time of this research.[5]

---

[4] _Ibid._, p. 65.

[5] Except as otherwise noted, data and other information presented on public housing, including the housing projects map and a reprint of the 1961 annual report advertisement in local newspapers (_Light_ and _News_, February 26, 1962, and _Express_, February 27, 1962), were obtained from

The San Antonio Housing Authority, supervised by a board of five commissioners, including one Mexican-American and one Negro, operated 12 public housing projects with a total of 5,154 apartment units, in which were housed 24,036 persons as of December 31, 1961. Details on the projects are shown in Table 47 and Map 1.

The first units occupied were in the Alazan-Apache project in 1942.

Mexican-Americans totaling 14,287 comprised 59.5% of total residents, as compared to 23.8% Negroes and 16.7% Anglos. Mexican-Americans also had the largest average number of persons per housing unit, 5.0 as compared to an average of 4.3 Negroes and 4.1 Anglos.

Applicants for housing were required to qualify as a family (at least two persons related by blood, marriage, or adoption), must have resided within a five-mile radius of San Antonio for six months immediately prior to making application, owned net assets of not more than $2,000, and had income within an established maximum. Preference was given to families displaced by urban renewal, code enforcement, and highway construction, and to all veterans.

Richard G. Jones, Executive Director of the San Antonio Housing Authority, during an interview in July, 1962.

TABLE 47

PUBLIC HOUSING PROJECTS
SAN ANTONIO HOUSING AUTHORITY, DECEMBER 31, 1961

Project Name	Number Units	Number Residents	*Ethnic Group
Alazan-Apache Courts	1,180	5,213	Mexican-American
Victoria Courts	796	3,796	Anglo
Wheatley Courts	236	999	Negro
Lincoln Heights Courts	342	1,330	Negro
Cassiano Homes	400	2,263	Mexican-American
East Terrace Homes	275	2,260	Negro
San Juan Homes and Annex	358	1,953	Mexican-American
S. J. Sutton Homes	202	1,139	Negro
Mirasol Homes	500	2,607	Mexican-American
Menchaca Homes	150	786	Mexican-American
Villa Veramendi	260	1,465	Mexican-American
Sutton Homes Addition	46	**	Negro
East Terrace Homes Addition	208	**	Negro
Wheatley Courts Addition	16	**	Negro
Victoria Plaza	185	225	Anglo
Totals	5,154	24,036	

Ethnic Distribution	Number Projects	Housing Units		Residents	
		Number	Percent	Number	Percent
Mexican-American	6	2,848	55.3	14,287	59.5
Negro	4	1,325	25.7	5,728	23.8
Anglo	2	981	19.0	4,021	16.7
Totals	12	5,154	100.0	24,036	100.0

*Executive director of housing authority maintained that all projects were both racially and ethnically integrated, but he conceded that occupancy was predominantly as shown and that ethnic total for number of residents for each ethnic group was a very close approximation.

**Residents included in number for original project.

Source: San Antonio Housing Authority Annual Report for 1961.

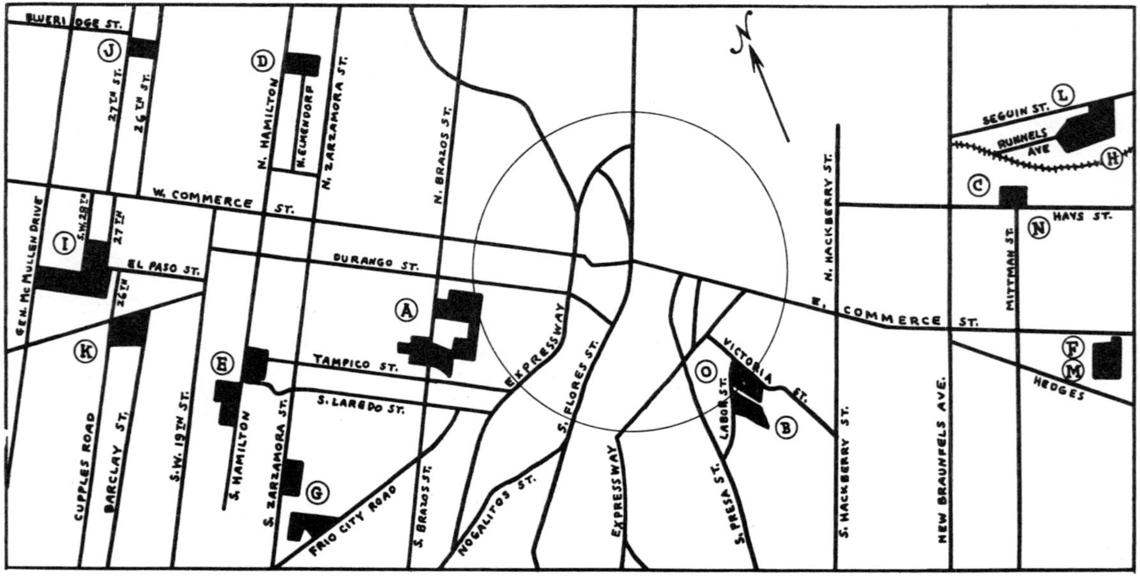

MAP 1

PUBLIC HOUSING PROJECTS
SAN ANTONIO HOUSING AUTHORITY, DECEMBER 31, 1961

	Units		Units		Units
A Alazan-Apache Courts	1180	F East Terrace Homes	275	K Villa Veramendi	260
B Victoria Courts	796	G San Juan Homes & Annex	358	L Sutton Homes Addition	46
C Wheatley Courts	236	H S. J. Sutton Homes	202	M East Ter. Homes Add.	208
D Lincoln Heights Cts.	342	I Mirasol Homes	500	N Wheatley Courts Add.	16
E Cassiano Homes	400	J Menchaca Homes	150	O Victoria Plaza	185

Rents were based on approximately 20 percent of net annual income for small families and 16-2/3 percent for large families, those with three or more minors. Average family rent was $27 per month.

The 5,154 housing project units had replaced 4,478 slum dwellings on a total of 376 acres, and a good majority of the leaders interviewed expressed satisfaction with the administration of the program as well as the benefits it provided to the very low income families. A referendum in 1963 resulted in approval for construction of 400 additional apartment units, a 200-unit addition to Victoria Courts and a 100-unit addition each to Cassiano Homes and San Juan Homes.

On the other hand, there was some strong opposition to public housing in general and others did not approve of the high concentration of families in the apartment type plan.

Mayor McAllister had been a foe of public housing from its inception, claiming that juvenile delinquency was heaviest in public housing areas. The assistant director of the San Antonio Housing Authority disputed this charge, stating that a survey she made from 1960 to 1962 showed that San Antonio police made 1.5 calls per 100 families in public housing projects annually, compared with a city-wide average of 2.2 calls per 100 families. Sister Mary Murray, a Catholic nun, in recording the results of her study of 118 families (10 percent random sample) at Alazan-Apache Courts, reported in 1952 that only three cases of juvenile delinquency among this group had ever been referred to the juvenile court.[6] The three cases involved one delinquent girl and two boys charged with truancy.

E. G. Luna, widely respected Mexican-American authority on the problems of this ethnic group, expressed the opinion that it was a mistake to concentrate people in large multiapartment housing projects, particularly young women with children.

Some critics charged that public housing projects' costs of construction and maintenance were too high, but the chairman of the housing authority pointed out that no comparable housing was being made available to low income families at anything like the rents of public housing units.

Two noteworthy recent alternative plans for housing for low-income families, both of which would provide for possible ultimate ownership by residents of the housing units, had been proposed.

---

[6](Sister) Mary John Murray, A Socio-cultural Study of 118 Mexican Families in a Low-Rent Public Project in San Antonio, Texas, unpublished Master's thesis, The University of Texas, Austin, 1952, p. 61.

One plan, originally developed in 1961 by the Bishops' Committee for the Spanish-speaking, was being submitted in 1964 for approval to the Federal Housing and Home Finance Agency under the sponsorship of the National Council on Agricultural Life and Labor, a private, nonprofit organization. The pilot plan called for the construction of an integrated community, including small commercial establishments as well as 120 concrete panel shell "row houses," which, complete with refrigerator and range, could be built at an average cost per house of about $6,400, to be amortized by payments averaging $46.63 to pay out in 40 years. A comprehensive program of job training and job placement would be provided to assist the project residents, chosen from among migrant families, to become economically independent. Families would pay 20 percent of their incomes until this became equivalent to the monthly payment. In the meantime, the balance above the 20 percent would be subsidized. Families would begin to build up equity in the houses when able to make the full amount of the monthly amortization payment and could ultimately acquire full ownership.

The other plan was developed by Amado E. Cavasos, vice-president and treasurer of the H. B. Zachry Co., a large contracting company.[7] The culmination of a comprehensive study for his master's thesis, Cavasos' plan also calls for ultimate ownership by the residents, and has two outstanding features: (1) all houses would be single family units separately constructed and with some variation in style, and (2) estimated cost for land and house with all standard, modern facilities would be only $5,000. The H. B. Zachry Company was making further cost studies in anticipation of probable promotion of a housing project along these lines.

Congressman Gonzalez announced in May, 1965, a grant to be administered by Action for Community Development, Inc., headed by Father John A. Wagner, part of which would provide transportation of donated building materials to the sites of homes of 7,300 migrant-owners, and supervision for such repairs as fixing windows, strengthening foundations, and repairing leaking roofs.[8]

Prior to a U.S. Supreme Court decision outlawing such provisions, it was common practice in San Antonio for developers of residential areas outside the West Side to include in title transfers restrictive covenants against

---

[7]Amado E. Cavasos, Adequate Housing for Low Income Families, unpublished Master's thesis, St. Mary's University, San Antonio, 1964.

[8]AFL-CIO Weekly Dispatch, May 14, 1965.

resale of the properties to persons of Mexican descent. Numerous complaints were made to the Fair Employment Practices Committees by Mexican-Americans of San Antonio during and immediately following World War II.[9]

For some years following invalidation of the legal barriers to mobility of Mexican-Americans to other San Antonio residential areas, difficulties still were placed in their way, and neighborhood acceptance was hard to achieve. Fortunately, according to statements to the writer by a number of Mexican-Americans who recently moved from the West Side to other sections of the city, such problems are now relatively small. The writer agreed with these men that moving out of the West Side is a major step toward rapid economic and social assimilation for members of this ethnic group.

Health

Handicapped by ignorance and superstition, weakened by malnutrition, living in crowded, dilapidated housing with primitive sanitary and other facilities, the Mexican-Americans inhabiting San Antonio's West Side slums have

---

[9]Perales, op. cit., pp. 139-149.

suffered horribly from disease and from debilitating health problems. Their plight was accentuated until the latter 1930's by an uncommonly inefficient and politics-ridden city health department.

Tuberculosis and intestinal diseases were massive causes of death among Mexican-American residents. Dr. St. Clair Drake, associate field director of the American Public Health Association, reported after his 1927 survey of health conditions in San Antonio that the tuberculosis death rate among the Mexican ethnic group was 343 per 100,000, 275% above the rate of other white persons and 48% higher than the Negro rate. The death rate among children of Mexican descent under two years of age from intestinal inflammation was characterized by Drake as a "positively appalling" 394 per 100,000, which was 300 percent higher than other white children in the city.[10]

Dr. K. E. Miller, senior surgeon of the U.S. Public Health Service, after analyzing the city's health situation, reported in June, 1935:

> As regards diarrhea and enteritis under two years of age, San Antonio not only has the highest death rate of all cities in Texas, but enjoys the unenviable

---

[10]Pat I. Nixon, *A Century of Medicine in San Antonio*, privately published, San Antonio, 1936, p. 308.

> distinction of having the highest death rate of all cities of the United States . . . . Aside from a few privies in the unsewered section of the city that conform to the state's standards, all the rest may be considered as highly dangerous health hazards. The overcrowded conditions, together with poor ventilation and lack of sunshine within the corrals and shacks naturally favor in a very large measure the development of tuberculosis and its spread to other members of the family . . . . It is plain to see, therefore, that in the family of American cities San Antonio does not occupy a very flattering position with respect to deaths from major preventable conditions.[11]

The gross inefficiency and mismanagement by the political appointees in the city health department finally became so bad that the county medical society refused to permit its members to serve on the city health board as long as political domination continued. This brought about some improvements, but it was not until 1943 that a city ordinance was adopted providing for a reorganization of the health board, to be composed of seven members, nominated by the San Antonio Chamber of Commerce and appointed by the mayor.[12] With the establishment of the new council-manager form of city government, administration and programs of the city health department continued to improve, but the department still suffered from inadequate funds and personnel to cope with the city's monumental health problems.

---

[11]Ibid., p. 309.

[12]Shapiro, op. cit., pp. 186, 191.

Table 48 presents selected vital statistics for the years 1952 and 1960, distributed according to Mexican-American, other white and nonwhite, taken from data reported by the San Antonio Public Health Department.

While the birth rates of all ethnic categories declined during the period, the ratio of Mexican-American birth rates to those of other white persons rose from 1.7 to 1 in 1952 to 1.9 to 1 in 1960. This pointed up the fact that expanded facilities would be needed for the education and housing of these additional Mexican-Americans as well as for expanded health facilities.

There is room for doubt as to the accuracy of the indicated reversal of death rates of Mexican-Americans (down from 7.5 to 6.0) and other whites (up from 7.0 to 7.9). The data are at least partially confirmed by analysis of the causes of death. Heart diseases, cancer, and cerebral lesions accounted for 85% of recorded Anglo deaths compared to only 50% of deaths of persons with Spanish surnames. When the number of deaths due to these three causes are deducted from the total deaths for the respective ethnic groups, the death rates found for other causes are 3.0 for Mexican-Americans and 1.1 for other whites. The increasing importance of San Antonio as a retirement center for Anglos is reflected in the high proportion of deaths due to the

TABLE 48

VITAL STATISTICS, BY ETHNIC GROUP
CITY OF SAN ANTONIO, 1952 AND 1960

Year	Total		Spanish Surname		Other White		Non-White	
	Number	Rate*	Number	Rate*	Number	Rate*	Number	Rate*
Live Births:								
1952	14,093	32.8	7,355	43.5	5,762	24.9	976	32.5
1960	15,946	27.1	8,952	36.7	5,786	19.2	1,208	27.9
Deaths from all Causes:								
1952	3,239	7.5	1,267	7.5	1,616	7.0	356	11.5
1960	4,186	7.1	1,467	6.0	2,293	7.9	426	9.8
Deaths from Selected Causes:								
Heart Diseases								
1952	1,178	27.4	294	17.4	773	33.5	111	37.0
1960	1,533	26.1	358	14.7	1,064	35.4	111	25.7
Cancer, all forms								
1952	622	14.5	160	9.5	415	18.0	47	15.7
1960	791	13.5	220	9.0	502	16.7	69	16.0
Cerebral Lesions								
1952	374	8.7	94	5.7	232	10.0	48	16.0
1960	600	10.2	158	6.5	378	12.6	64	14.8
Accidents								
1952	208	4.8	68	4.0	122	5.3	18	6.0
1960	268	4.6	98	3.7	162	5.4	17	3.9
Pneumonia								
1952	153	3.6	105	6.2	28	1.2	20	6.7
1960	224	3.8	83	3.4	120	4.0	22	5.1
Premature Births								
1952	164	3.8	81	4.8	67	2.9	16	5.3
1960	134	2.3	64	2.6	53	1.8	17	3.9
Tuberculosis								
1952	133	3.1	110	6.5	19	.8	4	1.3
1960	75	1.3	51	2.1	23	.8	1	.2

*For live Births and Deaths from all Causes, per 1000 population.
For Deaths from Selected Causes, per 10,000 population.

Source: Ten Years of Vital Statistics, 1952-1961, San Antonio Public Health Department, April, 1962.

three major causes, all of which occur most commonly during the later years of life.

The drop in the tuberculosis death rate of Mexican-Americans from 6.5 in 1952 to 2.1 in 1960 was encouraging, but the ravages among this ethnic group from the disease were far from stamped out. In 1961, San Antonio ranked eighth among 28 U.S. cities of over 475,000 population in the number of new active tuberculosis cases per 100,000 population, with 321 cases and a rate of 62.6.[13]

The LULACS began a very intensive and promising campaign against tuberculosis during the school year 1961-62. In cooperation with the city health department, they gave tuberculine skin tests to all school children in a 100-block area of census tract 43, in which Mexican-Americans comprised 93 percent of the population. Where positive reactions were indicated, follow-ups were made with X-rays, using mobile units, of the children and their parents. In a total of 7,510 X-rays taken, 33 definite cases and 146 probable cases of tuberculosis were found, plus 65 persons with cardiovascular (heart) problems and 55 other diseases.[14]

---

[13]Taken from data compiled by the National Tuberculosis Association, supplied by the managing director of the Bexar County Tuberculosis Association.

[14]Data provided by Bexar County Tuberculosis Association.

The project was so successful that an expanded program was planned for all 170,000 school children in Bexar County in 1963-64, with additional plans to X-ray all hospital admissions, school personnel, taxi drivers, and others most likely to spread the disease, with a follow-up compaign for treatment.[15] This promised to be among the most ambitious and valuable health programs ever carried out in San Antonio.

Percentage of births attended by midwives declined from 17.2 in 1952 to 5.4 in 1960, a definite sign of progress and an indication of some success in the continuing campaigns of the medical profession, the West Side settlement houses and others to convince Mexican-American expectant mothers of the importance of qualified medical attention. The Spanish language newspaper, La Prensa, in a blast against midwifery, pointed out that San Antonio was the only city of its size with such a large proportion of births attended by midwives, compared with less than one percent in Dallas and Houston. The write-up added: "Standard prescription of some midwives for women in great fear of pregnancy is a brew consisting of water in which a gold ring and a red ribbon have been boiled."[16]

---

[15] San Antonio Express, July 12, 30, 1963.

[16] La Prensa, September 21, 1961.

The planned new University of Texas Medical School, together with a new teaching hospital and clinic, will be a particular boon to the health care of indigent Mexican-Americans through alleviating the terribly inadequate facilities at the Robert B. Green Hospital. According to the hospital administrator, W. R. Forster, the standards of the U.S. Public Health Service call for 4.5 beds per 1,000. If grouped together, he reported, the medically indigent residents of Bexar County would form a city of 200,000, generating a need for 900 hospital beds as against the 300 currently operated at Green.[17]

The health problems of the masses of West Side residents of Mexican descent were still numerous and serious, but much had been done to alleviate them since mid-century, and the future showed promise of continued progress.

---

[17] San Antonio Express/News, Dec. 12, 1964.

CHAPTER XII

CULTURAL INHIBITIONS AND SOCIAL BARRIERS

The perspective of this chapter is based on the assumptions that maximum utilization of Mexican-American workers is desirable, that their cultural inhibitions to achievement of capacity employability should be eliminated or neutralized, and that social barriers erected by Anglos should be removed.

For the most part, deterrents to economic advancement attributed to Mexican cultural differences involve an order of values at variance with, and generally considered less materialistic than, that of Anglos. The first part of the chapter will be concerned with some of the institutional factors influencing these value relationships. This will be followed by a consideration of barriers to the full economic assimilation of persons of Mexican descent attributed to Anglo actions and attitudes.

The unity of the family and the patriarchal "extended family" organization has been the focus of the Mexican ethnic value system.[1] In the traditional family

---

[1]See Tuck, op. cit., pp. 157-158; Max S. Handman, "San Antonio," Survey Graphic, May, 1931.

relationship, the father exercises almost dictatorial power. The "extended family" encompasses relatives, and sometimes close friends of the family. To this is added the relationship of "compadre," or godfather, which imposes real responsibility on him who accepts it; an orphaned child is sure of a home and care equal to that given the other children of the family. The relationship often extends to business dealings.

The strength of this family system has been the collective protection of the group in times of personal or financial crisis of individual members, and in the maintaining of close personal relationships. On the other hand, this cohesion of the family organization has fostered the exaggerated individualism, petty jealousies and envy between family groups that has severely hampered Mexican-American cooperation toward political unity and the attainment of common goals.

An important source of value determination which inhibits assimilation is the concept of "La Raza," the Race, sometimes referred to as "Mexicanismo," by which the Mexican-American identifies himself with the glorious heritage of his Mexican ancestry. The proper recognition of his "dignidad" is more important than any monetary gain or practical advance; thus, he thinks differently than does the conventional Anglo on such fundamental concepts as time, work, and success.[2] Ozzie Simmons observed, "The Mexican's immediate goal with reference to the occupational system is the modest security of steady employment at a wage sufficient for attaining his primary goals."[3]

The family organization and the concept of "La Raza" are primary causes of the Mexican-Americans' persistent use of the Spanish language, with the resultant failure properly to learn and use English.

The average Mexican-American is strongly influenced by a curious admixture of Catholic religion, superstition, and fatalism.

He apparently has difficulty in reconciling any substantial increase in economic well-being with Catholic beliefs. Sister Mary Murray, in her study of public housing families, reported an interview with a local Catholic pastor in which the latter complained that as soon as the Mexican people move up the economic ladder, they tend to leave the Catholic Church in favor of a Protestant sect.[4]

---

[2]Marion P. Hardman, "The Contribution of Spanish Culture to the United States," Address, El Paso, October, 1947.

[3]Ozzie G. Simmons, Anglo Americans and Mexican Americans in South Texas, Unpublished Doctoral Dissertation, Harvard University, Cambridge, 1952, p. 262.

[4]Murray, op.cit., p. 79.

Ruth Tuck, on the other hand, saw the same result occurring from an opposite cause-effect relationship, stating

> The value of the settlement house lies in its introduction of the young to a cultural by-product of Protestantism: the idea that life is rewarded in this world, in the fruits of industry, sobriety, and thrift, in the tangible forms of success.[5]

A very large proportion of San Antonio's Mexican-Americans firmly believe that illness is caused by evil spirits, evil winds, and particularly the "evil eye."[6] Such superstitions retard assimilation in two important respects. In the first place, qualified medical doctors are reputed to have no power over such illness, and the person's health is jeapardized by his resort to the ministrations of herb doctors, sorcerers, and midwives. Secondly, the individual is absolved from personal responsibility for his failures and his success, thus minimizing the incentive to suceed.

---

[5]Tuck, op. cit., p. 150.

[6]Murray reported that approximately 80% of the families in her 1952 study believed in sickness resulting from the "evil eye" or "ojo." Diagnosis: rub entire body of the sick person with an unbroken egg, while chanting Our Father and Hail Mary and reciting the Apostles' Creed. When this ceremony is completed, break the egg and put it in a glass of water, then place the glass under the head of the patient's bed for several hours. If a round spot resembling an eye appears, the sickness is definitely "ojo." Cure: bury the egg and glass, and patient will recover. Murray, op. cit., p. 121.

Belief in fatalism has a significant effect on a person's sense of values. When the future is already irrevocably determined, one cannot gain much either from planning or concern about the future. With some justification, Anglos have charged such persons with laziness, lack of thrift, and frivolity.

In spite of the cultural inhibitions to assimilation mentioned above, increasing progress has been made toward acculturation of San Antonians of Mexican ethnic extraction. Authorities generally agree that assimilation is much easier and faster for third generation Mexican-Americans, and by 1960, already 55 percent were third generation and over in San Antonio. The LULACS, the settlement houses, church organizations, and other groups have been doing increasingly effective work, and the level of educational attainment is rising. There remains, however, a tremendous retardation among Mexican-Americans in the West Side because of the quagmire of their environment.

Until World War II, San Antonio's Mexican-Americans were treated as second-class citizens with a status little better than Negroes. Their employment was limited to unskilled jobs, and they were virtually restricted to living in the West Side because of restrictive covenants. Even after segregation of their children in the public schools was legally removed, they continued to attend de facto segregated schools. It was not uncommon for Mexican-American individuals and work crews to be paid less than their Anglo counterparts for identical work. In effect, discrimination against this ethnic group was so widely practiced that it was generally accepted by both Anglos and Mexican-Americans, and the term had little significance.

The series of major strikes by Mexican-Americans in the pecan, garment, and cigar industries during the 1930's served warning that their docility had limitations, but it was not until the middle of the next decade that factors incident to World War II led to a still evolving reassessment by the Anglo community of the economic role of the city's rapidly growing Mexican ethnic population.

With the aid of a few aggressive leaders dedicated to improvement of the lot of the Mexican-Americans, particularly at federal FEPC hearings, discrimination in employment and advancement at military installations and in other federal jobs was greatly reduced during the war, and, under the watchful eye of Congressman Gonzalez, it has since been virtually eliminated.

The shortage of skilled workers during the war forced the managements of private industrial firms to employ Mexican-Americans, and most came to realize that, with proper training, orientation and treatment, persons of Mexican extraction were able to compete with Anglos in higher skilled and other advanced occupations. This ethnic group has since comprised the majority of San Antonio's industrial skilled workers.

Very few Mexican-Americans had been accepted as members of local unions, with the exception of the hod carriers and common laborers union, prior to World War II. By 1963, however, Mexican-Americans were fairly well represented in all the major local organizations except the Asbestos Workers Union.

The increasing economic and political significance of the Mexican-American population, while far from reaching its potential, contributed to the virtual elimination of overt discrimination in employment policies of major industrial and business establishments of the city. Few claims and no specific evidence of current practice of unequal pay for the same work was found during this research. Evidence of discrimination against employment of persons of Mexican descent was found at the local telephone company branch and at the City Public Service Board, but, in general, ethnic bias in employment in plant and other skilled jobs by large firms was found only in the lower management positions.

Widespread discrimination still existed in managerial, office and sales positions, and some employers were still convinced that Mexican-Americans were inferior to Anglos in handling these jobs; however, most of the disparity in employment between Anglos and Mexican-Americans in such positions was due to the fact that relatively few of the latter had attained education, training, experience and other qualifications necessary to compete effectively.

By the mid-1960's, all of the legal barriers against Mexican-Americans had been long removed and overt discrimination had been nearly eliminated. The two major remaining barriers to economic assimilation of Mexican-Americans for which Anglos could be held largely responsible were sins of omission: namely, failure to facilitate assimilation of members of this group through gaining a better understanding of the Mexican ethnic culture, and failure of the dominant Anglo leadership to provide the necessary educational, housing and health facilities for more rapid acculturation of persons of Mexican descent.

CONCLUSIONS

For a hundred years prior to World War II, the Mexican-Americans of the Southwest were relegated to the status of second-class citizens, with possibilities for economic and social advancement little better than those of Negroes. Their somewhat higher legal position was offset by their language and other cultural problems. Stereotyped as intellectually inferior, lazy, and unreliable, they were restricted in employment to the most menial unskilled labor.

In 1960, a tremendous disparity still existed between Anglo employment and that of Mexican-Americans and Negroes. Data for six Texas cities, three with relatively high proportions of Mexican-Americans and three with relatively high proportions of Negroes, revealed that Anglos had superior labor force participation, much lower rates of unemployment, and substantially higher median family incomes than either of the other groups. Significantly, a comparison of the economic well-being of Mexican-Americans and Negroes in these six cities, based on the same three criteria, revealed that the most numerous minority group in each city was most disadvantaged. The single exception was the slightly higher Mexican-American median family income of $3,446 in San Antonio, only 59 percent that of Anglo families. Of the total Mexican-American families, 42.4 percent had incomes of less than $3,000; the lowest incomes were found in those census tracts in the heart of the West Side slums with the highest concentrations of Mexican-Americans. Although unemployment of Mexican-Americans relative to that of Anglos had declined from 1950 to 1960, the rate of Mexican ethnic unemployment was still more than double that of Anglos.

San Antonio's economy has been distinguished by its heavy dependence on military bases, private industry dominated by wholesale and retail trades and service establishments, and a small manufacturing sector. Research revealed no reason to expect any substantial change in these relationships in the next several decades.

The city's industrial leaders have generally ascribed San Antonio's small manufacturing sector solely to circumstances associated with its geographical location, citing distance from national markets, high freight rates, limited supplies of raw materials, and lack of adequate water for heavy industries. This writer's research has convinced him that the major effect of geographical location on San Antonio's industrialization has been its role in the development of the massive military bases which have made a large manufacturing sector unnecessary to the city's economic growth. In effect, civilian military employment, particularly at Kelly Air Force Base, has served as a substitute for more extensive private industry.

With no strong economic pressure to expand San Antonio's productive base, many of the city's business and political leaders have given only lip service to efforts towards expanding manufacturing, especially in heavy industries, because they feared that expansion would result in greater union power, with consequent increases in wages and prices. This lukewarm approach to enticing additional manufacturing, in competition with the aggressive tactics of other cities, promised limited prospects for any material expansion of industrialization.

San Antonio's labor force has been characterized by a large and growing supply of Mexican-American workers, deficiency in both diversity and degree of skills, low wages and incomes, and weak labor organizations.

Since the worker shortage during World War I lured the first massive twentieth century immigration to fill agricultural, railroad, and unskilled labor jobs, San Antonio has had an oversupply of persons of Mexican descent who have been willing to work for meager wages because even such low pay was better than they could obtain in Mexico. The resultant constant downward pressure on wage rates discouraged inflow of skilled workers, and the absence of skilled labor acted as a further deterrent to industrialization.

Conditions resulting from World War II combined to mark the beginning of the slow and painful liberation of San Antonio's Mexican-Americans from their limitation to unskilled jobs and other strictures of their second-class citizenship. Forced by the shortage of Anglo workers, employers hired and trained large numbers of Mexican-Americans for the first time in skilled jobs, and they were agreeably surprised to find the Mexican-Americans compared favorably with Anglos in competence and responsibility. By 1963, Mexican-Americans were commonly found throughout plant departments and engaged in substantially all types of skilled occupations. Half of all Mexican-Americans, as compared to one-third of Anglos, were employed in skilled and semiskilled occupations, 20 percent were working in formerly almost unattainable professional and white collar jobs, and only 30 percent remained engaged in service and common labor work.

The rate of growth of the Mexican-American segment of the population in Texas cities has been greater than for Anglos and for Negroes, and this relationship is likely to continue. The sustained trend is due to the relatively high Mexican-American birth rate (nearly double that of Anglos in San Antonio in 1960), direct migration from Mexico to Texas' urban centers, and movement of

The Texas state poll tax has been a major deterrent to political participation by the masses of low income Mexican-American families. Efforts to abolish this archaic and discriminatory qualification for voting have been unsuccessful at the state level, but it is hoped that Congress will legislate the abolition of the poll tax.

Next to the availability of relatively well paid and nondiscriminatory employment at the huge military installations and the extension of private employment opportunities during World War II, the most important single influence in improvement of the incomes and standard of living of San Antonio's Mexican-Americans has been the implementation of the Fair Labor Standards Act. This was particularly noteworthy in the cigar and pecan shelling industries. Extension of the minimum wage provision of the act should be made to include laundries and dry cleaners, hotels and restaurants, and a larger proportion of the retail establishments. The writer also has agreed with Congressman Gonzalez that a Texas minimum wage law would be highly desirable. A state minimum wage of $1.00 per hour would be beneficial to San Antonio's general economy as well as for the underpaid Mexican-Americans who filled most of the jobs not covered by the Fair Labor Standards Act.

It is true that some unemployment would result from extension of FLSA coverage and/or establishment of a state minimum wage; however, past experience in San Antonio has shown that the great majority of the workers who would lose their jobs would be from multiworker families with at least one worker whose continued employment at increased pay would substantially, if not entirely, make up the difference in family income. Those persons who lost their jobs would be free to get further education or training for other employment or to give their time to family responsibilities. Furthermore, as employers became more selective, the inflow of unskilled workers from Mexico would be discouraged.

On the other hand, neither immediate substantial increase in the FLSA minimum wage, decrease in the standard work week, nor increase of overtime pay to double time are recommended as desirable for San Antonio's economy and particularly her Mexican-American workers. Widespread unemployment would result in this preindustrial city.

The labor movement in San Antonio has always been weak. This has been partly because of the small industrial base made up largely of old, basic manufactures in which unionization has been traditionally low. Organized labor has also been strongly opposed by organized employers continuously since 1900. The constant supply of Mexican workers at lower than union scale has been a factor in the low level of unionization in San Antonio. Before 1940, employers used, and threatened to use, Mexican strikebreakers as a means of maintaining low wage rates. As a consequence, Anglo union locals rarely took Mexican-Americans into membership prior to World War II.

The preponderance of evidence since the 1930's has indicated that Mexican-Americans, women as well as men, have been at least as receptive as Anglos to unionization. Lacking in leadership of their own ethnic group and ignored by local Anglo unionists, Mexican-Americans were nevertheless aggressive in organized action in the textile, cigar, and pecan industries in the 1930's. During and after World War II, the major building trades unions have taken in substantial numbers of Mexican-Americans, many of whom learned their trades at Kelly Air Force Base. Mexican-Americans have been particularly active in industrial unions.

The passage of the Texas "Right-to-Work" law was a greater psychological blow to the labor movement in San Antonio than in other large cities. Its effect was most strongly felt by the industrial unions, notably in the deterioration of the virtually all Mexican-American local organization of the International Ladies Garment Workers'

Union. On the other hand, it is unlikely that repeal of section 14-b of the Taft-Hartley Act would materially strengthen the labor movement in San Antonio or have any significant effect on the economic conditions of Mexican-Americans.

Inadequate education has constituted the greatest single barrier to economic advancement of San Antonio's Mexican-Americans, who rank far behind Anglos at all educational levels. The median number of school years completed by persons 25 years old or over in 1960 was only 5.7 in San Antonio, compared to 8.9 in Los Angeles. The median for the other five Texas cities surveyed ranged from 4.5 in Corpus Christi to 7.1 in Fort Worth. Comparative data indicated, on the other hand, that the proportions of Mexican-Americans graduating from high school and from college were increasing substantially. Education of this ethnic group has been severely handicapped by widespread deficiency in the English language, a problem intensified by de facto segregation in schools and by the almost universal practice of Mexican-Americans to converse in Spanish.

The Manpower Development and Training projects were developing rapidly and appeared to be well planned and administered. About three-fourths of the trainees were Mexican-Americans.

The three local projects inaugurated under the Economic Opportunity Act of 1964--preschool education, improvements in migrant worker neighborhoods, and a neighborhood youth corps--were all found to be well planned, capably staffed programs serving important needs of Mexican-American slum families. To maximize the use of funds, however, a comprehensive and thorough study of the broad spectrum of educational, housing, and health needs should be made, and projects should be developed according to a central plan.

The most urgent current need under the poverty program was for a massive attack on adult illiteracy. Three-fourths of the estimated 109,000 functional illiterates in Bexar County in 1964 were Mexican-Americans. The local literacy council and other agencies were doing a good work in this field, but they were handicapped by lack of funds.

Only 49.7% of Mexican-American residences in San Antonio in 1960 were in sound condition with all standard plumbing facilities, as compared to 94.0% for other whites, and 59.5% of nonwhites. A comprehensive program of further replacement of slum housing with decent, modern dwellings should be implemented. Careful consideration should be given to utilization of both conventional public housing units and the several promising alternative plans. Mexican-Americans should be encouraged to move from the West Side, including more thorough integration of the various housing projects. A comprehensive study should be made of availability of sanitary and other public facilities to residential areas, and a program instituted to assure their availability to all dwellings.

By 1965, overt discrimination against Mexican-Americans had been eliminated by virtually all large employers and most small ones. Evidence of broad covert discrimination was found at the local branch of the telephone company and at the City Public Service Board. Otherwise, ethnic bias in skilled jobs by large firms was found only in the lower management positions. Widespread covert discrimination still existed in managerial, office, and sales positions; however, most of the disparity in employment between Anglos and Mexican-Americans was due to inadequate education, training, experience or other necessary qualifications.

Mexican-Americans had been quick to lodge charges of discriminatory practices at military installations, yet they had failed to use available measures against discrimination at the local telephone company and the City Public Service Board. Whether they will utilize the provisions of Title VII of the Civil Rights Act of 1964, effective July 2, 1965, remains to be seen.

The well organized, aggressive and effective nationwide campaign for equal opportunity by Negroes has benefitted the Mexican-Americans of San Antonio and throughout the southwest in four significant ways: (1) the relatively poorly organized Mexican-Americans have been encouraged to make stronger and more cohesive efforts on their own behalf, (2) the pressures for racial equality have caused Anglos to give greater attention to equality of opportunity for Mexican-Americans, (3) political cooperation between the two minorities has been fostered, and (4) while they contributed relatively little to the push for its enactment, Mexican-Americans share the advantages provided in the Civil Rights Act.

Employers who have sought to understand the cultural distinctions, background, and motivations of Mexican-American employees have been able to help them solve problems of assimilation. Some have promoted the establishment of credit unions as a means of keeping Mexican-Americans out of the clutches of loan-sharks. Many have found it practical to ignore minor police records when honestly reported. Still others have provided augmented orientation programs, which included special attention to importance of regular attendance and punctuality, and a few have helped Mexican-American employees secure good housing away from the West Side.

Full economic utilization of the masses of San Antonio's Mexican-Americans is still far from realization in 1965. The necessary education and cultural accommodations are slow and sometimes painful. However, much has been accomplished since World War II, and, with a well-planned and executed development of projects under the "War on Poverty," together with better interethnic understanding and appreciation, increasing numbers of Mexican-Americans will attain economic advancement commensurate with their abilities.

BIBLIOGRAPHY

Books

Allen, Ruth A. Chapters in the History of Organized Labor in Texas. Austin: The University of Texas Publications, 1941.

__________. The Great Southwest Strike. Austin: The University of Texas Publications, 1942.

Benjamin, G. G. The Germans in Texas. Philadelphia: University of Pennsylvania Publications, 1909.

Biesele, R. L. The History of the German Settlements in Texas, 1831-1861. Austin: Von Boeckmann-Jones Co., 1930.

Bogardus, Emory S. The Mexican in the United States. Los Angeles: University of Southern California Press, 1934.

Burma, John H. Spanish-speaking Groups in the United States. Durham: Duke University Press, 1954.

Chabot, Frederick, C. San Antonio and Its Beginnings. San Antonio: Artes Graficas Printing Co., 1936.

__________. With the Makers of San Antonio. San Antonio: Artes Graficas Printing Co., 1937.

Curtis, Albert. Military San Antonio. San Antonio: Standard Printing Co., 1943.

__________. Fabulous San Antonio. San Antonio: The Naylor Co., c. 1955.

Gamio, Manuel. Mexican Immigration to the United States. Chicago: The University of Chicago Press, 1930.

Handy, Mary Olivia. History of Fort Sam Houston. San Antonio: The Naylor Co., c. 1951.

Heusinger, Edward W. A Chronology of Events in San Antonio. San Antonio: Standard Printing Co., 1951.

House, Boyce. City of Flaming Adventure. San Antonio: The Naylor Co., 1949.

Johnston, Leah Carter. San Antonio, St. Anthony's Town. San Antonio: The Naylor Co., 1947.

Kibbe, Pauline R. Latin-Americans in Texas. Albuquerque: The University of New Mexico Press, 1946.

Lozano, Reuben R. Viva Tejas. San Antonio and Houston: Southern Literary Institute, 1936.

McWilliams, Carey. North from Mexico, the Spanish-speaking People of the United States. Philadelphia: J. B. Lippincott, 1949.

Manuel, H. T. The Education of Mexican and Spanish-Speaking Children in Texas. Austin: The University of Texas, 1930.

Nixon, Pat I. A Century of Medicine in San Antonio. San Antonio: Privately published, 1936.

Oberste, William H. Texas Irish Empresarios and Their Colonies. Austin: Von Boeckmann-Jones Co., 1953.

Perales, Alonza. Are We Good Neighbors? San Antonio: Artes Graficas, 1948.

Picnot, T. N. An Economic and Industrial Survey of San Antonio, Texas. San Antonio: Public Service Co., 1942.

Ramsdell, Charles. San Antonio, A Historical and Pictorial Guide. Austin: The University of Texas Press, 1959.

Saunders, Lyle. The Spanish-Speaking Population of Texas. Austin: The University of Texas Press, 1949.

Talbert, Robert H. Spanish Name People in the Southwest and West. Fort Worth: The Manney Co., 1955.

Taylor, Paul S. An American-Mexican Frontier. Chapel Hill: University of North Carolina Press, 1934.

Tuck, Ruth D. Not With the Fist. New York: Harcourt Brace and Co., 1946.

Waugh, Julia Nott. Castroville and Henri Castro--Empresario. San Antonio: Standard Printing Co., 1934.

Wertenbaker, Green Peyton. San Antonio, City in the Sun. New York: McGraw-Hill Book Co., Inc., 1946.

Woods, Frances J. Mexican Ethnic Leadership in San Antonio, Texas. Washington: Catholic University Press, 1949.

WPA, Federal Writers' Project. San Antonio, An Authoritative Guide to the City and Its Environs. San Antonio: The Clegg Co., 1938.

Writers' Program, Texas. San Antonio, A History and Guide. San Antonio: The Clegg Co., 1941.

Articles

"Coyotes Bite," Time, LXV (May 2, 1955), 36.

Handman, Max S. "Economic Reasons for the Coming of the Mexican Immigrant," American Journal of Sociology, XXXV (Jan., 1930), 601-611.

Lucey, Robert E. "Badge of Infamy," Extension, June, 1958, reprint.

__________. "Justice for the Mexicans," Commonweal, XLIX (Nov. 12, 1948), 117.

Manuel, H. T. "The Mexican Population of Texas," Southwestern Social Science Quarterly, XV, 1 (June, 1934), 51.

McWilliams, Carey. "Mexicans to Michigan," Common Ground, II (Autumn, 1941), 5-18.

Meyers, Frederic. "Employment and Relative Earnings of Spanish-Name Persons in Texas Industries," Southern Economics Journal, XIX (April, 1953), 494-507.

Perry, George Sessions. "San Antonio," Saturday Evening Post, (Nov. 24, 1945), 23, 108, 110, 113-114.

"San Antonio," Business Review, Federal Reserve Bank of Dallas, June, 1959, reprint.

Taylor, Paul S. "Mexicans North of the Rio Grande," Survey Graphic, (May, 1931), 201-202.

"A West Side Story," The Texas Observer, Sept. 9, 1961.

Monographs, Bulletins, and Pamphlets

American G.I. Forum of Texas and Texas State Federation of Labor. What Price Wetbacks? Austin: 1953.

American Public Welfare Association. Public Welfare Survey of San Antonio, Texas. 1940.

Belo, A. H., Corporation. Texas Almanac, 1961-1962. Dallas: 1962.

Bexar County Tuberculosis Association. Like a Sore Thumb. San Antonio: 1945.

Catholic Council for the Spanish Speaking. Tenth Conference. St. Louis: April, 1960.

Chramosta, Sharon. Directory of Community Services in the Southwest Area of San Antonio, Texas. San Antonio: Bishops' Committee for the Spanish Speaking, 1961.

City of San Antonio, Municipal Advertising Commission. Romantic San Antonio. C. 1948.

Community Welfare Council of San Antonio. Directory of Community Services, San Antonio and Bexar County. March, 1960.

League of United Latin American Citizens. LULAC Handbook. San Antonio, 1961.

Little, Wilson. Spanish-speaking Children in Texas. Austin: University of Texas Press, 1944.

Menefee, Seldon, and Cassmore, C. C. _The Pecan Shellers of San Antonio_. Works Progress Administration. Washington, D.C.: Superintendent of Documents, 1940.

Meyers, Frederic. _Right to Work in Practice_. New York: The Fund for the Republic, 1959.

Murray, Mary John. _Socio-Cultural Study of 118 Mexican Families Living in a Low Rent Public Housing Project in San Antonio, Texas_. Washington, D.C.: Catholic University of America Press, 1958.

New York World Telegram and Sun. _World Almanac_. New York: 1963.

San Antonio Chamber of Commerce. _San Antonio Plant Location Facts_. June, 1962.

San Antonio Department of Housing and Inspections. _Our Slum and Blighted Areas_. 1957.

San Antonio Manufacturers Association. _1962 Directory of San Antonio Manufacturers_.

San Antonio Public Health Department. _Vital Statistics_, 1957.

__________. _Ten Years of Vital Statistics, 1952-1961_. April, 1962.

Sánchez, George I. _Wetbacks_. Preliminary Report to Advisory Committee, Study of Spanish-speaking People. Austin: 1949.

__________. _Concerning Segregation of Spanish-speaking Children in the Public Schools_. Inter-American Occasional Paper IX, The University of Texas. Austin: Dec., 1951.

Texas Committee on Migrant Farm Workers and the Good Neighbor Commission of Texas. _Proceedings of the Texas Conference on Education for Adult Migrant Farm Workers_. Austin: March 8, 1962.

Texas Education Agency, Division of Research. _Report of Pupils in Texas Public Schools having Spanish Surnames, 1955-56_. (Mimeo) August, 1957.

Texas Employment Commission. Texas Labor Market. Austin: June, 1962.

Texas State Employment Service. Origins and Problems of Texas Migratory Farm Labor. Austin: 1940.

Texas State Federation of Labor. Down in the Valley. Austin: 1955.

University of Texas, Bureau of Business Research. Directory of Texas Manufacturers, 1962. Austin: 1963.

Unpublished Materials

Bradshaw, Benjamin S. Some Demographic Aspects of Marriage: A Comparative Study of Three Ethnic Groups. Master's thesis, The University of Texas, 1960.

Brookshire, Marjorie. The Industrial Pattern of Mexican-American Employment in Nueces County, Texas. Doctoral dissertation, The University of Texas, 1954.

Cavasos, Amado E. Adequate Housing for Low Income Families. Master's thesis, St. Mary's University, San Antonio, 1964.

Hardman, Marion P. "The Contribution of Spanish Culture to the United States." Address delivered in El Paso, Texas, on October 21, 1947. (Mimeo)

Knox, William J. The Economic Status of the Mexican Immigrant in San Antonio, Texas. Master's thesis, The University of Texas, 1927.

Madisen, William. "Cultural Factors in Migratory Labor Education." Address delivered at the Texas Conference on Education for Adult Migrant Farm Workers, Austin, March 8, 1962.

Marshall, Ray. "Equal Employment Opportunity: Problems and Prospects." Address delivered to the Industrial Relations Research Association, Buffalo, New York on May 3, 1965. (Mimeo)

Meyers, Frederic. "Estimated Proportions of Total Eligible Jobs in Texas Manufacturing Industry Covered by Collective Bargaining, by Industry, April, 1953." (Ditto)

Mullenix, Grady Lee. A History of the Texas State Federation of Labor, 1955. Doctoral Dissertation, University of Texas. Austin: 1955.

Picnot, T.N. "Socio-Economic Status of Low Income Groups in San Antonio." Address before the San Antonio Social Workers Association, 1943. (Mimeo).

Rogers, Thomas Guy. The Housing Situation of the Mexicans in San Antonio, Texas. Master's Thesis, University of Texas. Austin: 1927.

Saunders, Lyle. "A Study of Spanish speaking People." Speech before the National Convention of the League of United Latin American Citizens. June 11, 1949. (Mimeo).

Shapiro, Harold A. The Workers of San Antonio, Texas 1900-1940. Doctoral Dissertation, University of Texas. Austin: 1952.

Simmons, Ozzie G. Anglo-Americans and Mexican-Americans in South Texas. Doctoral Dissertation, Harvard University. Cambridge: 1952.

U. S. Immigration and Naturalization Service. "Number of Immigrants of Mexican Birth Destined to San Antonio, Texas, Years Ended June 30, 1956-62." Letter from E.A. Loughran, Associate Commissioner, Management, June 18, 1963.

Wagner, John A. "Community of Tomorrow." Address delivered at Christ the King Church, Lubbock, Texas, July 9, 1961. (Mimeo).

White, Jean. Time Orientation as a Factor in the Acculturation of the Southwestern Spanish Speaking Groups. Master's Thesis, University of Texas. Austin: 1955.

U. S. Government Publications

President's Committee on Equal Employment Opportunities. Statistical Summary, Minority Groups in Federal Employment, June 1962, Spanish Speaking and Total Employment by Grade and Salary Groups. 1963.

U. S. Bureau of the Census, U. S. Census of Population, 1950. Vol. I. Number of Inhabitants, Texas.

_________. Vol. II. Characteristics of the Population, Part 43, Texas.

_________. Special Reports, Persons of Spanish Surnames.

U. S. Bureau of the Census, U. S. Census of Population, 1960. General Social and Economic Characteristics, Texas.

_________. Persons of Spanish Surnames.

U. S. Bureau of the Census, U. S. Censuses of Population and Housing, 1960. Census Tracts: Corpus Christi, Dallas, El Paso, Fort Worth, Houston, San Antonio.

U. S. Bureau of the Census, Statistical Abstract of the United States, 1963.

U. S. Department of Labor, Bureau of Labor Statistics. 1962 Statistical Supplement, Monthly Labor Review. 1963.

_________. Employment and Earnings Statistics for States and Areas, 1939-62. 1963.

U. S. Immigration and Naturalization Service. Annual Report, Comissioner General of Immigration. 1928.

Newspapers

AFL-CIO Weekly Dispatch. San Antonio: 1962-1965.

La Prensa. San Antonio, 1960-1964.

San Antonio Express. San Antonio: 1900-1965.

San Antonio Light. San Antonio: 1930-1964.

APPENDIX A

POPULATION, TOTAL AND SPANISH-SURNAME, BY CENSUS TRACTS FOR CENSUS TRACTS WITH MORE THAN 400 SPANISH-SURNAMES BEXAR COUNTY, TEXAS, 1960

Tract Number	Total	Spanish Surname	Percent Spanish-Surname	Tract Number	Total	Spanish Surname	Percent Spanish-Surname
1	2,141	407	19.0	53	2,830	1,030	36.4
3	4,664	1,031	22.1	54	9,539	5,146	53.9
5	16,161	1,447	9.0	55	2,032	685	32.2
6	14,730	1,126	7.6	56	9,354	7,637	81.6
8	7.189	436	6.1	57	4,517	2,784	61.6
9	10,607	1,105	10.4	58	12,372	11,803	95.4
10	4,522	2,204	48.7	59	10,223	8.729	85.4
13	4,965	463	9.3	60	7,544	7,010	92.9
15	3,776	456	12.1	61	8,789	3,383	38.5
16	10,248	2,182	21.3	62	5,402	2,056	38.1
17	7,953	823	10.3	63	5,987	2,060	34.4
21	6,111	3,302	54.0	64	5,804	4,453	76.7
22	6,509	6,122	94.1	65	5,817	4,183	71.9
23	5,064	998	19.7	66	8.518	1,683	19.8
24	5,441	2,153	39.6	69	8,857	3,279	37.0
25	4,482	1,479	33.0	71	15,211	1,289	8.5
26	6,884	2,126	30.9	72	2,059	1.227	59.6
27	11,165	606	5.4	75	6,059	408	6.7
28	4,478	1,530	34.2	76	1,596	583	36.5
29	4,274	1,481	34.7	77	6,193	1,984	32.0
30	2,253	822	36.5	78	4,918	3,193	64.9
31	4,744	1,187	25.0	79	10,859	9,618	88.6
32	3,000	2,016	67.2	80	8,742	4,224	48.3
33	9,746	8,738	90.0	81	6,675	3,688	55.3
34	12,294	9,716	79.0	82	3,340	951	28.5
35	14,193	8,909	62.8	85	7,966	1,887	23.7
36	1,951	1,599	82.0	86	503	411	81.7
37	2,519	2,360	93.7	87	3,002	1,529	50.9
38	8,927	5,302	59.4	88	8.959	589	6.6
39	3,808	3,136	82.4	91	4,080	784	19.2
40	8,775	8,455	96.4	92	6.928	4,948	71.4
41	9,053	8.038	88.9	93	11,432	555	4.9
42	12,042	11,383	94.5	101	3,150	653	20.7
43	13,794	12,845	93.1	106	1,136	944	83.1
44	7,406	6,956	93.9	109	19,403	538	2.8
45	6,342	4,500	71.0	110	3,642	1,747	48.0
46	6,378	2,860	44.9	115	2,522	522	20.7
47	2,724	1.077	39.5	117	1,952	580	29.7
48	6,128	2,067	33.7	119	2,668	885	33.2
49	6,807	588	8.6	120	2,770	1,244	44.9
50	8,959	979	10.9	121	5,158	2,150	41.7
52	4,341	826	19.0				

Source: U.S. Censuses of Population and Housing: 1960 Census Tracts, San Antonio, Texas, pp. 13-22, 54-60.

APPENDIX B

CLASS ACT AND WAGE BOARD SCHEDULE
MILITARY INSTALLATIONS
SAN ANTONIO, TEXAS

Effective Date: GS - First Pay Period after January 1, 1964
WB - First Pay Period after August 1, 1963

GS No.	Annual Salary Starting	Annual Salary Maximum
1	$ 3,305	$ 4,250
2	3,620	4,565
3	3,880	4,900
4	4,215	5,475
5	4,690	6,130
6	5,235	6,810
7	5,795	7,550
8	6,390	8,280
9	7,030	9,100
10	7,600	9,985
11	8,410	10,650
12	9,980	12,620
13	11,725	14,805
14	13,615	17,215
15	15,665	19,270
WB No.	Hourly Rate	
1	$ 1.43	$ 1.58
2	1.52	1.68
3	1.62	1.79
4	1.70	1.88
5	1.80	1.98
6	1.94	2.14
7	2.08	2.30
8	2.22	2.46
9	2.37	2.61
10	2.51	2.77
11	2.65	2.93
12	2.78	3.08
13	2.93	3.23
14	3.14	3.47
15	3.41	3.77

Source: Public Information Office, Kelly AFB

Map 2. Concentration of Mexican-American Population by Census Tracts, San Antonio, Texas, 1960

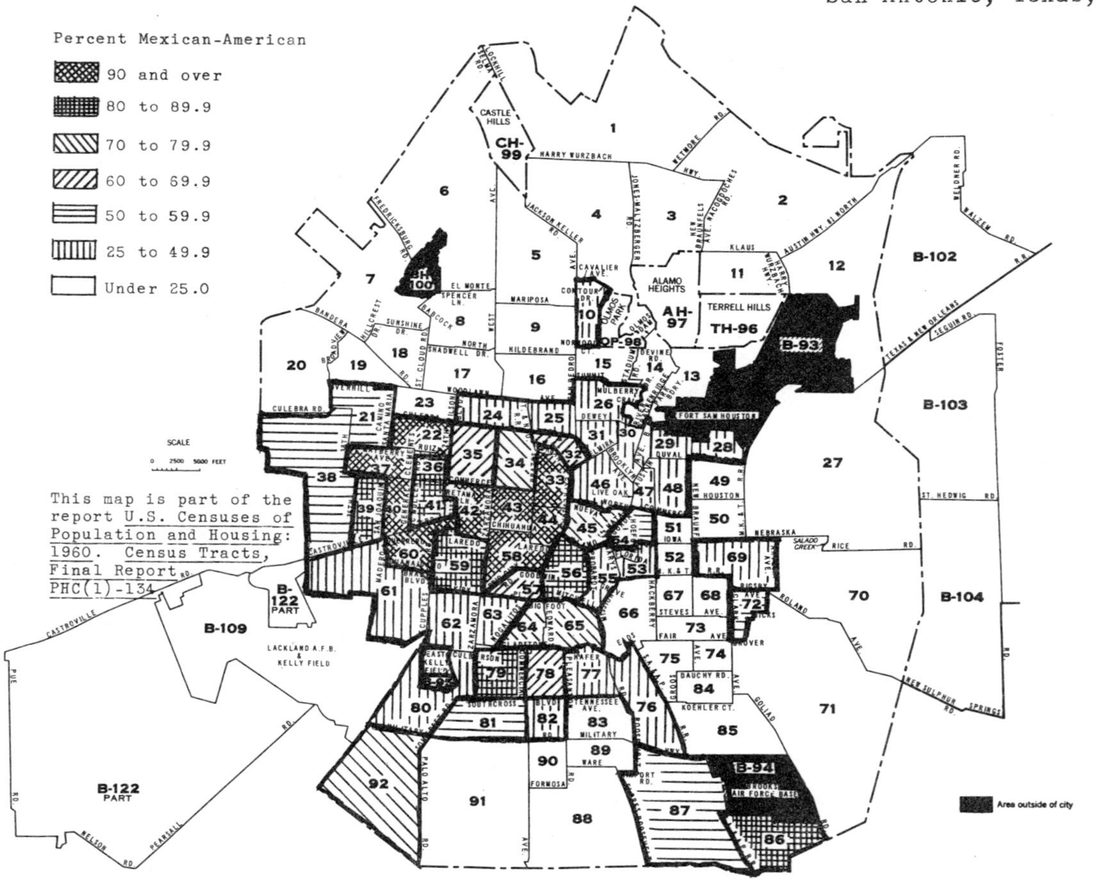

This map is part of the report U.S. Censuses of Population and Housing: 1960. Census Tracts, Final Report PHC(1)-134

Map 3. Concentration of Mexican-American Population by Census Tracts, San Antonio SMSA, 1960.

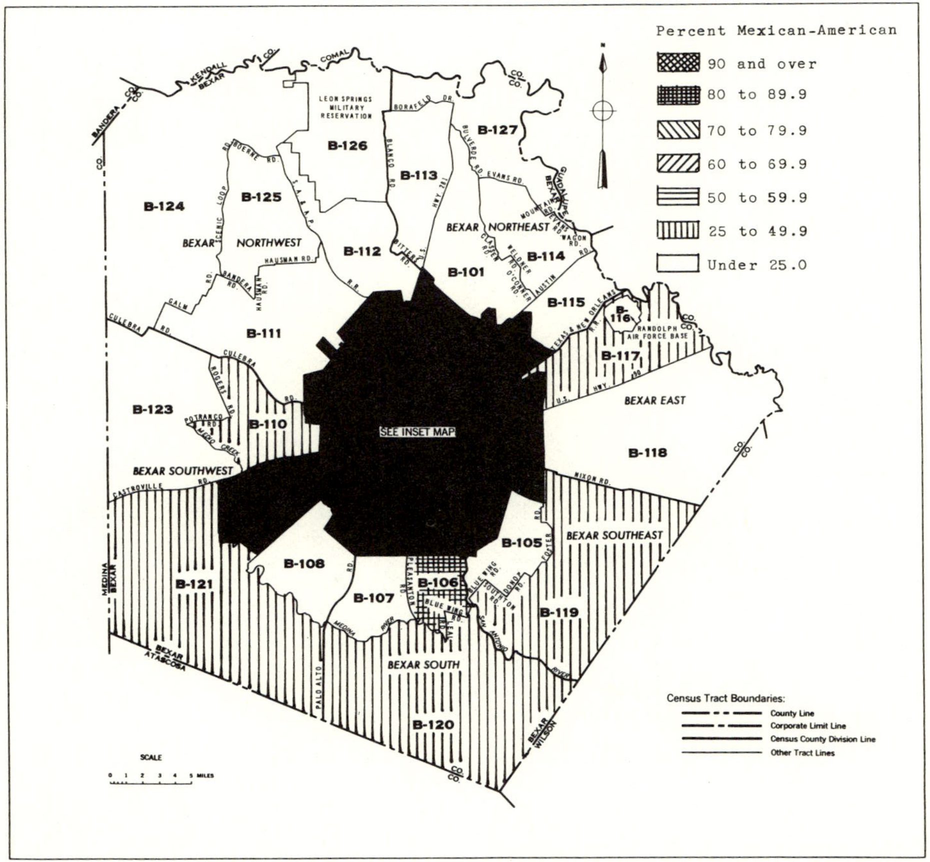

V I T A

Robert Garland Landolt was born in Somerville, Texas, on October 28, 1913, the son of William Landolt and Lonie Massey Landolt. He was graduated from Somerville High School in 1931, and in the summer of that year attended South Park College, Beaumont, Texas. He enrolled at Austin College, Sherman, Texas, in the fall of 1931, and he received the degrees of Bachelor of Arts in 1934 and Master of Arts in 1937 from that institution. Early employment included: bookkeeper and bursar, Austin College, 1934-37; junior accountant with a public accountant and a business machines company, 1937-40; interviewer and employer relations man for the Texas Employment Commission, Houston, Texas, 1940-42; personnel officer, Todd Shipyards Corp., Houston and Galveston, Texas, 1942-47; business manager, First Presbyterian Church, Ft. Worth, Texas, 1947-49. From 1949 to 1958, he served as president of Lees Junior College, Jackson, Kentucky. He was enrolled in the graduate school of the University of Texas from 1958 to 1962, during which time he served as teaching assistant in the department of economics and instructor in the extension division. Since 1962, he has been professor of economics and business administration at Morris Harvey College, Charleston, West Virginia, and he was made head of the departments of business administration and economics in 1963 and 1964, respectively. In 1938, he married Mary Campbell Landolt. They have three sons, Robert George, John Charles, and William Joseph, and one daughter, Mary Elizabeth.

Permanent address: 2934 Phillips Street
South Charleston, West Virginia

THE CHICANO HERITAGE

An Arno Press Collection

Adams, Emma H. **To and Fro in Southern California.** 1887

Anderson, Henry P. **The Bracero Program in California.** 1961

Aviña, Rose Hollenbaugh. **Spanish and Mexican Land Grants in California.** 1976

Barker, Ruth Laughlin. **Caballeros.** 1932

Bell, Horace. **On the Old West Coast.** 1930

Biberman, Herbert. **Salt of the Earth.** 1965

Casteñeda, Carlos E., trans. **The Mexican Side of the Texas Revolution (1836).** 1928

Casteñeda, Carlos E. **Our Catholic Heritage in Texas, 1519-1936.** Seven volumes. 1936-1958

Colton, Walter. **Three Years in California.** 1850

Cooke, Philip St. George. **The Conquest of New Mexico and California.** 1878

Cue Canovas, Agustin. **Los Estados Unidos Y El Mexico Olvidado.** 1970

Curtin, L. S. M. **Healing Herbs of the Upper Rio Grande.** 1947

Fergusson, Harvey. **The Blood of the Conquerors.** 1921

Fernandez, Jose. **Cuarenta Años de Legislador:** Biografia del Senador Casimiro Barela. 1911

Francis, Jessie Davies. **An Economic and Social History of Mexican California** (1822-1846). Volume I: Chiefly Economic. Two vols. in one. 1976

Getty, Harry T. **Interethnic Relationships in the Community of Tucson.** 1976

Guzman, Ralph C. **The Political Socialization of the Mexican American People.** 1976

Harding, George L. **Don Agustin V. Zamorano.** 1934

Hayes, Benjamin. **Pioneer Notes from the Diaries of Judge Benjamin Hayes, 1849-1875.** 1929

Herrick, Robert. **Waste.** 1924

Jamieson, Stuart. **Labor Unionism in American Agriculture.** 1945

Landolt, Robert Garland. **The Mexican-American Workers of San Antonio, Texas.** 1976

Lane, Jr., John Hart. **Voluntary Associations Among Mexican Americans in San Antonio, Texas.** 1976

Livermore, Abiel Abbot. **The War with Mexico Reviewed.** 1850

Loyola, Mary. **The American Occupation of New Mexico, 1821-1852.** 1939

Macklin, Barbara June. **Structural Stability and Culture Change in a Mexican-American Community.** 1976

McWilliams, Carey. **Ill Fares the Land:** Migrants and Migratory Labor in the United States. 1942

Murray, Winifred. **A Socio-Cultural Study of 118 Mexican Families Living in a Low-Rent Public Housing Project in San Antonio, Texas.** 1954

Niggli, Josephina. **Mexican Folk Plays.** 1938

Parigi, Sam Frank. **A Case Study of Latin American Unionization in Austin, Texas.** 1976

Poldervaart, Arie W. **Black-Robed Justice.** 1948

Rayburn, John C. and Virginia Kemp Rayburn, eds. **Century of Conflict, 1821-1913.** Incidents in the Lives of William Neale and William A. Neale, Early Settlers in South Texas. 1966

Read, Benjamin. **Illustrated History of New Mexico.** 1912

Rodriguez, Jr., Eugene. **Henry B. Gonzalez.** 1976

Sanchez, Nellie Van de Grift. **Spanish and Indian Place Names of California.** 1930

Sanchez, Nellie Van de Grift. **Spanish Arcadia.** 1929

Shulman, Irving. **The Square Trap.** 1953

Tireman, L. S. **Teaching Spanish-Speaking Children.** 1948

Tireman, L. S. and Mary Watson. **A Community School in a Spanish-Speaking Village.** 1948

Twitchell, Ralph Emerson. **The History of the Military Occupation of the Territory of New Mexico.** 1909

Twitchell, Ralph Emerson. **The Spanish Archives of New Mexico.** Two vols. 1914

U. S. House of Representatives. **California and New Mexico:** Message from the President of the United States, January 21, 1850. 1850

Valdes y Tapia, Daniel. **Hispanos and American Politics.** 1976

West, Stanley A. **The Mexican Aztec Society.** 1976

Woods, Frances Jerome. **Mexican Ethnic Leadership in San Antonio, Texas.** 1949

Aspects of the Mexican American Experience. 1976

Mexicans in California After the U. S. Conquest. 1976

Hispanic Folklore Studies of Arthur L. Campa. 1976

Hispano Culture of New Mexico. 1976

Mexican California. 1976

The Mexican Experience in Arizona. 1976

The Mexican Experience in Texas. 1976

Mexican Migration to the United States. 1976

The United States Conquest of California. 1976

Northern Mexico On the Eve of the United States Invasion: Rare Imprints Concerning California, Arizona, New Mexico, and Texas, 1821-1846. Edited by David J. Weber. 1976